THE

Wolfgang Puck Cookbook

THE
Wolfgang Puck
Cookbook

RECIPES FROM SPAGO, CHINOIS
AND POINTS EAST AND WEST

WOLFGANG PUCK

RANDOM HOUSE
NEW YORK

Library of Congress Cataloging-in-Publication Data

Puck, Wolfgang.
The Wolfgang Puck Cookbook.

Includes index.
1. Cookery.   2. Spago (Restaurant)   3. Chinois
(Restaurant)   I. Title.
TX715.P952   1986   641.5'09794'94   86-10155
ISBN 0-394-53366-6

Manufactured in the United States of America
24689753
First Edition

Designed by Jo Anne Metsch
Illustrations by Wolfgang Puck

*I will always remember Joan Hoien laughing warmly,
cooking something new and exciting or wonderfully familiar
and comforting. Joan faithfully tested all the recipes for this book,
and my first, as well. She always lifted my mornings with her
enthusiasm for life—she made mine happier, more organized,
and much better for having known her. We know
heaven's aroma must now be divine—
and why the angels look so well fed.*

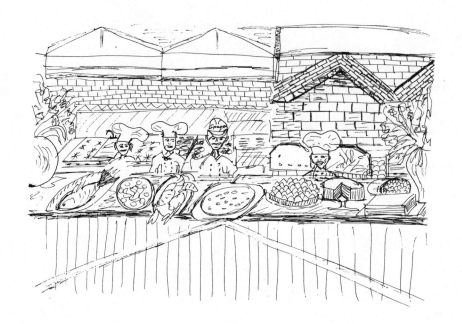

Acknowledgments

I would like to thank

Jason Epstein, my editor, who had confidence in me and always believed that one day or another I would finish this book;

Becky Saletan, for her patience and perseverance and her always pleasant spirit;

Barbara Figueroa, talented writer and chef, whose collaboration on the introductions was indispensable;

Spago chefs Mark Peel, Nancy Silverton, Hiro Sone, Beatrice Keech, and Annie Breuer, and Chinois chefs Kazuto Matsusaka and Fred Iwasaki for their loyalty and hard work;

Tom Kaplan, Mickey, Kenji, Bernard, Janice, Joseph, Nancy, Laura, Margaret, Bella, Serge, Luis, and all the rest of both staffs—office, kitchen, and dining room alike—that keep Spago and Chinois running so smoothly;

Pam Slate at Spago—a special thanks for typing, suggestions, and keeping me organized;

Judy Gethers and Maida Heatter for their valuable contributions professionally and personally;

all of our customers, whose appetites helped inspire most of these recipes; Barbara Lazaroff, my wife, who designed Spago and Chinois, my fantasy playgrounds, for her support and her assurance that she did not marry me for my cooking—but adds, it didn't hurt.

Foreword

hey asked me to write a few introductory words for Wolfgang Puck's new cookbook. Why, do you suppose? Surely not because I am a culinary maven. It must be because I am both a friend of his and a *Landsmann*.

Of course we all know the other guy can cook up a storm. But can he write *not just another cookbook*? Well let me tell you—it ain't easy.

There are millions of lovers around, considering themselves summa cum laude, black belt virtuosos. They all think they can write manuals on that subject. Nonsense. It takes both a poet and a *Feinschmecker* like Dr. Ruth Westheimer to put down definitive rules, guidelines and suggestions on sex (including footnotes on how to do it in high altitudes, on express trains, and in case of a head cold).

How do you evaluate a cookbook? Simple enough. The proof of the pudding is in the eating, right? On page 249 he has a recipe for a chocolate bread pudding with hazelnuts. Well, I got all the ingredients—brioche, bittersweet chocolate, ground hazelnuts, almond liqueur. I separated the eggs, I started preheating the oven to 350°. Then I noticed that I was making enough for twelve servings. So I called eleven of my friends to come over. Six were at Spago's, four at Chinois, and one was still at the office with his secretary, practicing for that black belt no doubt.

Well I am glad they did not show up. It turned out delicious, I ate it all.

Obviously the book works like magic. In fact the guy is magic. It seems, once every 200 or 300 years that erstwhile *Vaterland* of ours comes up with a *Wunderkind*. I wouldn't be surprised if we looked up Wolfgang Puck's birth certificate and found out he had a middle name—Amadeus.

Billy Wilder

Contents

Introduction   xiii

Appetizers, Salads and Soups   1

Pasta   73

Pizza   105

Fish and Shellfish   129

Meat and Poultry   147

Vegetables   191

Bread   203

Desserts   217

Menus   279

Glossary   293

Index   295

Introduction

The past few years will go down in history as the rebirth of American cooking. I speak of neither a fad nor a passing fancy, but rather the result of a culinary evolution. Decades ago, the general population did not think along the same lines as James Beard and other such visionaries. The French dominated the restaurant scene, and all else was looked down upon as second class. But time marches on, and change has brought us back to the food belonging to this land and its unique inhabitants. Past and present join forces as time-tested classics combine with new concepts and techniques. There are still some who laugh at this progressiveness, as they stand clutching their Escoffiers. Maybe they don't change the water in their bathtubs for years at a time either!

That is not to say that a solid understanding of basics has become outdated. It is a necessary foundation for further creative development, much as it is in painting or music. But these branches of the arts are also continually moving into new areas. And as Picasso's style became less complicated later in life, so has cuisine in America left behind the showing-off typical of youth, maturing to a greater simplicity. We have the security of knowing that this country's resources are second to none and can stand on their own in preparations that expose natural character, instead of altering it so that you have to guess at what you're eating.

One of the most dramatic of today's food trends is the revival of regionalism. In the name of authenticity and absolute freshness, local products are being used whenever possible, as we learn to depend less and less on imported goods. Indigenous methods, too, are making a comeback. Mesquite grilling, a Southwestern technique employing the wood of a native plant, has made its way into a great many of the nation's leading restaurants. Regional cooking, which started out on a very homey, modest level, has become the favorite of fashionable circles!

Another major breakthrough, whose originators were once thought to be crazy, is the mixing of ethnic cuisines. It is not at all uncommon to find raw fish listed next to tortillas on the same menu. Ethnic crossovers also occur when distinct elements meet in a single recipe. This country is, after all, a huge melting pot. Why should its cooking not illustrate the American transformation of diversity into unity?

All these principles come together in the philosophies of Spago and Chinois, my two playgrounds where I can excel at doing what I like best to do. Both are reflections of southern California, but in different ways. The feeling at Spago is American, with suggestions of Italy and southern France: visitors from these countries often tell us that we have captured the spirit of their homelands better than a lot of their own restaurants. The Spago client dictates whether the tone of the meal will be casual or elegant, whether it will be a night for pizza or for foie gras and Champagne.

Chinois, by contrast, is the modern application of dining in the Chinese manner, from my wife Barbara's very original decor to the contemporary menu standards: all ingredients are fresh and locally purchased and no dried products, cornstarch, or MSG are ever seen in our kitchen. When Chinois first opened, people weren't quite ready for it; they didn't know what to think of a menu without *moo shu pork* or *egg foo yung*. Two years later, with the public not only accepting but demanding our version of this cuisine, I predict that the Chinese themselves will be modernizing not too far in the future.

A change in our attitude toward dining out calls for high-quality food in a more relaxed ambience. However, the "ambience of the people" is more important than the furniture and decoration. People want to feel the presence of other people. Going to a restaurant has come to be regarded as a social event. The atmospheres of Spago and of Chinois promotes this sociability, in the lion-hearted informality of the background music and interior design, in the openness of the seating arrangements. The kitchens are open, too, located right out in the dining area, where you can watch what's going on. We have nothing to hide!

How fortunate we all are to be part of such an adventurous age. No longer fearing to cross boundaries, the cook goes into unexplored territory without intimidation. You don't need to be a Cordon Bleu graduate to do it. Think of cooking as an outlet for your ideas, a release for the artist in you. It took me nearly eight years to break away from the traditions of my European training and feel free to experiment with new ways. But you can start now. Your American heritage is a wonderful one. Let the world know you're proud of it!

Appetizers, Salads and Soups

When our customers at Spago and Chinois walk through the front door, they are greeted by large, stunning floral arrangements, another aspect of my wife Barbara's inspired restaurant design. To start the evening on such a note is to be filled with optimism for what lies ahead. How could dining not be heightened by the sight of such lovely bouquets?

In the same manner, the appetizer acts as a spectacular entrance into the meal. An eye-catching, colorful presentation is essential here. The dish should be well seasoned to excite and awaken the sense of taste. And the portion must not be too large; the object is to ready the palate for the next course, to leave you wanting more. Success at this stage can give your guests a positive feeling throughout the entire meal. I cannot emphasize too strongly the importance of a good start.

To strive for a "symphony" of flavors between the appetizer and the entrée is to defeat the purpose of a first course. The transition should be one of clear contrast, which keeps things more interesting than similarity of main ingredients or sauces would. Actually, it is easier to achieve contrast, as there are so many ways to do it. Flavor is only one consideration. Temperature is another; a summertime meal that opens with a cold appetizer before a hot entrée is more welcome at that time of year than a succession of hot dishes. Heavy and light foods also work very well side by side; a rich appetizer can be placed before a clean, simple main course, and vice versa. Plan with these factors and others in mind, and it will be a dramatic, fascinating menu from beginning to end.

This chapter includes several soups and salads, since they are so often chosen as first courses nowadays. Soup is appropriate as a starter throughout the year, hot or cold. (Some of our recipes, as you will soon read, work well either way.) Salads cover a wider range than they used to, from the familiar mixed greens to complex arrangements with sautéed or grilled items and warm sauces. With so many possibilities to choose from, I sometimes find myself making an entire meal of appetizers. You enjoy more sensations with less food, and it's something you can do even in better restaurants, where today's movement away from a weighty diet is understood.

So whether you're talking about a single first course or about a feast of appetizers, give this part of the menu lots of character. Make the food play a lively tune, and keep the tastebuds dancing.

FOIE GRAS WITH SAUTÉED APPLES

Serves 4

1 duck liver
2 small Granny Smith or Pippin apples
juice of 1/2 lemon
4 tablespoons (2 ounces) unsalted butter
2 tablespoons almond or safflower oil
1 tablespoon flour
salt
freshly ground pepper
1/2 cup port
1 tablespoon green peppercorns, rinsed

1.   Clean the livers of all nerves and vessels that may be attached. Cut them into ⅜-inch slices.

2.   Peel and core the apples. Cut them into thin slices, about ¼-inch. Toss with the lemon juice and set aside.

3.   Heat a sauté pan. Add 2 tablespoons of the butter and sauté the apples until they are slightly browned but still slightly crunchy. Transfer the apples to a plate and keep warm.

4.   Melt the remaining 2 tablespoons of butter in the same pan with the oil. Season the liver slices with salt and pepper and dip them lightly in the flour. Sauté them over high heat for about 30 seconds on each side. The liver slices should be medium-rare, no more. (Sauté the livers in separate batches so that they are not crowded.) Transfer to a warm plate.

5.   Deglaze the pan with the port, stir in the peppercorns, then reduce the sauce by one third. Remove the pan from the heat and stir in the butter. Season to taste.

PRESENTATION: Divide the apples among the four warm appetizer plates. Top them with the liver slices and spoon the sauce over the top.

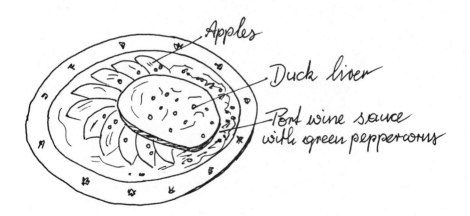

Apples

Duck liver

Port wine sauce
with green peppercorns

CHINOIS SPECIAL SCALLOPS

Serves 2

Yellow Tomato Relish

2 *shallots*
6 to 8 *small yellow tomatoes*
10 *oba leaves (plum leaves)*
1 *red jalapeño pepper, seeds removed*
2 *-inch piece hothouse cucumber, peeled*
1 *-inch piece carrot*
1 *-inch piece daikon*
1 *-inch piece red bell pepper*
1/4 *cup peanut oil*
2 *tablespoons rice wine vinegar*
1 *tablespoon fresh lemon or lime juice*
1 *tablespoon soy sauce*
2 *tablespoons sake*

Scallops

10 to 12 *sea scallops*
1 *teaspoon minced garlic*
1 *teaspoon minced fresh ginger*
1 *teaspoon minced onion*
1/2 *teaspoon minced jalapeño pepper*
peanut oil
salt
freshly ground pepper
1/4 *cup fine strips of daikon, carrot and red bell pepper, (store in ice water until ready to use, then shake off the excess water)*

1.   Prepare the relish: Cut all the ingredients into very fine cubes, ⅛ inch or smaller.

2. Combine the vegetables with the peanut oil, rice wine vinegar and lemon or lime juice. Add the soy sauce and sake and chill. This vinaigrette should have the consistency of a light relish with not much liquid.

3. Prepare the scallops: If necessary, remove the muscle—the small, white, rounded protuberance on the side of the scallops. They should be peeled off and discarded because they become like hard rubber when cooked and make the scallops unpleasant to eat.

4. Heat a small sauté pan. Add a little peanut oil and in it sauté the garlic, ginger, onion, and pepper for a few seconds over high heat to release the flavors. Remove from the heat.

5. Spread a little of the sautéed mixture on the top of each scallop, then sprinkle the scallops with a little salt and pepper.

6. Heat a medium sauté pan. Add peanut oil to coat the bottom of the pan. In it sauté the scallops over high heat for 30 to 40 seconds on each side, just until they are springy to the touch. Do not overcook.

PRESENTATION: Nap the plates with the relish. Place the scallops attractively on top. Garnish with a small nest of the fine strips of daikon, carrot and red bell pepper.

STIR-FRIED SCALLOP SALAD

Serves 6

Chinese Vinaigrette

3 tablespoons rice wine vinegar
1 tablespoon sesame oil
2 tablespoons peanut oil
2 tablespoons soy sauce
   juice of ½ lemon
   salt
   freshly ground pepper

Scallops

2 bunches watercress
4 ounces corn lettuce
1 bunch enoki mushrooms, approximately 3 to 4 ounces
18 sea scallops, side muscles removed (see page 7)
   salt
   freshly ground white pepper
2 tablespoons peanut oil

1. Prepare the vinaigrette: In a small bowl, whisk together the vinegar, oils, soy sauce, lemon juice, and salt and pepper to taste.
2. Wash the watercress and corn lettuce in two or three changes of water until the greens are absolutely clean and pat dry. Remove the large stems from the watercress.
3. Combine the watercress, corn lettuce and *enoki* mushrooms and toss with the vinaigrette.
4. Season the scallops with salt and pepper. Heat a wok or large sauté pan until very hot. In it stir-fry the scallops until they are lightly brown but slightly underdone.

PRESENTATION: Mound the salad on individual plates or on a large platter. Arrange the hot scallops on the greens and serve immediately.

BAY SCALLOPS AND SHRIMP SEVICHE IN TORTILLA CUPS

Serves 4 to 6

almond or peanut oil for frying
4 to 6 *small, thin corn tortillas, approximately 8 inches in diameter (recipe follows)*
½ *pound fresh baby bay scallops, side muscles removed (see page 7)*
½ *pound fresh shrimp, peeled and deveined*
¼ *cup extra-virgin olive oil*
3 to 4 *tablespoons fresh lime juice*
6 *tablespoons chopped fresh cilantro, plus 6 sprigs for garnish*
½ *medium red onion, cut into ¼-inch cubes*
1 *medium, ripe tomato, peeled, seeded and cut into ¼-inch cubes*
salt
freshly ground pepper

1. In a large heavy saucepan, heat 5 to 6 inches of the almond or peanut oil to 375 degrees F. Fry the tortillas, one by one, in the hot oil until they are soft, about 10 seconds and drain on paper towels. Reserve, covered, in a warm spot. Heat wire "potato nest" baskets in the hot oil for several minutes, or until they are very hot. Fit a soft tortilla into the bottom basket and place

the smaller basket on top of the tortilla. Immerse the basket in the hot oil and cook until the tortilla cup is crispy and golden brown. Remove the tortilla cup from the basket and invert on paper towels to drain. Repeat the procedure with the remaining tortillas. (If you don't have a potato nest basket, you can also lay the tortillas one by one on the surface of the hot oil, then immediately push the center to the bottom of the pan with a small empty tin can, thus creating a freeform cup. Be sure to use tongs and heat resistant gloves to protect yourself.)

2.   Cut the shrimp into pieces the same size as the bay scallops. (If you are using sea scallops, cut them as well as the shrimp into ¼- or ⅜-inch cubes.) Refrigerate the scallops and shrimp separately until serving time. This may be done several hours ahead.

3.   In a bowl mix together the olive oil, lime juice, cilantro, red onion and tomato and add salt and pepper to taste. To make a spicier version, add chopped jalapeño peppers to taste.

4.   At serving time, toss the scallops and shrimp with enough of the olive oil mixture to coat well.

PRESENTATION: Place the tortilla cups on appetizer plates. Divide the seviche among the cups and garnish each appetizer with small sprigs of cilantro.

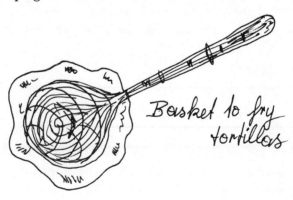

Basket to fry tortillas

TORTILLAS

Makes 8, about 7 inches in diameter

1 cup masa harina (6 ounces)
⅔ to ¾ cup water

1.   Mix the masa harina with enough water until it forms a ball.

2.   Cut it into 8 equal pieces and roll into balls. Keep the balls covered with plastic wrap or a damp towel.

3.   Heat a griddle or heavy skillet on top of the stove until very hot.

4.   While the griddle is heating press the tortillas: Place a ball of the dough between 2 sheets of plastic wrap on a tortilla press. Press hard to make a very thin tortilla. (You can also use the bottom of a pie tin as a press or you can roll the tortillas out with a rolling pin.) Remove the plastic carefully.

5.   Bake the tortillas on the hot griddle or in the skillet for 30 seconds on each side. They should still be soft and pliable.

6.   Stack the tortillas, on a plate, covered, until ready to use.

Tortilla cup

MARINATED TUNA WITH MAUI ONIONS AND AVOCADO

This was one of the first dishes on the menu at Spago. The combination of the Far East and the West makes this probably one of the most popular and most imitated appetizers at the restaurant.

Serves 4

Ginger Lime Vinaigrette

3 tablespoons soy sauce
juice of 2 limes
4 tablespoons extra-virgin olive oil
1 teaspoon minced fresh ginger
salt
freshly ground white pepper

Salad

8 ounces fresh tuna (blue fin or yellowtail)
1 small sweet Maui or Bermuda onion
1 bunch daikon sprouts (or any sharp salad leaves like arugola)
1 large avocado
2 generous teaspoons Sevruga caviar or golden caviar

1.   Prepare the vinaigrette: Combine all the ingredients for the vinaigrette in a blender and blend well. Set aside.
2.   Prepare the salad: Slice the tuna into 3-inch triangles, ¼ inch thick.
3.   Finely mince the onion.

PRESENTATION: Place the daikon sprouts in the center of each plate. Slice the avocado thinly and arrange it in a fan on one side. Arrange the tuna on the other side. Put the onion on top of the tuna and garnish each serving with ½ teaspoon caviar. Mix the vinaigrette well and spoon it over the tuna and avocado.

SMOKED SALMON AND CAVIAR ON BUCKWHEAT CAKES

Serves 4

Buckwheat Cakes

3 tablespoons buckwheat flour
4 tablespoons all-purpose flour
½ teaspoon salt
½ teaspoon freshly ground pepper
1 tablespoon minced fresh dill
½ cup good-tasting beer at room temperature
2 tablespoons unsalted butter, melted
1 egg, separated

Topping

thinly sliced red onion
3 to 4 ounces Scotch or Norwegian smoked salmon, cut into paper-thin slices
sour cream
2 ounces domestic golden caviar
minced fresh dill, plus additional sprigs for garnish

1. Prepare the buckwheat cakes: In a mixing bowl, combine the flours, salt, pepper and dill. Slowly stir in the beer, melted butter and the egg yolk. In a small bowl, whip the egg white until stiff. Carefully fold it into the buckwheat batter.

2. Heat a heavy skillet, griddle or blini pan until a small piece of butter dropped on the surface foams. Using a two-ounce ladle, pour the batter into the skillet, griddle or blini pan. (There is sufficient batter to make twelve to sixteen 2- or 3-inch cakes.) Cook the cakes over medium heat until brown on one side, about 2 to 3 minutes, then turn and brown the other side. Transfer the cakes to a tray or baking sheet large enough to hold them in one layer and keep them warm.

3. To assemble: On each of the cakes place a thin layer of the red onion. Cover the onion with a slice of salmon. Spoon a little sour cream over the salmon and top with a teaspoon of caviar. Sprinkle with the dill and grind a little pepper over each.

PRESENTATION: Place 3 or 4 finished buckwheat cakes on warm appetizer plates. Garnish each plate with a sprig of fresh dill. Serve with flutes of chilled Champagne.

CURED FRESH SALMON WITH GOLDEN CAVIAR SAUCE ON TOASTED BRIOCHE

This is an ideal party dish as it may be done well ahead of time.

Serves 4 to 6

4 ounces Cured Fresh Salmon per person (recipe follows)

Sauce

½ cup sour cream or Crème Fraîche *(page 293)*
1 tablespoon domestic golden caviar
  freshly ground pepper
2 thin slices Spago's Brioche Loaf per person (page 208)
1 tablespoon minced fresh dill

1. Slice the salmon paper thin as for smoked salmon.
2. Prepare the sauce: Gently mix together the sour cream or *crème fraîche*, caviar, and pepper to taste. Correct the seasonings as desired.
3. At serving time, toast the brioche lightly.

PRESENTATION: Arrange the salmon slices in a circular pattern on large appetizer plates. Spoon some of the sauce in the center and sprinkle it lightly with the fresh dill. Serve the brioche on separate napkin-lined plates.

CURED FRESH SALMON

Cured salmon may be kept up to one week under refrigeration. Since one salmon serves up to 15 people, I find this is an ideal appetizer for larger parties.

> *1 whole salmon 5 to 6 pounds, cleaned*
> *1 cup chopped fresh dill*
> *¼ cup kosher salt*
> *¼ cup freshly ground coarse black pepper*
> *2 tablespoons sugar*

1.   Remove the head and backbone from the salmon. Place the fillets, skin side up, on a work surface and make 1½-inch-long horizontal cuts that are ½ to ¾ inch deep every 2 inches for the length of the fish.

2.   Combine the dill, salt, pepper and sugar. Spread about ⅓ of the mixture in the bottom of a glass dish or stainless steel casserole large enough to hold the salmon in one layer. Place one half of the salmon, skin side down, in the casserole. Spread half the remaining dill mixture on the flesh of the fish. Top with the remaining salmon, skin side up, and spread it with the remaining dill mixture. Cover the fish, not the pan, tightly with plastic wrap, then with foil.

3.   Weight the salmon with 2 or 3 foil-wrapped bricks.

4.   Let the salmon marinate in the refrigerator 3 to 4 days. (After 4 days the salmon may become too salty.)
5.   Remove the fish from the dish and scrape off the excess dill mixture. Trim the edges of the salmon and remove any small bones with tweezers.
6.   If you don't wish to use the salmon immediately, wrap it securely in plastic wrap and refrigerate it for up to 1 week.

PRESENTATION: Slice the flesh thinly, as for smoked salmon. Serve with toast and a caviar, dill or mustard sauce.

BAY SCALLOPS WITH SAUTÉED APPLES

Baby bay scallops are preferable to sea scallops because they are sweeter and more succulent.

Serves 6

2 *Pippin or Granny Smith apples*
2 *tablespoons unsalted butter*
1 *pound fresh baby bay scallops*
  salt
  freshly ground white pepper
1 *tablespoon almond or safflower oil*
1 *tablespoon chopped fresh Italian parsley or cilantro*

1.   Peel, halve, and core the apples. Slice them thinly or cut them into ¼-inch julienne strips.
2.   Heat a large sauté pan and add the butter. In it sauté the apples over moderate heat 2 to 3 minutes, or until they are slightly brown but still crispy. It is better to sauté the apples

(and scallops) in several small batches than to crowd your sauté pan.

3. Season the scallops with salt and pepper. Heat another large sauté pan and add the oil. In it sauté the scallops over high heat until just springy to the touch, from 30 seconds to 1 minute, depending on their size. Remove from the heat.

4. Stir in the parsley or cilantro and correct the seasonings.

PRESENTATION: Arrange the apple slices in a wreath on warm appetizer plates and place the scallops in the center of the wreaths. Garnish with sprigs of Italian parsley or cilantro.

TWICE FRIED RICE

Don't confine yourself to the vegetables listed below. Use any fresh vegetables in season.

Serves 3 to 4

> *1 cup long-grain rice*
> *¾ cup Chicken Stock (page 69)*
> *¾ cup water*
> *1 red or yellow pepper, seeded and cored*
> *1 green pepper, seeded and cored*
> *1 cup sliced Napa cabbage*
> *½ cup mushrooms, sliced*
> *¼ cup snow peas, strings removed*
> *1 to 2 tablespoons peanut oil*
> *1 egg, beaten*
> *2 tablespoons mushroom soy (Superior)*
> *2 tablespoons regular soy (Kikkoman)*

1.   Place the rice in a saucepan and add the stock and water. Bring the liquid to a boil, reduce the heat, cover and cook slowly for 15 to 18 minutes. It is important to cook the rice until dry. Turn the rice out onto a large platter or baking sheet and let it air-dry for several hours or overnight.

2.   Shake the air-dried rice through a Chinese wire ladle or a wire fry basket to fluff it up and to separate the grains.

3.   Chop the peppers into 1-inch squares and add to the other vegetables.

4.   Heat a wok until it is very hot, pour the oil in around the edges, and then stir-fry all the vegetables for 30 seconds. Add the rice and continue to stir-fry for another 30 seconds. Pour the egg in around the edges of the wok and quickly stir it into the rice and vegetables.

5.   Stir in the soy sauces.

PRESENTATION: Turn the rice out onto a heated platter. Serve with chopsticks.

Variation: Add leftover duck, lamb, pork or chicken to the vegetables to make an entrée.

CURRIED OYSTERS WITH CUCUMBER SAUCE AND SALMON PEARLS

Edible flowers, such as nasturtiums add to the beauty and overall flavor of the dish.

Serves 6

24 *fresh oysters in their shells*
 1 *medium cucumber, hothouse variety*

⅓ to ½ cup rice wine vinegar
     salt
     freshly ground white pepper
  2 egg yolks
  ¼ cup light sesame oil
  ¼ cup almond oil
   1 tablespoon curry powder
   2 tablespoons flour
     peanut oil
     unsalted butter
   4 tablespoons salmon caviar
   1 bunch watercress
     lemon wedges
   6 small flowers for garnish

1.   Clean the oysters and shuck them, reserving the liqueur and the bottom shells. Place the oysters in their liqueur.

2.   Cut ⅜-inch slices from around the outside of the unpeeled cucumber and chop coarsely. Discard the remaining cucumber. In a blender, purée the cucumber with the rice wine vinegar, salt and pepper. In a bowl whisk the egg yolks and add the oils very gradually, whisking, as for mayonnaise. Whisk in enough of the puréed cucumber to make a sauce the consistency of very lightly whipped cream. (The sauce should be a light, refreshing green.) Season with more salt, pepper and rice wine vinegar if necessary.

3.   Combine the curry powder and flour on a plate. Coat the oysters with the mixture.

4.   Arrange 4 oyster shells on each plate on a bed of watercress "so the oysters stay straight and the sauce doesn't run out." Spoon a little sauce into each shell.

5.   Heat a pan over high heat. Add a little oil and butter and in it sauté the oysters for 15 seconds on each side. Arrange 1 oyster in each of the shells.

PRESENTATION: Top each oyster with a spoonful of salmon caviar or "pearls." Garnish with lemon wedges and a small flower in the center of each plate.

GOAT CHEESE CROUTONS

We served this in Williamsburg as a cheese course.

Serves 6

> 6 *ounces fresh Montrachet or* chèvre *(log-shaped goat cheese) cut into twelve equal slices*
> *extra-virgin olive oil*
> 2 *cloves garlic, peeled*
> 1 *branch fresh thyme leaves (about 1 teaspoon leaves), plus fresh thyme sprigs for garnish*
> *freshly ground coarse pepper*
> *twelve ½-inch slices French bread, cut from a baguette*
> 3 *tablespoons unsalted butter, melted*

1.   Place the cheese in a small plastic or glass container and add enough of the olive oil to cover it. Add 1 of the garlic cloves, the thyme and pepper to taste. Cover and let the cheese mellow in the refrigerator for 1 or 2 days.

2.   Brush 1 side of the bread slices with some of the melted butter. Arrange the croutons, buttered side up, on a heavy baking sheet.

3.   Heat a broiler or salamander until very hot, or preheat the oven to 450 degrees F. Broil or bake the croutons until the tops are lightly browned. Remove from the heat and reserve.

4.   At serving time, preheat the oven to 450 degrees F. Place

a slice of the marinated cheese on each crouton, and bake in the oven until the cheese begins to melt.

PRESENTATION: Allow 3 croutons per person and decorate each serving with sprigs of fresh thyme.

SWISS CHARD AND GOAT CHEESE RAMEKIN

This is a hearty, colorful appetizer or a wonderfully filling luncheon dish to serve with crusty French bread.

Serves 4

     ½ cup heavy cream
     3 eggs
     2 egg yolks
     ½ teaspoon chopped fresh thyme leaves
     ¼ teaspoon ground coriander
     pinch cayenne pepper
     salt
     freshly ground white pepper
     12 large Swiss chard leaves
     3 tablespoons unsalted butter
     1 large shallot, minced
     10 ounces fresh chèvre (log-shaped goat cheese)
     4 perfect fresh basil leaves

     Vinaigrette

     2 medium ripe tomatoes, peeled, seeded and diced
     4 fresh basil leaves, finely chopped
     2 tablespoons extra-virgin olive oil
     1 tablespoon sherry vinegar
     salt
     freshly ground pepper

1.   In a bowl, mix together the cream, eggs and egg yolks. Whisk in the thyme, coriander, cayenne, and salt and pepper.

2.   Wash the chard leaves carefully. Cut off the rib sections at the bottom and slice these into fine julienne. Cut the remaining parts of the leaves medium fine.

3.   Heat a large skillet and in it melt the butter. When foaming, add the shallot and cook over medium heat for 4 to 5 minutes. It should be soft but not brown. Add the chopped chard leaves and sauté them until just wilted.

4.   Crumble the *chèvre* into pea-size pieces, reserving approximately ⅓ of it for later use. Mix the remaining cheese with the egg/cream mixture and the chard mixture.

5.   Generously butter 4 ramekins or individual custard cups and fill each ¾ full with the mixture. Place the ramekins in a *bain-marie* (see page 293), cover loosely with buttered foil, buttered side down, and simmer gently on top of the stove for 15 to 20 minutes, or until a small knife inserted in the center of the ramekins comes out clean.

6.   While the ramekins are cooking, prepare the vinaigrette: Combine all the ingredients and set aside.

7.   When the ramekins are done, invert them on to an oven-proof plate or baking sheet and top each with some of the reserved cheese. Preheat a broiler or salamander and broil the custards for approximately 2 minutes, or until the cheese has softened and is beginning to brown.

PRESENTATION: Make a pool of vinaigrette in the center of each plate and place one custard in the center of the vinaigrette. Top each custard with a perfect basil leaf.

SCRAMBLED EGGS WITH
FRESH TRUFFLES

Serves 2

    4 fresh eggs
    2 fresh truffles, 4 nice slices reserved
  ¼ pound (4 ounces) Puff Pastry Baumanière (page 228)
    1 egg, beaten lightly, for egg wash
    2 tablespoons unsalted butter
    3 tablespoons heavy cream
    salt
    freshly ground white pepper

1. Place the truffles and the eggs *in their shells* in a small bowl and seal it hermetically with plastic wrap. Refrigerate. The truffles will impregnate the eggs with their wonderful perfume.

2. Roll out puff pastry on a floured surface ⅜ inch thick and cut it into 2 rounds 5 inches in diameter. Brush the tops with egg wash, taking care not to drip any of it down the sides of the rounds, which will cause the layers to stick together and the pastry to rise unevenly. With a small, sharp knife, cut another circle in each round, about halfway through the pastry ½ inch from the edge. Place the 2 pastry rounds on a baking sheet and let the dough rest in the refrigerator or freezer for 1 hour. This resting time allows the gluten to relax and results in a more delicate pastry.

3. Preheat the oven to 400 degrees F.

4. Bake the pastry for 15 minutes, or until it is golden brown and remove it from the oven. Using the small knife, cut around the incisions and remove the centers, keeping the "lids" intact. Scrape out the soft insides of the shells and discard. Keep the shells warm in a low oven.

5. Remove the truffles from the bowl, chop them and sauté

them over low heat in 2 tablespoons of the butter in a non-stick skillet.

6.   In the small bowl, beat the eggs with a fork and beat in the cream and salt and pepper. Pour the eggs into the skillet with the truffles and cook them over medium heat, stirring constantly with a wooden spoon to assure even cooking. When the eggs are just creamy, remove them from the heat and stir in the remaining butter.

PRESENTATION: Spoon the eggs and truffles into the warm pastry cases and decorate with the reserved truffle slices. Set the lids at an angle. Serve immediately.

Variation: The eggs can also be served in small bowls and garnished with toasted bread sticks. To make breadsticks: Cut a homemade-type bread into ½-inch slices. Cut off the crusts and cut the bread into sticks the size of your middle finger. Place on a baking sheet and toast them in a 400 degree F. oven until they are golden brown.

SPICY HONEY-GLAZED
BABY PORK RIBS

Baby pork ribs can be found in supermarkets or Chinese meat markets. Young ribs are more tender and juicy. Generally they come in sides; 2 sides should be enough for this recipe.

Serves 4 to 6

Marinade

1 cup soy sauce
1 cup sake

1 teaspoon ground dried chili flakes
4 tablespoons honey
2 tablespoons minced fresh ginger
2 tablespoons minced fresh garlic
6 tablespoons sesame oil

2 sides (about 3 pounds) baby pork ribs

1.   In a bowl, mix together all the ingredients for the marinade.
2.   Place the ribs in a container just large enough to hold them one side on top of the other. Pour the marinade over the ribs, cover with plastic wrap or tin foil and let marinate in the refrigerator overnight.
3.   Preheat the oven to 300 degrees F.
4.   Place half the marinade in a baking pan with the ribs and bake, turning the ribs frequently, for 2 hours, or until the meat is tender.
5.   Under a preheated broiler or on a wood-fired grill glaze the ribs for 3 to 4 minutes on each side. Watch carefully so they do not burn.
6.   Remove the ribs and cut each side into individual pieces.

PRESENTATION: Arrange the ribs in an overlapping fashion on each plate or on a large serving platter. Spoon the warm marinade over them.

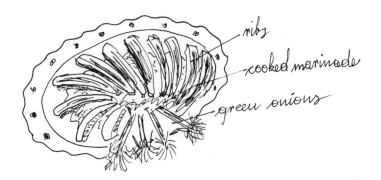

CHINOIS SEA SCALLOPS WITH
SPICY VINEGAR

Serves 6

1 pound sea scallops, sliced in half horizontally
1 tablespoon curry powder
salt
freshly ground pepper

Sauce

1 small cucumber
1 small bunch dill
4 tablespoons honey vinegar
2 egg yolks
1 tablespoon water
salt
freshly ground pepper

2 bunches watercress
12 oyster shells
4 tablespoons peanut oil
6 tablespoons salmon caviar

1.   Sprinkle the scallop slices with the curry powder and salt and pepper and let rest for 1 hour.
2.   Prepare the sauce: Peel the skin with ⅜ inch of the flesh attached from the cucumber. Discard the remaining flesh and seeds or reserve for another use. Coarsely chop the cucumber with the skin and the dill, place in a blender with the honey vinegar and purée.
3.   In a pan over very low heat or over a *bain-marie*, whisk the egg yolks and water together constantly until the mixture doubles in volume. Be sure to keep the heat very low to prevent the yolks from curdling. Remove from the heat, add the cu-

cumber purée, and season with salt and pepper to taste. Mix
well and set aside.

4. Divide the watercress among 6 appetizer plates, making a
bed for the oyster shells so they won't tip and the sauce won't
spill over. Place 2 shells on each plate and fill each with some
of the cucumber/vinegar sauce.

5. In a sauté pan, heat the peanut oil until it is hot and in it
sauté the scallops over high heat, turning once, for about 1
minute. Remove the scallops from the pan and drain on paper
towels.

PRESENTATION: Arrange the scallops slices in the oyster shells
and garnish each shell with a spoonful of the salmon caviar and
serve warm.

MANDARIN STEAK SALAD

This salad from the Spago menu is ideal for a summer barbecue
or as a winter appetizer. The New York steaks can be replaced
by flank steak, which is also very tasty.

Serves 4

Mandarin Marinade

    2 tablespoons orange or mandarin marmalade
    1 teaspoon minced fresh ginger
    1 clove garlic
    ½ teaspoon freshly ground white pepper
        salt
    ¼ cup fresh lemon juice
    ¼ cup wine vinegar

¼ cup fresh orange juice
½ cup extra-virgin olive oil

Ginger Vinaigrette

1 medium shallot
one ½-inch piece fresh ginger, peeled and minced
⅓ cup almond or extra-virgin olive oil
1 tablespoon dark sesame oil
½ cup rice wine vinegar or ⅓ cup Chinese black vinegar
salt
freshly ground pepper

Salad

two 8-ounce New York steaks
salt
freshly ground pepper
4 cups mixed salad greens, such as mâche, *arugola, and* radicchio
2 tablespoons unsalted butter
1 large shallot, minced
½ pound shiitake *mushrooms, sliced*

1.   Prepare the mandarin vinaigrette: In a saucepan, combine all the ingredients, except the olive oil, and reduce over low heat to ½ cup. Remove from the heat and let cool. Stir in the olive oil and reserve.

2.   Prepare the ginger vinaigrette: In a bowl, mix together all the ingredients and correct the seasonings as necessary. Reserve.

3.   Brush the steaks with some of the mandarin marinade and season them with salt and pepper. Grill the steaks to medium rare and set them aside in a warm spot.

4.   Toss the salad greens with the ginger vinaigrette, adding any collected meat juices to the dressing and set aside.

5.   In a large sauté pan, heat the butter until it is foamy and in it sauté the shallot and mushrooms over high heat for several minutes, or until *al dente*. Season with salt and pepper to taste.

PRESENTATION: Mound the salad greens in the center of 4 dinner plates. Slice the steak thinly on the diagonal and fan the slices around one side of the greens. Arrange the mushrooms decoratively on the opposite side. Serve immediately.

LAMB SALAD MONDAVI

I created this Provençal-style salad while I was giving a weekend of classes at the Robert Mondavi Winery. I was inspired by the array of fresh herbs and vegetables growing in the gardens there.

Serves 6 to 8

> *1 baby lamb shoulder*
> *salt*
> *freshly ground pepper*
> *5 or 6 fresh basil leaves*
> *2 tablespoons pine nuts, toasted*
> *½ head garlic, peeled and blanched*
> *2 tablespoons extra-virgin olive oil*
> *1 head chickory*
> *1 bunch red-leaf lettuce*
> *4 bunches arugola,* mâche *(lamb's lettuce) or a mixture of both*
> *2 heads* radicchio
> *¼ cup julienne strips sun-dried tomatoes*
> *1 tablespoon freshly grated Parmesan cheese*

Vinaigrette

6 tablespoons extra-virgin olive oil
1 to 2 tablespoons sherry vinegar or other strong vinegar
2 tablespoons minced mixed fresh herbs
salt
freshly ground pepper

1. Remove all the bones from the lamb shoulder except the "shin" bone.
2. Preheat the oven to 450 degrees F.
3. Season the inside of the meat with salt and pepper and arrange the basil leaves on top. Spread the pine nuts and garlic in the center, then tie the meat up in a roll. Season the outside with salt and pepper to taste.
4. In an ovenproof sauté pan, heat the olive oil until hot and in it brown the lamb over high heat on all sides. Then transfer the lamb to the oven and roast for 20 to 25 minutes, or until it is medium rare. Remove the lamb from the oven and let rest 15 minutes in a warm spot.
5. Wash and dry all the lettuces and place in a large bowl.
6. Prepare the vinaigrette: In a bowl, mix together all ingredients and correct the seasonings. (If the vinegar is too strong, cut the sauce with a little water.) Toss with the salad greens.

PRESENTATION: Divide the salad greens among the plates. Slice the lamb ½ inch thick and arrange on the greens, allowing 3 slices per person for appetizer salads; 4 per person for a luncheon dish. Arrange several "strips" of sun-dried tomatoes on top of each salad and sprinkle lightly with Parmesan cheese. Serve immediately.

GARLIC LAMB IN LETTUCE LEAVES

This dish is also delicious prepared with ground pork or chicken as a substitute for the ground lamb.

Serves 4 to 6

> *1 head iceberg lettuce*
> *1 sprig fresh mint, leaves only*
> *1 pound fine ground lamb*
> *5 cloves garlic, minced*
> *½ small onion, minced*
> *salt*
> *freshly ground pepper*
> *peanut oil*
> *2 tablespoons chili oil (recipe follows)*
> *¼ cup plum wine*
> *red, yellow and green bell peppers, cut into small* brunoise *(see page 293)*
> *4 to 6 scallions, green parts only, blanched*

1. Select 4 to 6 inner iceberg lettuce leaves that form natural cups and set aside. Cut some of the remaining lettuce into julienne strips (enough to make 1 to 1½ cups). Cut the mint into julienne strips and toss with the lettuce. Reserve.
2. Mix the lamb, garlic, onion, and salt and pepper.
3. Heat a wok until really hot. Add a little peanut oil around the edges and in the wok stir-fry the lamb until it is cooked through. Add a little chili oil, the plum wine and the *brunoise* of peppers and stir-fry 30 to 45 seconds more.

PRESENTATION: Fill the lettuce cups with the julienned strips of lettuce and mint. Spoon the lamb mixture over the greens and tie the lettuce bundles with the blanched scallions. Place the bundles in the center of salad plates.

CHILI OIL

Makes 1 cup

1 cup peanut, light sesame or olive oil
1/4 cup dried red chili flakes

1.   In a saucepan, heat the oil until very hot but not smoking. Add the chili flakes and remove from the heat. Let stand until cool.
2.   Pour into a bottle and use as desired.
3.   Store the oil in the refrigerator for up to 3 months, keeping in mind that the longer it sits, the hotter it gets.

SQUAB SALAD ROLLS

Serves 4

2   *squabs*
     salt
     freshly ground pepper
1   *tablespoon peanut oil*
1   *head Napa cabbage*
4   *very long chives or 8 shorter chives*
12   shiitake *mushrooms, diced*
3 to 4   *ounces* enoki *mushrooms, trimmed*
1   *large clove garlic, minced*
2   *thin slices fresh ginger, minced*
8   *very small young scallions, cut into 1/4-inch slices*
1 to 2   *tablespoons dark sesame oil*

⅛ teaspoon dried red chili flakes

2 tablespoons duck or brown demi-glace *(below or 294)*

1. Preheat oven to 500°.

2. Place the duck bones, onion, and celery in a roasting pan and roast until the bones are a dark golden brown, about 30 minutes. Turn the bones once or twice as they cook.

3. Transfer the duck bones and vegetables to a 6-quart stockpot. Deglaze the roasting pan with the white wine and pour it into the stockpot. Add the tomatoes, thyme, bay leaf, peppercorns, and enough water to cover all the ingredients by 1 inch. Bring the stock to a boil, reduce the heat, and simmer for 3 hours. Skim off the foam and fat as it rises to the top.

4. Strain into a clean pot or saucepan and carefully skim away any remaining fat.

5. Over high heat, reduce the stock until only half remains.

Note: *Demi-glace* is the result of cooking a stock until it is reduced by half; *glace* is the result of cooking it to a syrup.

1. Preheat the oven to 400 degrees F.

2. Season the squabs with salt and pepper. In a sauté pan heat the peanut oil and in it brown the squabs on both sides. Transfer the squabs to the oven and roast for 10 to 12 minutes, or until medium rare. Reserve in a warm spot.

3. Separate the cabbage leaves carefully and reserve 4 of the tender inner leaves that form natural cups.

4. Blanch the chives in boiling water just a few seconds, until they are limp, then remove to paper towels to dry. If you are using short or medium-length chives, tie the thick ends together to form 1 long chive. (The chives must be long enough to tie around the cabbage bundles.) Lay them across the center of the salad plates.

5. Combine the mushrooms, garlic, ginger and scallions.

6. In a heavy sauté pan or wok, heat the sesame oil until it is

very hot. Add the chili flakes, then the vegetables and stir-fry them for 45 seconds to 1 minute.

7.   Pour in the *demi-glace*, remove the pan from the heat and add the soy sauce. (Adding the soy sauce while the pan is on the heat causes it to become very salty.) Stir quickly to combine and season with salt and pepper to taste.

8.   Cut the squab breasts into *aiguillettes* (see page 293) and add them to the pan, tossing to combine.

PRESENTATION: Spoon the hot squab mixture into the cabbage leaves and tie each leaf loosely with a chive. Serve immediately.

Duck Stock

For this stock you can use bones from cooked or uncooked ducks.

    2 *duck carcasses, roughly chopped*
    1 *unpeeled onion, quartered*
    1 *stalk celery, coarsely sliced*
 1½ *cups dry white wine*
    2 *ripe tomatoes, quartered*
  ¼ *teaspoon dried thyme or 1 branch fresh thyme*
  ½ *bay leaf*
  ½ *teaspoon whole peppercorns*
    Water

SPINACH SALAD WITH
DUCK LIVER ON CROUTONS

The duck livers in this recipe are prepared two days in advance; the salad is then easily assembled at the last moment.

Serves 4

4 small duck livers
freshly ground pepper
1 sprig fresh thyme leaves
2 tablespoons port
salt
4 ounces clarified butter

Shallot Vinaigrette

2 shallots, finely chopped
2 tablespoons balsamic vinegar
salt
freshly ground pepper
¼ cup almond or safflower oil

12 slices French bread, cut ¼ inch thick
1 clove garlic, peeled
1 pound (about 2 bunches) spinach, washed, stemmed and dried

1.   Marinate the duck livers with the pepper, thyme leaves and port, covered, overnight.
2.   Drain the livers and place them in an earthenware crock just large enough to hold them. Add salt and pepper to taste, then cover with some of the clarified butter.
3.   Preheat the oven to 300 degrees F. Cover the crock with foil, place it in a *bain-marie* (see page 293) and bring the water to a boil on top of the stove. Transfer the crock to the oven and bake for 30 minutes. The duck livers should only be warmed

through, no more than rare. Remove the crock from the *bain-marie* and refrigerate overnight.

4.   In a bowl, combine all the ingredients for the vinaigrette and set aside.

5.   In a skillet, sauté the bread slices in 1 to 2 tablespoons of the clarified butter until they are crisp and golden. Rub both sides with the garlic. Reserve.

6.   Toss the spinach leaves with the vinaigrette to coat them lightly.

7.   Transfer the duck livers to a cutting board and cut them into ¼-inch slices.

8.   In the skillet sauté the livers for a few seconds on each side; or dust them lightly with flour and sauté them in a non-stick pan over high heat for about 10 seconds. Place 1 slice of duck liver on each crouton.

PRESENTATION: Divide the spinach among large salad plates and arrange 3 croutons on each serving of salad.

SWEETBREADS WITH VINEGAR BUTTER AND MÂCHE

Serves 4

1 to 1½ pounds sweetbreads
juice of 1 lemon
salt
freshly ground pepper
2 tablespoons extra-virgin olive oil
1 shallot, finely chopped
¼ cup red wine vinegar

½ *cup dry red wine*
½ *cup double-strength Chicken Stock (page 69)*
   salt
8 *tablespoons (4 ounces) unsalted butter, slightly softened*
4 *ounces* mâche *(lamb's lettuce)*

1. Soak the sweetbreads overnight in cold water. Drain and rinse.
2. Place the sweetbreads in a large saucepan with the lemon juice, a little salt and water to cover. Bring to a boil over high heat, reduce the heat, and simmer for 3 minutes. Remove the sweetbreads and plunge them into a bowl of ice water until cool. Pat dry and remove any membranes or fat parts.
3. Cut the sweetbreads horizontally into ½-inch scallops. Season both sides with pepper and brush with olive oil. Reserve.
4. In a saucepan, reduce the shallot, vinegar, wine, and stock to ⅓ cup. Over low heat whisk in the butter, a little at a time. Season with salt and pepper to taste and strain the mixture into a small clean saucepan. Keep warm.
5. Season the sweetbreads with a little salt and grill them over hot charcoal until they are crispy on the outside and still a little moist in the center; or, dust them lightly with flour and sauté them in a little olive oil over high heat.

PRESENTATION: Arrange the *mâche* nicely on salad plates. Divide the sweetbreads in overlapping slices on the *mâche* and spoon sauce over them.

I prefer the texture of the calf's sweetbreads to that of the lamb's sweetbreads.

ROASTED DUCK LEGS WITH NAPA CABBAGE AND PANCETTA

Serves 4

4 *duck legs*
salt
freshly ground pepper
3 *sprigs fresh thyme leaves*
1 *small head Napa cabbage (8 to 10 ounces)*
4 *ounces pancetta, cut into ¼-inch dice (bacon can be used as a substitute)*
4 *tablespoons Zinfandel vinegar, or a good, strong red or sherry wine vinegar*
2 *tablespoons extra-virgin olive oil*
4 *sprigs fresh thyme for garnish*

1.   Preheat the oven to 400 degrees F.
2.   Season the duck legs with salt, pepper and the thyme leaves. Heat an ovenproof sauté pan, in it place the duck legs, skin side down, and brown them on all sides until golden. Transfer the legs to the oven and roast them for 50 to 60 minutes, or until tender. Remove the duck legs from the oven and drain off the fat.
3.   Reserve 4 nice cabbage leaves. Cut the remaining cabbage into ⅜-inch "stripes," or strips. Reserve.
4.   In the skillet, sauté the pancetta over moderate heat for 8 to 10 minutes, or until it is crisp on the outside. Pour off half the rendered fat from the pan, add the sliced cabbage and sauté it over high heat until heated through. Transfer the cabbage and pancetta to a bowl and deglaze the pan with 4 tablespoons of the vinegar. Remove the pan from the heat, add the olive oil and season with salt and pepper to taste. Toss the liquid with the cabbage.

PRESENTATION: Arrange the reserved cabbage leaves on warm salad plates. Fill the leaves with the sautéed cabbage and pancetta. Place the duck legs on the cabbage and garnish each serving with a sprig of fresh thyme.

The skin of the duck should be crispy and the inside should be tender.

SONOMA LAMB SALAD

Serves 4

   1 baby lamb shoulder (less than 1 pound), boned
   2 tablespoons strong Dijon mustard
   2 branches fresh thyme (about 2 teaspoon thyme leaves)
      freshly ground pepper
      salt
   2 bunches arugola
   2 bunches mâche *(lamb's lettuce)*
   1 small head curly endive
 ½ cup mustard vinaigrette (page 40)
   4 tablespoons julienne-cut sun-dried tomatoes
   1 ounce freshly grated parmesan cheese

1.   Brush both sides of the lamb with the mustard and sprinkle it with the thyme leaves and pepper. Cover and let marinate overnight.
2.   Preheat the oven to 450 degrees F.
3.   Sprinkle the lamb with salt and place it on a rack in a small roasting pan. Roast for 20 minutes, or until it is medium rare. Remove from the oven and let the lamb rest for 10 to 15 minutes.

4.   Wash the salad greens, pat them dry and tear them into bite-size pieces if necessary. Place in a bowl and toss with enough vinaigrette to coat them lightly.

PRESENTATION: Arrange the salad greens in the center of 4 salad plates. Slice the lamb thinly and arrange the slices attractively on the greens. Divide the sun-dried tomato slices over the lamb and sprinkle each serving with some of the parmesan.

GOAT CHEESE SALAD WITH ARUGOLA AND RADICCHIO

Serves 4

Mustard Vinaigrette

   1 tablespoon Dijon mustard
   1 teaspoon finely chopped fresh tarragon
   1 tablespoon sherry wine vinegar
       salt
       freshly ground white pepper
   1 cup almond or extra-virgin olive oil (or a mixture of both)

Salad

   4 ounces fresh Chèvre *(log-shaped goat cheese), cut into 4 equal slices*
 1/4 cup extra-virgin olive oil
1 1/2 teaspoons fresh thyme leaves
   1 clove garlic, peeled and crushed
       freshly ground pepper
   2 small heads radicchio
 1/2 pound arugola or mâche *(lamb's lettuce)*

1.   Prepare the vinaigrette: Combine the mustard, tarragon, vinegar, salt and pepper in a small bowl. Slowly whisk in the oil. Correct the seasonings, including the mustard and vinegar, and set aside.

2.   In a bowl, let the cheese marinate in the olive oil overnight with 1 teaspoon of the thyme leaves, the garlic and pepper.

3.   Wash the *radicchio* and arugola and pat them dry with clean paper towels.

4.   In a bowl, toss the salad greens with enough of the vinaigrette to coat them lightly. Divide the greens among 4 large salad plates.

5.   Heat a non-stick sauté pan until very hot and add 2 tablespoons of the goat-cheese marinade. Add the cheese and sauté it over medium heat for 30 seconds on each side; or place the cheese in a preheated 450 degree F. oven for 1 minute.

PRESENTATION: Top each salad with a slice of hot goat cheese. Garnish the cheese with the remaining thyme leaves. Serve immediately.

Fresh goat cheese is necessary because old goat cheese tastes rough and salty.

SALAD OF GRILLED
CHANTERELLES OR CÊPES

Cêpes are wonderful if barbecued or grilled, but chanterelles must be seasoned and sautéed over high heat in some olive oil.

Serves 4

1 pound cêpes *or fresh chanterelles*
1 very ripe medium tomato, peeled, seeded and chopped
2 to 3 tablespoons wine vinegar
2 medium shallots, minced
salt
freshly ground pepper
6 tablespoons extra-virgin olive oil
1 tablespoon chopped fresh Italian parsley, chervil or tarragon
1 head radicchio, *separated into leaves*

1.   Clean the mushrooms with a soft, dry brush or a damp cloth. Trim as necessary, and, if they are large, cut them into halves or quarters.
2.   In a bowl, combine the tomato, vinegar, shallots, salt, pepper and 4 tablespoons of the olive oil. Reserve the vinaigrette.
3.   Toss the mushrooms with salt, pepper, the remaining olive oil and the chopped herbs.
4.   Grill the mushrooms over hot charcoal; or, in a skillet, sauté them over high heat in a little oil for 4 minutes.

PRESENTATION: Nap 4 appetizer plates with the vinaigrette. Arrange the *radicchio* leaves and grilled mushrooms on top.

Note: To serve as a luncheon dish or as an appetizer, you can add 4 to 5 slices of Duck Sausage (page 113) to each plate.

RACK OF LAMB CHINOIS

Our friend Bart Ehman raises the best lamb, which he then hand-selects for Spago and Chinois.

Serves 4

3 *racks of lamb (about 1 pound each), trimmed*
   salt
   freshly ground pepper
10 *Belgian endives*
   sesame oil
2 to 3 *heads tender young lettuce*

Marinade

1 *cup soy sauce*
1 *cup mirin (sweet sake)*
½ *cup chopped scallions*
1 *tablespoon dried red chili flakes*
2 to 3 *garlic cloves, finely chopped*

Sauce

¼ *cup each of coarsely chopped mint, cilantro and parsley*
½ *cup peanut oil*
½ *cup rice wine vinegar*
2 *egg yolks*
   a little Chili Oil (page 32)
   salt
   freshly ground pepper

Vinaigrette

½ *cup peanut oil*
¼ *cup rice wine vinegar*
1 *teaspoon miso (soy bean paste)*
   salt

freshly ground pepper
1 teaspoon finely chopped fresh ginger

1.   Prepare the marinade: In a bowl, mix together all the marinade ingredients. Pour them over the lamb and let it marinate
for 30 minutes. Remove from the marinade and let stand until
ready to cook. Reserve the marinade for later use.
2.   While the lamb is marinating, prepare the sauce and the
vinaigrette. To make the sauce, combine all the sauce ingredients in a blender and purée. Strain into a bowl. To make the
vinaigrette, in a bowl whisk together all the ingredients. Correct
the seasonings.
3.   Season the lamb with salt and pepper and place it on a hot
grill. Grill medium rare, about 15 to 20 minutes; or cut the rack
into chops and sauté them in a pan over high heat for about 2
minutes on each side. (Cook the chops in several batches if
necessary, but don't crowd the pan.)
4.   Meanwhile cut the endives in half lengthwise and brush the
halves with sesame oil. Sprinkle with salt and pepper and grill
or sauté them in a pan for about 2 minutes on each side.
5.   Toss the salad greens with enough dressing to coat them
lightly.

PRESENTATION: Make an island of sauce on each plate. Place the
lamb in the center and the salad to the side. Serve the remaining
sauce in a separate bowl.

A whole, live baby lamb should weigh 40 to 50 pounds... no more. The carcass weighs about half of the live weight.

ROAST SADDLE OF LAMB SALAD

Sonoma County is one of the best regions for raising fine lamb as well as for producing fine wine.

Serves 4 for lunch or 8 as an appetizer

1 saddle of lamb (about 2 pounds)
salt
freshly ground pepper
6 tablespoons extra-virgin olive oil
2 teaspoons coarsely chopped fresh thyme leaves
2 tablespoons red wine vinegar
2 teaspoons Dijon mustard
4 heads of Kentucky limestone lettuce or 3 heads of Boston bibb lettuce
freshly grated Parmesan cheese

1.   Preheat the oven to 400 degrees F.
2.   Pull and cut away all the surface fat from the lamb. The lamb remaining should weigh about 1½ pounds.
3.   Place the lamb in a baking dish and sprinkle it with salt, pepper, 2 tablespoons of the olive oil and the thyme.
4.   Roast the lamb in the oven for 30 to 35 minutes. Remove the lamb and let it stand for 20 minutes to allow the juices to redistribute.
5.   Meanwhile, in a bowl whisk together the vinegar and mustard with salt and pepper to taste and whisk in the remaining olive oil.
6.   Place the greens in a salad bowl and toss them with the dressing. Arrange the greens on salad plates.

PRESENTATION: Place the lamb on a flat surface and cut it lengthwise into very thin slices. Arrange 4 to 6 slices of lamb over each serving of greens and sprinkle each serving with a little of the freshly grated Parmesan. Serve immediately.

WATERCRESS SALAD WITH BARBECUED CHICKEN BREAST

An ideal luncheon dish for spring or summer.

Serves 6

Mustard Vinaigrette

1 tablespoon Dijon mustard
1 teaspoon finely chopped fresh tarragon
1 tablespoon sherry wine vinegar
  salt
  freshly ground white pepper
1 cup almond or extra-virgin olive oil (or a mixture of both)

Salad

3 small whole chicken breasts
15 cloves garlic
1/4 cup fresh Italian parsley leaves
  salt
  freshly ground pepper
3 tablespoons extra-virgin olive oil
3 bunches watercress
1/2 pound mushrooms such as chanterelle, porcini or shiitake

1. Prepare the vinaigrette: In a small bowl, combine the mustard, tarragon, vinegar, salt and pepper. Whisk in the oil in a slow, steady stream. Taste carefully and correct the seasonings, including the mustard and vinegar. Set aside.
2. Preheat a grill or barbecue.
3. Cut the chicken breasts in half and set aside.
4. Peel the garlic, place it in a saucepan with water to cover

and bring the water to a boil. Drain and slice the garlic thin. Mix the garlic with the parsley and spread it underneath the skin of the chicken. Season the chicken with freshly ground pepper and salt, then brush it with olive oil.

5. Place the chicken, skin side down, on the grill and cook it for about 6 minutes on each side.

6. Wash and dry the watercress and remove the tough stems. In a big bowl toss the watercress with enough vinaigrette to coat it lightly.

7. Heat a large skillet and add 1 to 2 tablespoons olive oil. In it sauté the mushrooms over high heat about 4 minutes and season them with salt and pepper.

PRESENTATION: Divide the watercress among 6 salad plates. Arrange the mushrooms around it. Cut each chicken breast on the diagonal into 6 slices and arrange the slices over each plate of watercress.

WARM LOBSTER SALAD WITH WHITE TRUFFLES

This is an expensive but splendid salad that can be served as a luncheon entrée or as a first course at an elegant dinner. Using the lobster while it is still warm maximizes its flavor. If truffles are out of season, make a *beurre blanc* with fresh herbs to replace the truffle butter.

Serves 6

> *6 firm white truffles (black ones can also be used)*
> *6 small heads limestone lettuce or Boston bibb lettuce*
> *1 large ripe avocado, peeled*
> *2 medium tomatoes, peeled, seeded and coarsely chopped*
> *1 pound* haricots verts *(small French green beans), cooked* al dente *(see page 293)*
> *2 gallons* Court Bouillon *(see page 50)*
> *six live 1-pound lobsters*
> *2 tablespoons dry vermouth*
> *6 tablespoons heavy cream*
> *½ pound unsalted butter at room temperature*
> *salt*
> *freshly ground white pepper*
> *fresh lemon juice*

1.   Cut 24 nice slices from the truffles to garnish the plates. (If you are using the black truffles, sauté them in a skillet in a little butter over low heat and reserve them. If you are using white truffles, reserve them without sautéeing them first.) Cut the remaining pieces of truffle into julienne strips for the sauce, cover and set aside. In the center of 6 soup plates, arrange a mound of lettuce. Around each mound, arrange avocado slices, tomatoes, green beans and truffle slices.

2.   In a large pot, bring the *court bouillon* to a rapid boil, add

the lobsters and cook them for 5 minutes, or until the shells are bright red. Remove the lobsters from the liquid and let them cool slightly.

3.   While the lobsters are cooling, in a saucepan reduce the vermouth with the julienne strips of black truffles (white truffle should be added when the sauce is finished) and the cream until the mixture coats the back of a spoon. Whisk in the butter, a little at a time, until all of it has been incorporated. Season the sauce to taste with salt, pepper and lemon juice. If you are using white truffles, add them at this point. Keep the sauce warm.

PRESENTATION: Slice the lobster tails and arrange 1 over each mound of lettuce. Place the claw meat (in 1 piece if possible) in each corner of the plate and spoon the warm sauce over the salads.

Black truffles are best eaten warm, but white truffles are at their best at room temperature and not cooked.

COURT BOUILLON

Court bouillon is excellent for poaching fish for the health- and weight-conscious. I also like to use it as the liquid for steaming fish.

Makes approximately 2 quarts

> 2 *medium carrots*
> 2 *stalks celery*
> 1 *leek*
> 1 *sprig of fresh thyme or a pinch of dried thyme*
> 1 *bay leaf*
> 1 *teaspoon salt*
> ½ *teaspoon freshly ground pepper*
> 2 *quarts water*
> 2 *cups dry white wine*

1.   Slice carrots, celery, and leek into ¼-inch pieces. Place in the bottom of a saucepan.

2.   Add the remaining ingredients and bring to a boil. Boil for 20 minutes. Use as needed.

ASPARAGUS WITH DUCK PROSCIUTTO

The vinaigrette will lose color if made too much in advance. Use a good Italian prosciutto if you cannot get duck prosciutto.

Serves 4

> *Watercress Vinaigrette*
>
> 2 *bunches watercress*
> ¼ *cup strong red wine vinegar*

> 2 *tablespoons Dijon mustard*
> 1 *egg yolk*
> 1 *cup extra-virgin olive oil*
> *salt*
> *freshly ground pepper*

Salad

> 1 *pound large asparagus, trimmed and peeled*
> 6 *ounces duck prosciutto*

1. Prepare the vinaigrette: Blanch the watercress in boiling water for 10 seconds. Drain thoroughly and separate the leaves from the stems. In a blender blend the vinegar, mustard and egg yolk, then add the watercress leaves. Slowly add the olive oil. Season with salt and pepper to taste. Set aside.

2. Blanch the asparagus in a large quantity of rapidly boiling salted water for 5 to 7 minutes, or until *al dente*. Remove from the pot and plunge immediately into ice water to stop the cooking process. When cold, lift from the water and dry carefully on paper towels.

3. Slice the prosciutto paper thin and set aside.

PRESENTATION: Make a pool of watercress vinaigrette in the middle of each plate. Arrange the asparagus in the center of the plates, aligning the tips. Cover the bases of the asparagus with overlapping slices of the prosciutto. Serve immediately.

CHICKEN SALAD CHINOIS

Makes 2 entrée salads

Chinese Mustard Vinaigrette

　　1 egg yolk
　　2 teaspoons dry Chinese mustard
　¹/₄ cup rice wine vinegar
　　1 teaspoon soy sauce
　　2 tablespoons light sesame oil
　2 to 3 tablespoons peanut oil
　　　salt
　　　freshly ground pepper

Chicken Salad

　　　*one 3-pound chicken, its cavity filled with celery, carrot,
　　　　onion, garlic, bay leaf, thyme, salt and pepper*
　　2 ounces unsalted butter, melted
　　2 small heads or 1 medium head Napa cabbage
　　1 cup romaine lettuce, cut into ¹/₄-inch julienne strips
　8 to 10 snow peas, cut into ¹/₄-inch julienne strips
　　1 teaspoon black sesame seeds

1.　Prepare the vinaigrette: Place all the vinaigrette ingredients in a blender and blend until smooth. Correct the seasonings.

2.　Preheat the oven to 425 degrees F.

3.　Place the chicken on a rack in a roasting pan and baste it with some of the butter. Roast for about 1 ½ hours, or until just done. (The meat near the joints should still be very slightly pink.) Baste every 15 or 20 minutes with the butter and the drippings.

4.　Select 4 to 8 nice leaves from the Napa cabbage and reserve them. Slice the remaining cabbage into ¹/₄-inch julienne strips.

5.　Shred the meat from the breasts and thighs of the chicken.

6. Combine the chicken, cabbage, romaine and snow peas in a bowl and toss with enough of the vinaigrette to coat the salad nicely.

PRESENTATION: Arrange the reserved Napa cabbage leaves around the edge of a large serving plate. Mound the salad in the center and sprinkle it with the sesame seeds.

WILD MUSHROOM SOUP

Serves 4

½ *pound chanterelles or* shiitake *mushrooms*
½ *pound white mushrooms*
1 *lemon, cut in half*
1½ *tablespoons unsalted butter*
2 *medium shallots, minced*
1 *small sprig thyme, leaves only*
½ *bay leaf*
   salt
   freshly ground pepper
2 *cups heavy cream*
1½ *cups Chicken Stock (page 69)*
1 *teaspoon cornstarch dissolved in 1 tablespoon water*

1. Sprinkle all the mushrooms with the lemon juice. Slice ¼ cup of the chanterelles or *shiitake* mushrooms thinly and reserve. Cut the remaining mushrooms into very small cubes.
2. Melt 1 tablespoon of the butter in a heavy saucepan and in it lightly sauté the shallots. Add the chopped mushrooms, thyme

leaves and bay leaf and sauté the mixture over moderate heat for 10 minutes, or until the liquid disappears.

3.   Add salt, pepper, the cream and chicken stock and bring the liquid just to a boil. Reduce the heat and simmer the soup for 20 minutes.

4.   Whisk in the cornstarch mixture and simmer the soup, stirring constantly, for 10 minutes. Correct the seasonings.

5.   In a skillet, sauté the reserved sliced mushrooms in the remaining butter and season them with salt and pepper to taste.

PRESENTATION: Serve the soup in warm bowls and garnish with the sautéed sliced mushrooms.

FISH SOUP

Serves 6 to 8

1/4 *cup extra-virgin olive oil*
  3 *pounds fish bones, such as red snapper, sea bass or halibut*
  2 *medium onions, sliced*
  2 *carrots, peeled and sliced*
 10 *cloves fresh garlic, peeled*
  2 *branches fennel, sliced*
 10 *ripe tomatoes, sliced*
  1 *stalk celery, sliced*
  1 *large potato, peeled and sliced*
  2 *cups dry white wine*
large *pinch saffron threads*
2 to 3 *sprigs fresh thyme*
1/2 *bunch fresh basil, chopped*

> *light Fish Stock (page 70) or water to cover (about 3*
> *cups)*
> 2 *tablespoons Pernod*
>   *salt*
>   *freshly ground pepper*
>   *cayenne pepper*
>   *twelve ½-inch slices French bread. 1 per person plus*
>   *extras*
> 3 *small lobsters, and/or 1 pound medium shrimp or fish*
>   *fillets, or 36 to 48 mussels or clams—enough for 6 to*
>   *8 people*
>   *Rouille (page 60)*

1.   Heat a large heavy stockpot and to it add the olive oil. Add the fish bones and cook them over low heat, covered, until any flesh on them flakes from the bones. Add the vegetables and any shells from the shrimps, cover and cook over low heat until the vegetables sweat, about 10 minutes.

2.   Deglaze the pot with the wine, scraping up any particles sticking to the bottom of the pan. Stir in the saffron, thyme, basil.

3.   Add the fish stock or water, and let the mixture gently boil for 1 hour, then purée it in a food processor or pass it through a food mill. Pass the purée through a medium strainer into a clean stockpot. Stir in the Pernod. Season the base to taste with salt, pepper and cayenne. The soup should have a full-bodied flavor: If it seems weak reduce it over low heat to concentrate the flavor.

4.   Skim any fish oil from the top of the soup and reserve it to stir into the rouille.

5.   Toast the croutons in a preheated 350 degree F. oven until golden and then brush with rouille.

6.   Bring the soup to a boil. Add the shellfish and/or uncooked fish fillets to the soup, one variety at a time. Cook each until done, then remove from the soup and keep warm. (The lobsters

will take about 10 minutes and their shells will be bright red when done; medium shrimp will take 3 or 4 minutes to cook; fish fillets from 1 to 7 minutes, depending on their thickness [they should remain slightly underdone]; and the mussels and clams cook only for 3 to 5 minutes, until their shells open.)

PRESENTATION: Place 1 crouton in the bottom of large, shallow, heated soup plates. Then arrange the fish and/or shellfish around each crouton. Ladle the hot soup over all. Serve immediately. Pass additional rouille in a separate serving bowl.

CREAM OF LEEK AND CHERVIL SOUP
WITH WHITE TRUFFLES

White truffles should be cut at the last moment, or better yet, grated on top of the soup in front of your guests.

Serves 6 to 8

3 *leeks*
   one 6- to 8-ounce baking potato, peeled
2 *tablespoons unsalted butter*
5 *cups double-strength Chicken Stock (page 69)*
½ *cup fresh chervil leaves (reserve 2 tablespoons for dec-*
   oration)
1 *cup heavy cream*
   salt
   freshly ground white pepper
   fresh lemon juice
1 *large white truffle or 1 teaspoon Sevruga caviar per*
   serving

1.   Wash the leeks carefully and cut the white part into ¼-inch slices.

2.   Quarter the potato, then cut it into ¼-inch slices.

3.   In a large saucepan, melt the butter, add the leeks and cook over low heat for 5 minutes. Add the potato slices and cook 15 minutes more.

4.   Stir in the stock thoroughly, then bring it to a boil. Reduce the heat and simmer the soup base until the vegetables are very soft, approximately 45 minutes. Add the chervil and cook 15 minutes more.

5.   While the vegetables are simmering, in a small saucepan reduce the cream by half and reserve it.

6.   When the vegetables are done, remove them with a slotted spoon and purée them in a food processor or blender with a little of the cooking liquid. Return the purée to the rest of the liquid, and stir in the reduced cream. If necessary, reduce the soup over low heat to concentrate the flavors. Season to taste with salt, pepper and drops of lemon juice.

7.   Mince the remaining chervil leaves.

PRESENTATION: Ladle the soup into warm soup bowls and garnish each serving with chopped chervil leaves and shaved truffles, or Sevruga caviar.

Variation: This soup is also delicious served cold, but it must be thinned with a little chicken stock or milk and seasoned more highly. Serve in chilled bowls.

CREAM OF CORN SOUP WITH GULF OYSTERS

Serves 8

12 to 16 Gulf oysters, scrubbed clean
2 *cups* Mirepoix *(see page 294)*
1 *cup dry white wine*
4 *tablespoons (2 ounces) unsalted butter*
2 *cloves garlic, peeled and lightly crushed*
1/4 to 1/2 teaspoon dried red chili flakes
6 *cups double-strength Chicken Stock (page 69)*
4 to 6 ears fresh sweet corn, husked
1 *baking potato (6 to 7 ounces), peeled and diced*
1 *cup heavy cream*
salt
freshly ground white pepper
fresh lemon juice

1.   Place the oysters in a saucepan with 1 cup of the *mirepoix* and the wine. Cover and steam for several minutes, or until the oysters open. Strain the liquid through a fine sieve into a bowl, reserving it, and discard any oysters that did not open. Remove the oysters from their shells and reserve.

2.   In a large saucepan, melt the butter and sweat the remaining *mirepoix* with the garlic and chili flakes over low heat for 10 minutes.

3.   Add the chicken stock and reserved oyster liquid to the pan and bring to a boil. When the stock is boiling, add the ears of corn and cook 5 to 7 minutes, or until the corn is tender. Remove the ears and let them cool slightly. Reduce the heat so that the stock simmers. Cut the kernels from the cobs and reserve. Add the corn cobs to the soup and cook it slowly for 45 minutes more.

4.   Remove the corn cobs and add the potato and all but 1 cup

of the corn. Simmer 30 to 45 minutes, or until the potato is soft.

5.   While the vegetables are cooking, in a saucepan reduce the cream by half and reserve.

6.   When the vegetables are tender, purée the soup in a food processor or blender until it is creamy but letting the corn still give it a little texture.

7.   Return the soup to the pan and add the reduced cream. Season to taste with salt, pepper and lemon juice. Chill the soup until serving time if you are making it in advance.

8.   At serving time, reheat the soup if it has been chilled. Dice the oysters and add them to the hot soup with the reserved 1 cup corn. Heat through, about 1 minute. Taste and correct the seasonings if necessary.

PRESENTATION: Ladle the soup into hot bowls making sure that there are some oysters and corn in each bowl. Serve immediately.

Notes: You can substitute clams, cockles, or mussels for the oysters.

Adjust the amount of chili flakes to your taste If you wish the soup to be a little thicker, make a *beurre manié* (page 293) using masa harina in place of flour. Add enough of it to the soup to bring it to the desired consistency.

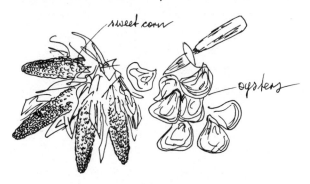

CRAYFISH BISQUE

Crayfish are native to the New Orleans and Sacramento areas, and fortunately they are shipped worldwide. In general, any good fish market will secure them for you if you order in advance.

Serves 6 to 8

Rouille

     2 *egg yolks*
3 or 4 *cloves garlic, finely minced*
     1 *tablespoon Dijon mustard*
   1/4 *teaspoon dried red chili flakes*
     1 *cup olive or almond oil*
   1/4 *teaspoon saffron*
3 to 4 *tablespoons crayfish stock*
       lemon juice
       salt
       freshly ground pepper

Crayfish Bisque

     5 *dozen live crayfish*
   1/4 *cup almond oil*
     1 *large carrot, chopped*
     1 *medium onion, chopped*
     1 *stalk celery, chopped*
2 or 3 *green leek leaves, sliced*
   1/4 *cup each of Cognac and Madeira*
     2 *cups dry white wine*
     1 *sprig fresh thyme*
4 to 6 *cloves garlic, unpeeled*
     1 *teaspoon whole black or white peppercorns*
     6 *tablespoons tomato paste*

2 *quarts Fish Stock (page 70) or Chicken Stock (page 69)*
1 *bay leaf*
1½ *cups heavy cream*
salt
pepper
lemon juice
cayenne pepper

1. Prepare the *rouille*: In a bowl, whisk together the egg yolks, garlic, mustard, and chili flakes. Whisk in the oil in a very slow steady stream until the sauce begins to emulsify. Add the remaining oil in a thin stream until all of it is incorporated. Add the saffron. Thin the sauce with the crayfish stock and season it to taste with lemon juice, salt and pepper.
2. Prepare the bisque: Remove the intestines of the crayfish by twisting and pulling the center section of the tail. Discard. Separate the head from the tails and reserve both.
3. Heat a heavy soup pot and to it add the almond oil. Add the crayfish tails and sauté them over high heat until they turn bright red, about 5 minutes. Transfer the tails to another container and set aside in a cool place.
4. Add a little more oil to the pot and sauté the crayfish heads with the carrot, onion, celery and leek leaves over moderate heat until the crayfish heads turn bright red and the vegetables are tender, about 10 minutes.
5. Deglaze the pot with the Cognac and Madeira. Then add the white wine, thyme, garlic, peppercorns and tomato paste. Stir over the heat for several minutes to mix well and add enough of the fish or chicken stock to make sure that the crayfish are swimming. Cover the pot and simmer rapidly stirring occasionally, for 1 hour. Add the bay leaf. Remove the heads with a slotted spoon to a food processor and purée them. Return the purée to the pot and simmer the mixture for another 10 minutes.

6.   While the soup is cooking, reduce the cream in a saucepan by half.

7.   Strain the bisque into a clean soup pot and reduce it until the flavor of the stock is quite strong.

8.   Remove the tail meat from the crayfish shells and reserve.

9.   Add the reduced cream to the base and continue to cook the soup for 15 minutes or so to blend the flavors. Strain the soup through a very fine *chinoise* or strainer lined with 2 layers of cheesecloth into another pot.

10.   Season the soup with salt, pepper, lemon juice and cayenne to taste and add the reserved crayfish tails. Heat for 3 to 4 minutes more.

PRESENTATION: Divide the crayfish tails among the soup bowls. Ladle the soup over the shellfish and put a spoonful of *rouille* in the center of each bowl.

CLAM AND MUSSEL SOUP

Serves 6 to 8

1 quart Fish Stock (page 70)
1 tablespoon unsalted butter
1 medium carrot, diced
½ medium onion, diced
2-inch piece celery, diced
1 quart heavy cream
18 to 24 fresh mussels, beards removed and scrubbed clean
12 to 16 small clams, cleaned
2 medium shallots, minced
½ bottle dry white wine

salt
freshly ground white pepper
lemon juice
1 cup mixed julienne strips of daikon, red pepper, cucumber skins and yellow or green bell peppers, stored in ice water until ready to use

1.   In a large saucepan, bring the fish stock to a boil and reduce it by half.
2.   In another saucepan, heat the butter, add the diced vegetables and sweat them over low heat, covered, for 10 minutes. Add the cream and bring it to a boil. Reduce the heat and simmer the mixture until the cream is reduced by half. Let the vegetables steep in the cream for another 30 minutes off the heat.
3.   Strain the cream into the fish stock and simmer for 10 to 15 minutes to marry the flavors. Season with salt, pepper and lemon juice to taste. Reserve.
4.   In a large saucepan, combine the mussels, clams, shallots and wine. Cover and steam over moderate heat for about 5 minutes. Remove any mussels or clams that have opened to a warm platter and continue to steam the shellfish, checking every few minutes to remove any that are open.
5.   When all the mussels and clams have been removed (discard any that do not open), reduce the liquid in the pan to almost a glaze. Strain the glaze into the stock along with any juices that have collected on the shellfish platter. Correct the seasonings.

PRESENTATION: Ladle the soup into warm soup bowls. Place 3 mussels and 2 clams in each bowl and arrange a nest of the vegetables, patted dry, in the center of each bowl. Serve immediately.

TORTILLA SOUP

This is our version of the tortilla soups typical of the American Southwest.

Serves 6 to 8

2 *tablespoons corn oil*
2 *Corn Tortillas (page 11), cut into 1-inch squares*
2 *tablespoons chopped fresh garlic*
1/4 *medium onion*
1 *small jalapeño pepper*
1 *pound ripe fresh tomatoes, peeled, seeded, and diced. (If tomatoes are out of season, use an equal portion of canned tomatoes.)*
2 *tablespoons tomato paste*
2 to 3 *teaspoons ground cumin*
2 *quarts double-strength Chicken Stock (page 69)*

Garnish

2 *Corn Tortillas (page 11)*
1 *avocado*
1 *large chicken breast, cooked*
1/2 *cup grated cheddar cheese*
1/3 *cup coarsely chopped fresh cilantro*

1. In a large soup pot, heat the oil, add the tortillas and cook them over low heat until they are slightly crisp.
2. Using a food grinder fitted with a medium disk, grind the garlic, onion, corn and jalapeño pepper together and add the mixture to the tortillas. Simmer until the vegetables are tender.
3. Add the tomatoes to the pot with the tomato paste and simmer the mixture for 10 minutes to bring out the flavor. Add the cumin and mix well.

4.   Slowly whisk in the stock, then simmer the soup until it is reduced by one third.

5.   Purée the soup in a blender until it is very smooth, then pass it through a fine strainer into a clean pot.

6.   Add salt, pepper and cumin to taste.

7.   Prepare the garnish: Preheat the oven to 350 degrees F. Cut the tortillas into julienne strips, place them on a baking sheet and bake them for 10 to 15 minutes, or until they are crisp. Peel and dice the avocado, cut the chicken into julienne strips, grate the cheese and chop the cilantro. Place each garnish in a separate bowl.

8.   At serving time, reheat the soup.

PRESENTATION: Add the chicken and avocado to the soup and heat. Pour the soup into a warm tureen, then ladle it into hot shallow soup bowls. Garnish with the cheese, tortilla strips and chopped cilantro. Serve immediately.

FRESH PUMPKIN AND OYSTER SOUP

Serves 6

>   *six ½-inch slices French bread, cut into small cubes*
> 2   *tablespoons clarified unsalted butter*
> 1   *pumpkin (6 to 8 pounds)*
>   *enough heavy cream to fill the pumpkin*
> 1   *teaspoon fresh thyme leaves*
>   *salt*
>   *freshly ground white pepper*
> 6   *oysters*
> ½   *cup finely chopped celery*

¼ cup finely chopped shallots
½ to 1 cup dry white wine
cayenne pepper
fresh lemon juice

1.   In a skillet, sauté the croutons slowly in the clarified butter. Reserve.

2.   Preheat the oven to 375 degrees F.

3.   Remove the top of the pumpkin, being careful not to pierce the shell, and remove the seeds.

4.   In a saucepan, bring the cream to a boil and pour it into the pumpkin. Add the thyme leaves, salt and pepper to taste.

5.   Place the pumpkin on a small towel in an ovenproof pan containing 1 inch of hot water. (The towel in the bottom is to prevent the pumpkin from sliding or tipping.) Bake the pumpkin in the oven for about 50 minutes, or until the flesh is soft. (Be careful not to puncture the shell when testing for doneness.)

6.   Meanwhile, in a covered saucepan steam the oysters, celery and shallots in the wine, covered, until the oysters open and render their juice. Remove the oysters from their shells and strain the juice through a fine sieve lined with cheesecloth into a bowl. Cut the oysters into 3 or 4 pieces if they are large and set aside.

7.   Pour the cream from the pumpkin into a food processor or blender. Scoop out the flesh of the pumpkin, leaving a ½-inch shell. Add the pumpkin flesh and oyster juice to the cream and blend until smooth. Put the purée in a saucepan, bring it to a boil and cook it over low heat for 15 to 20 minutes to concentrate the flavors. Season to taste with cayenne, lemon juice, salt and white pepper. Add the reserved oysters and let them heat in the soup for 30 seconds or so.

PRESENTATION: Place the pumpkin shell, firmly anchored on folded napkins or tea towels, on a platter. Fill the shell with the soup. At the table, ladle the soup into individual warmed soup bowls and serve the croutons on the side.

CRAB SOUP WITH FRIED
SPICY CRAB ROLLS

Serves 8

  2 *stone or rock crabs*
     peanut oil
  6 *ripe tomatoes, finely chopped*
  1 *onion, finely chopped*
  2 *carrots, finely chopped*
  1 *medium leek, finely chopped*
  4 *stalks lemongrass, finely chopped*
  3 *tablespoons chopped garlic*
  1 *tablespoon curry powder*
  2 *cups dry white wine*
  1 *gallon Fish Stock (page 70)*
½ *cup rice*

Crab Rolls

  2 *scallions*
  3 *cloves garlic*
     wonton skins for frying (16 small ones or 8 large ones)

Garnish

¼ *Japanese cucumber, cut into julienne strips*
  2 *stalks celery, peeled and cut into julienne strips*
  1 *leek, cut into julienne strips*
  1 *carrot, cut into julienne strips*
  2 *tablespoons peanut oil*

  1 *quart peanut oil*
  4 *tablespoons rice wine vinegar*
  3 *tablespoons sesame oil*
  1 *bunch cilantro, leaves only*

1. Preheat the oven to 450 degrees F.

2. Roast the crabs in a large heatproof casserole or roasting pan in a little peanut oil in the oven until red, about 15 minutes.

3. Add to the casserole all the finely chopped vegetables, garlic and curry powder and cook over low heat on top of the stove for 5 minutes, adding a little more oil if necessary.

4. Transfer the crabs and vegetables to a large soup pot. Deglaze the casserole or roasting pan with the white wine and pour the liquid into the soup pot. Add the fish stock and rice, bring to a boil and cook at a rapid simmer for 30 minutes. Remove the crabs and continue to simmer the mixture for 30 minutes more.

5. Strain the soup into another pot. In a blender purée the strained ingredients, then add the purée to the pot. Continue to simmer the soup slowly to concentrate the flavors.

6. Prepare the crab rolls: Crack the crabs and remove all the meat. Chop together the scallions and garlic cloves, mix with the crab meat and season with salt and pepper to taste. Divide the mixture among the wonton skins and roll them up like small cigars. Set aside.

7. Prepare the garnish: In a skillet, sauté the cucumber, celery, leek and carrot in the peanut oil until *al dente*. Remove from the heat and keep warm.

8. To fry the wontons: Heat the peanut oil in a large sauté pan until very hot, add the wontons, and fry until crispy and golden brown. Keep warm.

9. Taste the soup and correct the seasonings.

PRESENTATION: Finish the soup with the rice wine vinegar and sesame oil, then pour it into a warm tureen. Stir in the vegetable strips and sprinkle the soup with the cilantro leaves. Serve the warm crab rolls on the side.

CHICKEN STOCK

Makes 2 quarts

　　　　bones from 2 chickens, chopped into pieces
　　1　small carrot, peeled and sliced
　　1　small onion, quartered
　　1　small stalk celery, sliced
　　　　stems from 1 bunch parsley
3 to 4　green leek leaves, sliced (optional)
　　1　sprig fresh thyme or 1 pinch dried thyme
　　1　bay leaf
　　1　teaspoon white peppercorns
　　　　mushroom scraps (optional)
　　　　tomato scraps (optional)
　　4　quarts water, approximately

1.　In a stockpot, place the chicken bones, then add all the remaining ingredients, except the water. Add water to cover by 2 inches, bring it to a boil and reduce the heat. Simmer the mixture for 2 or 3 hours, skimming the surface scum from the stock as it collects.

2.　Strain the stock into a clean pot and degrease it thoroughly. Bring the stock to a boil and reduce it over moderate heat to 2 quarts.

3.　Use the stock immediately or let it cool to room temperature and refrigerate or freeze it until needed.

Note: To make *demi-glace* chicken, duck, veal, etc., reduce stock until it is slightly syrupy and the flavor is concentrated.

FISH STOCK

Use the skeletons of saltwater fish such as sole, John Dory, turbot, halibut or other very fresh non-oily fish for stock.

Makes 1 quart

> 2 *pounds fish skeletons, cut into pieces*
> 2 *tablespoons vegetable or other flavorless oil*
> 1 *small carrot, peeled and sliced*
> ½ *onion, sliced*
> 1 *small stalk celery, sliced*
> 2 *cups dry white wine*
> 1 *bouquet garni (see page 293)*
> 1 *quart water, approximately*

1.   Clean the fish bones under cold running water, removing the gills from the head and any traces of blood on the frames.
2.   In a large saucepan, heat the oil. In it sweat the fish bones and vegetables over low heat, covered, for 10 minutes, stirring once or twice to prevent them from browning.
3.   Deglaze the pan with the wine, then add enough water to cover the bones and vegetables by 2 inches. Add the bouquet garni and bring the liquid to a boil. Skim the froth from the surface, reduce the heat and simmer the stock for 20 to 25 minutes.
4.   Strain the stock into a clean saucepan. Bring it to a boil and reduce it over moderate heat to 1 quart.

Note: Fish stock will keep in the refrigerator for 2 to 3 days or frozen for 2 to 3 weeks. After that time the flavor begins to fade.

BROWN VEAL STOCK

Makes ½ gallon stock,
or 1 quart demi-glace

10 pounds veal bones, cut into 2-inch pieces
2 onions, quartered
2 carrots, coarsely chopped
1 stalk celery, coarsely chopped
1 leek, coarsely chopped
2 tomatoes, quartered
2 bay leaves
1 teaspoon black peppercorns
2 sprigs thyme
1 head garlic, halved (optional)
1 gallon water

1.   Preheat the oven to 450 degrees F.
2.   Spread the bones and onions in a single layer in a large roasting pan and place in the oven. Turn the bones as they brown until they are a dark golden brown on all sides. Transfer the bones to a large stockpot. Add the vegetables, bay leaves, peppercorns, thyme and garlic, if desired.
3.   Pour off the fat from the roasting pan, then deglaze the pan with 2 cups of the water, scraping up any particles sticking to the bottom of the pan. Add this liquid to the stockpot and pour in enough water to cover the bones by 2 inches. Bring the water to a boil, reduce the heat and let the mixture simmer at least 6 hours and as long as 24 hours, skimming the foam and fat as necessary.
4.   Strain the liquid through a sieve into a clean stockpot. Remove any last traces of foam or fat. Bring the stock to a boil and reduce it over low heat until the flavor is full-bodied. There should be about 1 gallon. To make veal *demi-glace*, reduce the stock by half.

5.   Refrigerate the stock for 2 to 3 days or freeze it in small quantities. It will freeze well for 2 to 3 months. *Demi-glace* will keep up to 1 week in the refrigerator and in the freezer for 2 to 3 months.

Note: Veal stock can be used instead of brown duck stock or lamb stock. It has a neutral flavor.

Pasta

Gone are the days when pasta belonged to Italian menus alone. Actually pasta originated with the ancient Chinese. It appeared later in Italy and developed in a different direction. Many other nations have embraced it. Escoffier wrote recipes using macaroni, noodles, and ravioli in ways that practically shouted, "Vive la France!" Various forms of pasta are also traditional in Central and Eastern Europe, Greece, Spain, Israel, Japan, and elsewhere. It is without question a universal favorite.

There is no reason why pasta cannot reflect American culinary practices as well. For the daily special at Spago, we might present a rare mesquite-grilled duck breast fanned out around a savory tangle of fettuccine. (At Chinois, the same duck breast might be sautéed with sesame oil, garlic, scallions, and ginger, and matched up with spicy angel hair.) Another day could bring ravioli plump with gravlax from Columbia River salmon, or perhaps a fettuccine featuring California's homegrown baby vegetables and herbs. Meat, fish, fowl, vegetables—all take gladly to pairing with pasta.

This chapter deals with a number of techniques for and approaches to pasta that illustrate its great versatility, but it is far from exhaustive. A top-quality pasta machine is an invaluable piece of equipment. Of the many models on the market, I prefer those that shape the dough by rolling rather than extrusion, as the texture of rolled pasta tends to be smoother and more uniform. A good machine is an investment that, with proper care, will reward you with many years of service.

Certain procedures in pasta cookery are absolute law, designed to produce perfect results and to preserve the sanity of the cook. There must be plenty of well-salted water in your pot, about one gallon plus 1 teaspoon salt per pound of pasta, with a few tablespoons of olive oil added to help prevent the pasta from sticking. If you are a "well-stocked" cook, by all means, use chicken stock instead of water for a wonderful extra taste dimension (you can omit the olive oil in this case, as the stock already contains a bit of fat). Whichever you use, the liquid must be kept at a rapid boil throughout the cooking process; cover the pot if the boiling stops when you add the pasta. Stir the pasta when you drop it in and several times thereafter to keep it from sticking, and don't let it go past the "al dente" stage (remember that it will continue to cook a little after it has been drained). The last thing to do is to rinse the pasta with hot water—this is the final step in keeping the pasta noodles separated—and then to toss it with the sauce. Serve the pasta at once. Pasta is impatient; the thin types, in particular, soon tire of good behavior on the plate and conspire to cling together in a gooey, inedible glob!

This brings to mind an unforgettable moment in Spago history. I had just prepared some pasta for one of L.A.'s best-known food critics, who continued a conversation with her companion for about fifteen minutes after it was brought to table. When she finally dug in her fork, both pasta and plate lifted off the table! Then the plate fell back down with a thud. Needless to say, we replaced it in a hurry with hot, fresh pasta. When cooking for family and friends, tell them to throw etiquette to the wind and start eating their pasta right away when served. They will thank you for it.

Pasta is truly the dish that has it all: It can play the role of appetizer, entrée, or cold salad. It can be rustic or refined; it can impress the most discriminating dinner guest, or provide the basis for popular, nourishing family meals when combined with complete proteins. Let the season, the availability of ingredients, and your own pioneering spirit help you to explore its endless potential.

ANGEL HAIR PASTA WITH
GOAT CHEESE AND BROCCOLI

At Spago in the summertime we use fresh basil in this recipe instead of thyme.

Serves 4 to 6

12 *ounces Regular Pasta Dough (page 98), cut into ⅛-inch noodles*
   extra-virgin olive oil
½ *pound tiny broccoli flowerettes*
¾ *cup double-strength Chicken Stock (page 69)*
 1 *teaspoon fresh thyme leaves, plus 4 to 6 sprigs for garnish*
   freshly ground pepper
 3 *tablespoons unsalted butter*
 4 *ounces chèvre (goat cheese), crumbled*
   salt
 1 *tablespoon toasted pine nuts*

1. Bring a large pot of water to a boil with a little olive oil.
2. In a skillet, sauté the broccoli in a little olive oil for 1 minute, or until just crispy and add the stock. Bring it to a boil.
3. Add the thyme leaves, pepper, butter and goat cheese and whisk together until the cheese melts. Remove the skillet from the heat and keep the sauce warm.

4.   Add some salt to the boiling water, then the pasta and cook it until *al dente*. Drain the pasta and rinse it under hot water.

5.   Add the pasta to the sauce and toss to distribute the sauce and broccoli evenly. Season to taste with salt and pepper.

PRESENTATION: Divide the pasta among warm appetizer plates. Garnish each serving with a sprig of thyme and some of the toasted pine nuts.

ANGEL HAIR PASTA WITH SMOKED SALMON AND GOLDEN CAVIAR

Serves 4

> 8 *ounces Regular Pasta Dough (page 98), cut into* ⅛-*inch noodles*
> *extra-virgin olive oil*
> ½ *cup heavy cream*
> *freshly ground white pepper*
> *salt*
> 3 *ounces smoked salmon, cut into julienne strips*
> 2 *ounces golden caviar*
> 1 *tablespoon minced chives or chervil leaves*

1.   Bring a large pot of water to a boil with a little olive oil.

2.   Pour the cream into a large skillet. Add the pepper. Just before cooking the pasta, bring the cream to a boil and remove the skillet from the heat.

3.   Add a little salt to the boiling water, then the pasta and cook it until *al dente*. Drain and rinse the pasta quickly under hot water.

4.   Toss the pasta with the hot cream and the smoked salmon and heat the mixture through. Stir in half the caviar and correct the seasonings.

PRESENTATION: Divide the pasta among 4 warm appetizer plates and garnish each serving with the remaining caviar and a light sprinkling of minced chives or chervil leaves.

It is also very good to use black caviar like Sevruga or Oscetra to make this even more luxurious and colorful.

FETTUCCINE WITH MUSHROOMS

Serves 4

8 ounces *Regular Pasta Dough (page 98), cut into ¼-inch noodles or "stripes"*
1 *tablespoon extra-virgin olive oil*
2 *tablespoons unsalted butter*
1 *medium shallot, minced*
4 *ounces* shiitake *mushrooms, sliced*
4 *ounces oyster mushrooms, sliced*
2 *tablespoons port*
½ *cup Chicken Stock (page 69)*
½ *cup heavy cream*
   freshly ground white pepper
   salt
6 *ounces* enoki *mushrooms, ends trimmed*

1.   Bring a large pot of water to a boil with a little olive oil.

2.   Meanwhile, heat a heavy sauté pan large enough to hold the mushrooms, sauce and pasta. Add the butter and in it sauté the shallot, the *shiitake* and oyster mushrooms over high heat for 3 to 4 minutes.

3.   Add the port and continue to cook the mixture until the liquid evaporates. Add the stock and cream, bring the liquid to a boil and reduce it over moderate heat until slightly thickened. Season with salt and pepper to taste. Add the *enoki* mushrooms and keep the sauce warm.

4.   Add a little salt to the boiling water, then the pasta and cook it until *al dente*. Drain and rinse quickly under hot water.

5.   Add the pasta to the sauce, toss well and correct the seasonings.

PRESENTATION: Divide the pasta among warm appetizer plates and serve immediately.

Note: If fresh oyster or *shiitake* mushrooms are not available, substitute cultivated mushrooms, Japanese tree mushrooms, chanterelles or whatever wild mushrooms are available to you.

PIGEON BREASTS CHINOIS

Serves 6

3 ounces Regular Pasta Dough (page 98), cut into ⅛-inch noodles
1 small head iceberg lettuce
3 whole young pigeons
   extra-virgin olive oil
   salt

freshly ground pepper
1 *teaspoon minced fresh ginger*
light sesame oil
4 *tablespoons rice wine vinegar*
4 *tablespoons (2 ounces) unsalted butter*

1.   Core the lettuce and reserve 6 nice outside leaves. Cut the remaining lettuce into julienne strips and reserve.

2.   Remove the breast meat from the pigeons, reserving the bones for another use.

3.   Bring a pot of water to a boil with a little olive oil.

4.   As the water heats, season the pigeons with salt, pepper and ginger.

5.   Heat a heavy sauté pan and add the sesame oil. In it sauté the pigeon breasts over high heat until medium rare, approximately 4 minutes per side. Remove the breasts from the pan and keep them warm. Pour off any fat from the pan and deglaze the pan with the vinegar. Then whisk in half the butter, a little at a time, and correct the seasonings. Strain the sauce and reserve in a warm spot.

6.   Add a little salt to the boiling water, then the pasta and cook until *al dente*. Drain and rinse quickly under hot water. Melt the remaining butter in the pot and reheat the pasta in it.

PRESENTATION: Place the reserved lettuce leaves on each of 6 appetizer plates. Fill them with the julienne strips of lettuce. Top with the hot pasta. Slice each pigeon breast into 4 or 5 nice slices and place on top. Spoon a little sauce over each serving.

one of my original recipes for Chinois on Main, inspired by the traditional minced squab.

CHANTERELLE RAVIOLI WITH
GRILLED CHANTERELLES

Serves 4

¾ pound (½ recipe) Regular Pasta Dough (page 98)
1 pound chanterelles
5 tablespoons unsalted butter
4 sprigs fresh thyme leaves
2 medium shallots, minced
salt
freshly ground pepper
½ cup heavy cream
2 eggs
1 tablespoon extra-virgin olive oil
1 cup double-strength Chicken Stock (page 69) or Duck
Stock (page 34)
1 tablespoon fresh Italian parsley, finely chopped

1.   Clean the chanterelles with a soft brush or a clean, damp cloth. Reserve 12 small chanterelles or, if the mushrooms are large, cut 3 of them into quarters and reserve. Coarsely chop the remaining mushrooms.
2.   Heat a heavy sauté pan and add 1 tablespoon of the butter. In it sauté the chopped mushrooms with half the thyme, the shallots and a little salt and pepper over moderate heat until the liquid evaporates. Add the cream and reduce it to a thick purée. Remove the pan from the heat and stir in 1 of the eggs until well combined. Season to taste with salt and pepper.
3.   Beat the remaining egg lightly to make an egg wash. Then, on a floured surface roll out the pasta dough in 2 sheets as thin as possible. Brush 1 of the sheets with some of the egg wash.
4.   Using a teaspoon, space evenly 24 small mounds of the chanterelle mixture on the egg-washed pasta. Cover with the

second sheet of pasta and press the dough down around the mounds of chanterelle mixture to seal the dough.

5.   Cut the ravioli into two-inch squares with a special ravioli cutter, a pastry wheel or sharp knife and transfer the packets to a baking sheet heavily dusted with semolina and refrigerate until needed (2 days maximum).

6.   Bring a large pot of water to a boil with a little olive oil.

7.   As the water heats, season the reserved chanterelles with olive oil, salt and pepper. Then grill them over charcoal or sauté them over very high heat for 4 to 5 minutes. Reserve.

8.   In a saucepan reduce the stock by half. Add the remaining thyme leaves, the remaining butter and salt and pepper to taste.

9.   Add a little salt to the boiling water, then the ravioli and cook them for 4 to 5 minutes. Drain and rinse quickly under hot water. Add the ravioli to the sauce, bring it to a simmer and remove it from the heat.

PRESENTATION: Divide the ravioli and sauce among heated soup dishes. Garnish each serving with some of the grilled chanterelles and a little of the chopped parsley. Serve immediately.

When selecting mushrooms, make sure they are firm and dry.

PASTA WITH SWEETBREADS
AND ARTICHOKES

Serves 4

> 8 *ounces Regular Pasta Dough, (page 98), cut into ⅛-inch noodles*
> 4 to 6 *ounces sweetbreads*
> ½ *teaspoon peppercorns*
> ½ *bay leaf*
> ¼ *medium onion, chopped*
> ½ *medium carrot, chopped*
> ½ *stalk celery, chopped*
> 1 *sprig parsley*
> 1 *sprig thyme*
> *salt*
> *freshly ground white pepper*
> 4 *medium artichokes*
> 1 *lemon, halved*
> 2 *tablespoons olive oil*
> *flour*
> 3 *tablespoons unsalted butter*
> 1 *cup Chicken Stock (page 69)*
> 1 *ounce blue cheese or well-aged goat cheese, crumbled*

1.   Prepare the pasta: Let it dry on a tray dusted generously with semolina until you are ready to use it, as much as 24 hours in advance.

2.   Soak the sweetbreads in cold water overnight. Drain and rinse under cold water.

3.   Bring 6 cups of water to a boil in a large pot with the peppercorns, bay leaf, onion, carrot, celery, parsley, thyme and a pinch of salt. Add the sweetbreads and cook them 3 to 4 minutes, or until medium rare. Drain and plunge them into a bowl of ice water to stop the cooking. When they are cold, peel

away the membranes and remove the tubes and extra tissue. They will separate into pieces as you clean them. Reserve.

4.   With a small knife, trim the artichokes, removing leaves, to expose the bottoms and rub the bottoms with lemon juice. Cook the artichoke bottoms in boiling salted water until barely tender, then plunge them into cold water. When they are cool, drain and pat dry. Cut the bottoms into ¼-inch slices and reserve.

5.   Bring a large pot of water to a boil with 1 tablespoon olive oil.

6.   As the water heats, prepare the sweetbreads as follows: Cut each piece into 3 or 4 scallops and season both sides with salt and pepper. Dust lightly with flour, shake off the excess, and set aside.

7.   Heat a heavy sauté pan until very hot and add to it 1 tablespoon each of olive oil and butter. In it sauté the artichokes until lightly browned and remove from the pan. Season them with salt and pepper. Drain any excess oil from the pan, then deglaze it with the chicken stock. Add the cheese and reduce by one third. Keep the sauce warm.

8.   Heat another sauté pan and add the remaining butter. When the butter is very hot, sauté the sweetbreads in it until golden brown on both sides. Drain on paper towels. Keep hot.

9.   Add a little salt to the boiling water, then the pasta and cook until *al dente*. Drain and rinse quickly under hot water. Add the pasta to the sauce and heat through.

PRESENTATION: Fan a few artichoke slices around the edges of 4 warm appetizer plates. Arrange the pasta in the center of each plate and top with the sautéed sweetbread scallops.

SPICY PASTA WITH WILD MUSHROOMS AND GRILLED DUCK BREASTS

Serves 4

8 to 10 *ounces Spicy Pasta Dough (page 99), cut into ½-inch
            noodles
            extra-virgin olive oil*
      1 *large shallot, minced*
      1 *cup dry white wine*
      1 *sprig tarragon, plus a few whole leaves for garnish*
     ¼ *cup Chicken Stock (page 69)*
     ½ *cup heavy cream*
    10 *tablespoons (5 ounces) unsalted butter, softened*
      4 *duck breasts, boned
            salt
            freshly ground black pepper*
     ½ *pound fresh chanterelles,* cêpes, *porcini,* shiitake, *Jap-
            anese tree mushrooms, oyster or abolne mushrooms, or
            cultivated mushrooms*
     ¼ *teaspoon dried red chili flakes*

1.   Bring a large pot of water to a boil with a little olive oil.
2.   In a saucepan over medium heat reduce the shallot, wine and tarragon sprig to 2 tablespoons. Add the stock and reduce by half. Add the cream and reduce until slightly thickened. Whisk in 8 tablespoons of the softened butter, a little at a time and correct the seasonings. Strain the sauce into a clean sauce-pan, set aside and keep warm.
3.   Brush the duck breasts with olive oil and season them with salt and pepper. Grill or sauté the breasts over high heat for 4 to 5 minutes, or until they are medium rare. Slice the duck breasts in scallops. Keep warm.
4.   Season the mushrooms with a little salt and sauté them in a skillet in the remaining butter over high heat. Add the chili

flakes and combine well. Remove the skillet from the heat and keep warm.

5. Add some salt to the boiling water, then the pasta and cook it until *al dente*.

6. Drain the pasta and rinse it quickly under hot water. Return the pasta to the pan and toss it with the sauce and mushrooms, adding any juices rendered from the duck.

PRESENTATION: On each of 4 warm plates arrange the 1 sliced duck breast, like petals, around a serving of the pasta.

FRESH HERB PASTA WITH GRILLED TROUT

Serves 4

½ *recipe Fresh Herb Pasta Dough (page 100), cut into ½-inch "stripes" or noodles*
2 *whole trout or salmon trout*
extra-virgin olive oil
freshly ground black pepper
2 *sprigs fresh thyme*
1 *small red bell pepper, cut into ¼-inch julienne strips*
1 *small yellow bell pepper, cut into ¼-inch julienne strips*
1 *cup dry white wine*
1 *shallot, minced*
½ *cup Fish Stock (page 70)*
¼ *cup heavy cream*
4 *tablespoons (2 ounces) unsalted butter*
salt
freshly ground white pepper

1.   Skin and bone the fish and rub them with olive oil. Sprinkle with freshly ground pepper and half the thyme leaves, cover and refrigerate until cooking time.

2.   Bring a large pot of water to a boil with a little olive oil.

3.   Heat a skillet and add 1 to 2 tablespoons olive oil. When it is hot, sauté in it the red and yellow peppers until tender-crisp. Transfer the peppers to a plate and keep them warm.

4.   In a saucepan, reduce the wine with the shallot to a glaze. Add the fish stock, reduce it by half, then add the cream and reduce it slightly.

5.   Whisk in the butter, a little at a time. Strain the sauce, add the remaining thyme leaves and season to taste with salt and white pepper. Set the sauce aside.

6.   On a heated grill or in a hot broiler, cook the fish for 2 to 3 minutes per side. Do not overcook. Transfer the fish to a plate. Keep warm.

7.   Add a little salt to the boiling water, then the pasta and cook until *al dente*. Drain and rinse it quickly under hot water. Return the pasta to the pan and toss with the sauce and the peppers.

PRESENTATION: Divide the pasta among 4 warm dinner plates. Place half a fish on each plate. Serve immediately.

Note: Sometimes the pasta absorbs the sauce; if it is too dry add a little more cream or fish stock.

Strong herbs like the ones we use at Spago give the pasta a nice green color and a pleasant flavor.

LOBSTER RAVIOLI WITH FRESH DILL SAUCE

Serves 6 to 8

1 recipe Regular Pasta Dough (page 98)
1 or 2 eggs, beaten lightly, for egg wash
  semolina

Mousse

1 pound fresh sea scallops, side muscles removed (see page 7)
1 egg
1 cup very cold heavy cream
½ teaspoon cayenne pepper
1 tablespoon chopped fresh dill
1 teaspoon salt
1 teaspoon freshly ground white pepper
1 small lobster, cooked

Sauce

2 cups dry white wine
1 bunch fresh dill
2 large shallots, minced
1 cup heavy cream
1 pound unsalted butter
  salt
  freshly ground white pepper
  fresh lemon juice

Vegetables

2 tablespoons unsalted butter
1 carrot, cut into julienne strips
1 stalk celery, cut into julienne strips
1 leek, white part only, cut into julienne strips

salt
freshly ground white pepper
reserved dill and lobster meat

1.   Prepare the mousse: In a food processor purée the scallops with the egg. With the motor running, slowly pour in the cream, then add the cayenne, dill, salt and pepper. Transfer the mousse to a bowl and chill, covered.

2.   Remove the meat from the lobster tail and claws and dice it fine. Fold ¼ of the meat into the mousse. Reserve the remaining meat for the sauce.

3.   On a floured surface, roll the pasta as thin as possible. Brush half of the dough with the egg wash. On it place 30 mounds of the mousse, 3 inches apart. Cover the mounds with the unegg-washed pasta sheet and press the dough together around each ravioli. With a ravioli cutter or a large, sharp knife cut the ravioli apart. Dust a tray with semolina and place the ravioli on the tray. Refrigerate.

4.   At dinnertime, while you make the sauce, bring a large pot of water to a boil with a little oil.

5.   Prepare the sauce: In a saucepan, reduce the wine with 1 sprig of the dill and the minced shallot until ¼ cup liquid remains. Add the cream and reduce it by half. Slowly whisk in the butter, a little at a time, until all of it is incorporated. Season to taste with salt, pepper and lemon juice. Set the sauce aside and keep it warm.

6.   Chop the remaining dill sprigs into ¼-inch pieces, reserving 6 small sprigs for the final garnish. Set aside.

7.   Prepare the vegetables: Heat a sauté pan over medium heat and add the butter. When it foams, add the julienne strips of vegetables and sauté them until *al dente*. Season to taste with salt and pepper and reserve.

8.   Add a little salt to the water, then the ravioli and cook for 5 to 6 minutes. Cut 1 ravioli open to see if the mousse is done.

It should be barely cooked through as it will continue to cook in the sauce. Drain the ravioli.

9. Add the ravioli to the sauce with the vegetables and the reserved lobster meat and the chopped dill and heat just to the boiling point.

PRESENTATION: Divide the ravioli among heated dinner plates. Spoon the sauce over them and garnish each plate with a small sprig of dill in the center. Serve immediately.

RAVIOLI WITH FOIE GRAS AND TRUFFLES

Serves 6

   8 *ounces fresh foie gras*
      salt
      freshly ground white pepper
   1 *cup dry sherry*
   6 *black truffles*
   1 *recipe Regular Pasta Dough (page 98)*
1 or 2 *eggs, beaten lightly, for egg wash*
      semolina
      extra-virgin olive oil
   1 *cup Chicken Stock (page 69)*
  16 *tablespoons (8 ounces) unsalted butter at room temperature*
  ½ *cup julienne strips of carrots*
  ½ *cup julienne strips of leeks, white part only*

1.   Cut the foie gras into 30 small slices. Sprinkle it with salt and freshly ground white pepper and let the slices marinate in ½ cup of the sherry.

2.   Using a small very sharp knife, peel the truffles and cut them into about 50 slices. Chop the peel finely and reserve for the sauce.

3.   On a floured surface, with a pasta machine, roll out dough as thin as possible. This is very important—if the dough is too thick the foie gras will melt as the ravioli cooks.

4.   Brush ½ of dough with the egg wash. Place 1 slice of foie gras every 3 inches on the dough and top it with a truffle slice. Cover the slices with the remaining sheet of pasta and press the dough around each mound to seal it. Cut with a ravioli cutter or sharp knife into 30 squares. Dust a tray liberally with semolina and place the ravioli on the tray.

5.   At serving time, bring a large pot of water to a boil with a little olive oil.

6.   In a saucepan, reduce the remaining sherry with the chopped truffle peelings until thickened slightly. Add the stock, bring it to a boil and reduce it to 1 cup liquid. Slowly whisk in all but 1 tablespoon of the butter, a little at a time, over very low heat. Season the sauce to taste with salt and freshly ground pepper, then purée it in a blender.

7.   In a skillet, sauté the julienne strips of carrots and leek in the remaining butter until *al dente*. Season to taste with salt and pepper.

8.   Add a little salt to the boiling water, then the ravioli and cook them for 5 minutes. Remove the ravioli with a large slotted spoon and drain it well.

9.   Pour the sauce into a large saucepan. Add the ravioli and bring it just to a boil. Correct the seasonings.

10.   In a small saucepan, heat the remaining truffle slices in a little butter.

.   .   .

PRESENTATION: Arrange the ravioli on warm dinner plates. Sprinkle each serving with the julienne strips of vegetables and garnish with the warm truffle slices.

Thin slices of black truffles need only to be warm to release their perfume.

PUMPKIN RAVIOLI

Serves 4 to 6

8 *tablespoons (4 ounces) unsalted butter*
1 *pound fresh pumpkin, peeled and cut in 1-inch cubes*
2 *cups heavy cream*
½ *bay leaf*
2 *tablespoons minced fresh sage, plus 6 small leaves for garnish*
2 *teaspoons fresh thyme leaves*
2 *eggs, beaten*
  salt
  freshly ground white pepper
½ *recipe Spinach Pasta Dough (page 101) or Regular Pasta Dough (page 98)*
1 *egg, beaten lightly, for egg wash*
  semolina
2 *cups Chicken Stock (page 69) or light duck stock*
2 *shallots, chopped*

1.   Heat a sauté pan over low heat and add 4 tablespoons of the butter. When the butter is foamy, add the cubed pumpkin

and cook, stirring often to stop it from sticking and burning, until it softens and falls into a purée.

2. Turn the pumpkin into a saucepan, add half the cream and half the herbs and cook over low heat for approximately 1 hour, or until the purée is thick and the liquid has evaporated. Stir occasionally to prevent scorching. Remove from the heat and beat in an additional 2 tablespoons butter.

3. Whisk in the beaten eggs. Season to taste with salt and pepper and set aside to cool.

4. On a floured surface, roll out the pasta as thin as possible. Cut it into 2 sheets and brush 1 of them with egg wash. Using a teaspoon, place 24 equal mounds of the pumpkin purée on the egg-washed dough, 2 inches apart. Cover the mounded dough with the second sheet of pasta and press around the mounds of pumpkin to seal the dough.

5. Using a ravioli cutter or a sharp knife, cut the ravioli. Dust a tray with semolina and place the ravioli on it.

6. Bring a large pot of water to a boil while you make the sauce.

7. Prepare the sauce: In a saucepan, reduce the stock with the shallots to ½ cup. Add the remaining cream and reduce by half. Over low heat, whisk in the remaining 4 tablespoons butter, a little at a time, over low heat. Strain the sauce into a clean saucepan and add the remaining sage and thyme. Season to taste with salt and pepper.

8. Add the ravioli to the rapidly boiling water and cook for 4 to 5 minutes. Remove with a slotted spoon and drain. Add the ravioli to the sauce and bring just to the boil. Correct the seasonings.

PRESENTATION: Divide the ravioli among preheated soup dishes and spoon the sauce over them. Garnish each serving with a fresh sage leaf. Serve immediately.

· · ·

Note: A simple but delicious alternative sauce can be made from fresh unsalted butter, minced fresh sage and a little freshly grated Parmesan cheese.

BLACK PASTA WITH SMOKED SCALLOPS

Serves 4

　2 *red bell peppers, cut into ³/8-inch slices*
12 *tablespoons (6 ounces) unsalted butter*
12 *ounces sea or bay scallops*
½ *cup dry white wine*
　2 *tablespoons chopped thyme leaves*
　6 *ounces unsalted butter*
　　salt
　　freshly ground black pepper
　1 *pound Black Pasta Dough (page 102), cut into ½-inch "stripes" or noodles*

1. Bring a large pot of water to a boil with a little olive oil.
2. In a large skillet, sauté the red peppers in a little butter until tender.
3. Add the smoked scallops and sauté them for approximately 1 minute, or until barely heated through.
4. Remove the peppers and scallops to a plate and deglaze the skillet with the white wine. Reduce the liquid by two thirds.
5. Whisk in the remaining butter, a little at a time, over very low heat. Return the scallops and peppers to the skillet and season them with thyme, salt and pepper. Set aside.
6. Add a little salt to the boiling water, then the pasta and cook it until *al dente*. Drain and rinse quickly under hot water.

7.   Add the pasta to the scallop mixture and toss it gently to mix.

PRESENTATION: Divide the pasta among 4 warm plates and serve immediately.

Note: I like to make this recipe with smoked scallops, which I prepare myself; you can easily make them, too. Simply marinate the scallops for a couple of hours with a little salt, pepper, and thyme (or other herb). Get a very small fire—just a few coals, you don't want it hot—going in a barbecue. When the coals are gray, scatter on some soaked wood chips. Cover the grill rack with aluminum foil, place the scallops on it, place the lid on the grill and let the scallops smoke for 30 to 45 minutes, or until they turn light yellow. Be sure there's plenty of smoke but not much heat.

DAVID HARTMAN'S FRESH PASTA SALAD WITH MUSSELS AND CLAMS

Serves 4

   2 *shallots, finely chopped*
   2 *cups dry white wine*
  24 *mussels, beards removed and scrubbed clean*
  24 *clams, scrubbed*
 1/2 *cup extra-virgin olive oil*
   1 *teaspoon dried red chili flakes*
   6 *ounces Regular Pasta Dough (page 98), cut in 1/4- or 1/2-inch noodles*
   2 *ounces snow peas, cooked until tender-crisp*

4   baby carrots, cooked tender-crisp (cut in half lengthwise
    if they are more than a ½-inch in diameter)
6   scallions
4   stalks asparagus, peeled and cooked until tender-crisp
2   tomatoes, peeled, seeded and chopped
2   ounces tiny broccoli flowerettes, cooked until tender-
    crisp
¼   cup red wine vinegar
4   cloves garlic, finely chopped

1.   In a medium saucepan, bring the shallots and wine to a
boil. Add the scrubbed mussels and cook, covered, for about 3
minutes, or until they open. Remove. Repeat the process with
the clams. Discard any mussels or clams that do not open after
5 minutes of cooking. Reserve 4 mussels and 4 clams in their
shells for decoration. Remove the rest from their shells and
chill.
2.   In a saucepan, heat the olive oil until hot and add the chili
flakes. Remove from the heat and let cool.
3.   Bring a large pot of water to a boil with a little oil. Add a
little salt, then the pasta and cook until *al dente*. Drain and rinse
quickly under hot water. Toss with the chili oil.
4.   Cut the carrots, snow peas, scallions and asparagus into nice
slices.
5.   In a large bowl, toss together the pasta, mussels, clams, all
the vegetables, vinegar and garlic. Taste carefully and correct
the seasonings.

PRESENTATION: Arrange the pasta on dinner plates and garnish
each serving with the reserved mussels and clams.

REGULAR PASTA DOUGH

It is best to have the pasta dough as dry as possible because the noodles have a better texture. If the dough is too soft, knead in more semolina or all-purpose flour until the dough becomes quite firm. Since it is hard for small machines to roll pasta that is very firm, the pasta may have to be dried after rolling on a rack made for that purpose or over a broomstick that hangs between 2 chairs.

Makes 1 ½ pounds

1 ½ *cups semolina flour, finest grind*
1 ½ *cups all-purpose flour*
  2 *teaspoons salt*
  4 *eggs*
  2 *tablespoons extra-virgin olive oil*

1.   Place the flours in a food processor fitted with a metal blade. Add the salt, eggs and olive oil.
2.   Process until the dough begins to mass on the blade (about 1–2 minutes).
3.   Remove the dough from the processor and press it into a ball. Wrap in plastic and let rest at least 2 hours in the refrigerator before rolling and cutting. (Rolling the dough by hand is extremely tedious; with a small pasta machine and cutting attachment, you will save time and produce a much more uniform product.)

Note: The pasta can also be made by hand or in an electric mixer fitted with a dough hook. For each of these methods, mix the dry ingredients together first, make a well in the center, add the wet ingredients and mix them together slowly until everything is combined well. Wrap the dough in plastic.

SPICY PASTA DOUGH

Makes 1½ pounds

1 small red bell pepper, cored and sliced
1½ cups all-purpose flour
1½ cups semolina flour, finest grind
1 teaspoon salt
2 eggs
2 tablespoons chili oil (page 32)

1.   In a food processor, purée the red pepper and transfer the purée to a small bowl.

2.   Place the flours in the food processor with the salt, eggs and chili oil. Process until mixed. With the motor running add the puréed pepper through the feed tube and process until the mixture begins to hold together—it should be dry and still a little crumbly. If the dough becomes too soft, add semolina flour, a little at a time, until it stiffens.

3.   Remove the pasta and knead it into a ball. Wrap the dough in plastic and let rest at room temperature for at least 2 hours.

4.   When ready to roll the dough out, cut it into 4 or 5 pieces. Dip 1 piece at a time in semolina, then roll and cut it as desired, keeping the remaining dough covered so that it does not dry out.

FRESH HERB PASTA DOUGH

Makes 1½ pounds

1 tablespoon fresh thyme leaves
1 tablespoon fresh rosemary needles
1 tablespoon fresh marjoram or oregano
1 tablespoon fresh sage (about 2 leafy sprigs)
½ cup water
1½ cups all-purpose flour
1½ cups semolina flour finest grind
1 teaspoon salt
2 tablespoons extra-virgin olive oil
3 eggs

1.   Chop the herbs very fine. Bring the water to a boil in a very small saucepan, add the herbs and bring to a boil. Reduce the mixture over low heat to ¼ cup. Remove the pan from the heat, cover and let the "tea" steep for 15 minutes.

2.   Place the flours, salt, olive oil, eggs and herb tea in a food processor fitted with the metal blade. Process until the dough holds together when pressed. (It will seem quite dry.) Turn the dough out on to a work surface and knead it by hand until it forms a ball. Wrap in plastic and let rest for at least 2 hours at room temperature, or for several hours in the refrigerator.

3.   Cut the dough into 4 pieces and roll out 1 piece at a time as desired.

fresh herbs

SPINACH PASTA DOUGH

Makes 1½ pounds

½ *pound fresh spinach (about 1 bunch)*
1½ *cups semolina flour, finest grind*
1½ *cups all-purpose flour*
  1 *teaspoon salt*
  3 *eggs*
  2 *tablespoons extra-virgin olive oil*

1.   Wash the spinach carefully in 2 or 3 changes of water. Cut off 1 inch of the stems. Chop the leaves and purée them in a food processor. Put the purée in the center of a linen towel or napkin and squeeze the juice into a measuring cup. (Use a towel or napkin that you won't mind using only for this purpose because spinach juice stains.) There should be about ¼ cup juice. Stir 2 tablespoons of the spinach purée into the spinach juice and reserve. Discard the remaining purée.

2.   Combine the flours in the food processor with the salt. With the motor running, add the eggs, olive oil and enough of the spinach mixture through the feed tube so that the dough forms a ball when pressed together. Wrap the dough in plastic and let it rest at room temperature for at least 2 hours.

3.   Divide the dough into 4 pieces and roll and cut 1 at a time as desired. Keep the unrolled dough covered to prevent it from drying. Place any cut pasta on baking sheets that have been liberally dusted with semolina.

Notes: The unrolled dough should be refrigerated after it has relaxed for 2 hours. Plan to use it within 24 hours for best results. Cut pasta may be refrigerated up to 24 hours before using or it may be left to air-dry. For longer storage, freeze the cut pasta, then wrap it tightly in plastic and return to the freezer. It will keep 3 to 4 weeks if carefully wrapped.

BLACK PASTA DOUGH

The cuttlefish is a large Mediterranean *calamari* that weighs about 4 or 5 pounds and has an ink pocket that weighs about 5 ounces.

It is sold in most fish stores and is generally sold frozen. (The meat itself can be grilled or fried for salads or pasta.) I still have some friends who are upset with me because when I gave them this recipe for a large party they were having I didn't explain to them about the large *calamari*. They bought I don't know how many local small ones to get enough ink to make their black pasta.

Makes 1½ pounds

> *ink pocket from 1 cuttlefish*
> *3 cups semolina flour, finest grind*
> *2 teaspoons salt*
> *3 eggs*
> *¼ cup extra-virgin olive oil*

1.   Remove the pocket carefully from the cuttlefish. Measure out the ink and add to it an equal amount of water. In a saucepan, bring the liquid to a boil, pass it through a fine strainer, then let cool until needed. Freeze any unused liquid for future use.

2.   Place the flour and salt in a food processor. With the motor running, add the eggs, olive oil and enough cuttlefish ink (about ¼ cup) so that the dough forms a ball when pressed together.

3.   Remove the dough and press it into a ball. Wrap in plastic and let rest at room temperature for at least 2 hours.

4.   Divide the dough in 4 pieces and roll out 1 at a time. Keep unrolled pasta covered to prevent drying. Cut as desired. Refrigerate until ready to use.

. . .

Notes: Roll and use the dough within 24 hours for best results. For longer storage, freeze the cut pasta, wrap in plastic and return to the freezer for 3 to 4 weeks.

Pizza

I have never met anyone who didn't like pizza. For many, each mouthful reaches back to childhood, when it seemed there was no better food on the face of the earth. In recent years, pizza has taken a giant step forward. It is now seen on the menus of many fine restaurants, offering the chance to relive memories but on a more sophisticated level. At Spago, we have regulars like Kenny Rogers, who comes in with prosciutto pizza on his mind, and Linda Evans, who never starts a meal without her duck sausage pizza.

Pizza's image has certainly come a long way. It began humbly in Italy as a kind of bread; in fact, it was often made on bread-baking day, from a piece of the reserved dough. The pizza margherita, a classic marriage of mozzarella, parmesan and fresh tomatoes—not tomato sauce—was only one of many regional variations. Some enclosed a filling the way a large, flat calzone would do, or had extra ingredients kneaded into the dough itself. Some were just dough plain and simple, either baked or deep fried, with a sauce spooned over afterwards. But topping the dough with tomato sauce and cheese and various other toppings, a formula that would become one of the world's best-loved luncheon and snack foods, did not occur until later.

My own taste for pizza was developed in France, at a restaurant in Salon-de-Provence called Chez Gu. I was working at L'Oustau de Baumanière with my friend Guy Leroy at the time.

On our days off together we would celebrate with a light, informal dinner at Chez Gu, and it always included one of their pizzas. It was here, as we sat relaxing and talking, that our visions of starting a restaurant in America came to include a pizzeria right next door to the restaurant. Imagine our disappointment when we moved to Los Angeles and found that such an idea was unheard of in the States. Who would have guessed that, some six years later, restaurants would be serving pizza from one end of town to the other?

Don't let the new seriousness about pizza scare you away from making it at home: It's just as easy as it was in the old days. The dough only asks that you follow a few basic rules, and it will cooperate beautifully. When mixing it, add the yeast last to prevent the other ingredients from harming the yeast. Salt, especially, can slow down its action or even kill it. After the dough has been worked, it should be rolled into portion-size balls, covered with a kitchen towel and left for two or more hours in the refrigerator to lose its elasticity, which it must do if you are to stretch it out thin. Just let it stand for an hour at room temperature, and it will be ready to go.

A very hot oven is essential to produce a crust that is crisp on the outside and chewy within. (If your pizza has been baked in a slow oven, you might as well try a slice of cardboard!) Our pizzas at Spago always seem to come out best after the fire in the oven has been heating the bricks for three hours or more. Even without a brick oven, the home cook can get excellent results with a pizza stone, which distributes the heat evenly and does not scorch the crust as a baking sheet might do. A minimum of 45 minutes preheating will give you a pizza of professional caliber. But make sure it's eaten immediately, or you'll have a steamy, soggy crust, tough rubbery cheese and lots of leftovers!

Fresh cheeses, such as mozzarella, fontina, and the mild goat cheeses, are what you need for your pizza; Avoid the hard, salty types. Your herbs, too, should be fresh: They will be far more pungent and flavorful than dried herbs when baked on a pizza.

The other toppings are up to you. Know which of them should be precooked (artichoke bottoms, wild mushrooms and zucchini, for example, which take longer to cook than the pizza will) and which should be used raw (such as shrimp tails cut in half lengthwise, tomato slices, onions, and leeks cut into julienne strips). Then create your own combinations. Making the pizza is half the fun!

Almost any wine—a Champagne, a hearty country red, a rosé, or a *vin gris*—can be served with pizza, depending on the toppings. I personally like a red wine in most cases, since it is such a natural partner with cheese. But a shrimp pizza, for instance, would be better off with a Chardonnay, and a smoked salmon pizza with a Puligny-Montrachet. Beer also has its place; it stands up to very full-flavored or spicy ingredients.

Pizza is one of the most sociable of foods; it loves going to a party. A festive array of pizzas will please any crowd, and it makes great finger food when cut into small wedges. It leaves you time to enjoy the party, too. Just bake the pizzas ahead, leaving them slightly underdone, and freeze them (they will keep well for several days). Pop them right out of the freezer onto a pizza stone preheated in a 500 degree F. oven. You'll know it is done when the cheese comes alive with bubbles, about ten minutes later.

But don't wait for your next party to try it. Any time is the right time to turn your kitchen into a private pizzeria. Find out what you've been missing.

PIZZA DOUGH

Makes four 7- to 8-inch pizzas

> 3 *cups all-purpose flour*
> 1 *teaspoon salt*
> 1 *tablespoon honey*
> 2 *tablespoons olive oil*
> ¾ *cup cool water*
> 1 *package fresh or dry yeast*
> ¼ *cup warm water*

1. Place the flour in a food processor.
2. Combine the salt, honey, olive oil and the ¾ cup cool water in a small bowl or measuring cup. Mix well.
3. Dissolve the yeast in the ¼ cup warm water and let proof for 10 minutes.
4. With the motor running, slowly pour the salt and honey liquid through the feed tube. Then pour in the dissolved yeast. Process until the dough forms a ball on the blade. If it is sticky, add sprinklings of flour.
5. Transfer the dough to a lightly floured surface and knead until it is smooth. Place in a buttered bowl and allow the dough to rest, covered, for 30 minutes.
6. Divide the dough into 4 equal parts. Roll each piece into a smooth, tight ball. Place on a flat sheet or dish, cover with a damp towel and refrigerate.
7. One hour before baking, remove the dough from the refrigerator and let it come to room temperature.
8. Lightly flour a work surface. Using the fleshy part of your fingertips, flatten each ball of dough into a circle, about 6 inches in diameter, making the outer edge thicker than the center. Turn the dough over and repeat. Lift the dough from the work surface and gently stretch the edges, working clockwise to form

a 7- to 8-inch circle. Repeat with the other 3 pieces. Place the circles on a wooden peel or on baking sheets, and build the pizzas as desired.

Notes: To make the dough in an electric mixer fitted with a dough hook, place the flour in the bowl and add the ingredients in the same order as when using a food processor. Knead the dough in the machine until it forms a smooth ball. Place the dough in a buttered bowl and allow it to rest, covered, for 30 minutes.

To prepare by hand, place the flour on a work surface and make a well in the center. Add the wet ingredients and proofed yeast. Slowly incorporate the flour into the wet ingredients working from the center outward. When a dough forms, knead it on a floured surface until smooth. Place in a buttered bowl and allow the dough to rest, covered, for 30 minutes.

Note: You can also roll out the pizzas with a rolling pin, then inch up the edges with your fingers to form a little ridge.

BLACK FOREST HAM AND GOAT CHEESE PIZZA

Makes 4 pizzas

1 recipe Pizza Dough (page 110), divided into 4 equal pieces
extra-virgin olive oil, about 2 tablespoons
1 teaspoon dried red chili flakes
1 cup grated Italian fontina cheese
2 cups grated mozzarella cheese or an equal amount of fresh, sliced mozzarella
2 baby Japanese eggplants, sliced lengthwise to ¼-inch slices and grilled or sautéed in olive oil
1 cup cubed goat cheese
4 ounces Black Forest ham, cut into julienne strips
1 bunch fresh basil, chopped, with 1 sprig reserved for garnish

1.   Before you are ready to bake the pizzas, preheat the oven with a pizza stone inside to 500 degrees F. for 30 minutes.
2.   Roll or stretch the pizza dough, a quarter at a time, into a 7- to 8-inch circle.
3.   One at a time, place the pizza on a wooden peel (paddle), dusted lightly with flour or semolina.
4.   For each pizza, brush the dough with olive oil and sprinkle it with dried chili flakes according to how spicy you like your pizza. Arrange a quarter of the fontina and mozzarella cheese on the dough. Then add a quarter of the eggplant, goat cheese and ham. Sprinkle some chopped basil on top. Assemble the 3 remaining pizzas in the same way.
5.   Slide the pizza onto the stone and bake it for 10 to 12 minutes, or until the cheese is bubbling lively.

.   .   .

PRESENTATION: Remove the pizza from the oven and transfer it to a warm plate. Garnish with the basil sprig. Serve immediately, cut into wedges.

PIZZA WITH DUCK SAUSAGE

Makes 4 pizzas

Duck Sausages

2 duck legs, boned
8 ounces lean pork
8 ounces pork fatback or smoked pancetta
2 shallots, minced
5 cloves garlic, minced
1 teaspoon fresh rosemary
2 tablespoons Cognac
3/4 cup dry white wine
   salt
   freshly ground white pepper

Pizzas

1 recipe Pizza Dough (page 110), divided into 4 equal pieces
1 large red bell pepper, cut into julienne strips
2 tablespoons extra-virgin olive oil
2 tablespoons Chili Oil (page 32)
1 cup grated fontina cheese
2 cups grated mozzarella cheese
4 large cloves garlic, blanched for 30 seconds in boiling water
4 sprigs fresh oregano, leaves only
4 sprigs fresh thyme, leaves only
1 medium onion, thinly sliced

1.   Prepare the sausages: Remove the skin from the duck legs and reserve it in the refrigerator.

2.   Cut the deboned duck meat, pork, and fatback or pancetta into small pieces and in a bowl mix with the shallots, garlic, rosemary, Cognac and ¼ cup of the wine. Cover and refrigerate overnight.

3.   Put the duck meat mixture through a grinder with medium-sized holes. Then shape the ground meat into 2 fat sausages and wrap each in a reserved duck skin. (The duck skin may not cover the sausages completely—that's O.K.) Tie each sausage securely with kitchen string.

4.   Place the sausages in a roasting pan with the remaining wine and roast them in a preheated 350 degree F. oven for 1 hour and 15 minutes to 1 hour and 30 minutes. The sausages should be cooked through, but not dry. Remove the sausages from the pan and let cool. Refrigerate until needed.

5.   Slice the sausages ¼ inch thick.

6.   Prepare the pizzas: In a sauté pan, sauté the bell pepper in a little olive oil over high heat for 2 to 3 minutes.

7.   Before you are ready to bake the pizzas, preheat the oven with a pizza stone inside to 500 degrees F. for 30 minutes.

8.   Roll or stretch the pizza dough, a quarter at a time, into a 7- to 8-inch circle and place it on a lightly floured wooden peel.

9.   Brush the dough with the chili oil, then top it with a quarter of the cheeses, sautéed pepper, chopped garlic, fresh herbs, onion and sliced sausages. Assemble the 3 remaining pizzas in the same way

10.   Slide the pizza onto the hot stone and bake it for 10 to 12 minutes, or until the cheese bubbles and dances.

PRESENTATION: Transfer the pizzas to heated appetizer plates and serve immediately.

PIZZA WITH SMOKED SALMON
AND GOLDEN CAVIAR

Makes 4 pizzas

    1 recipe Pizza Dough (page 110)
3 to 4 ounces smoked salmon
    1 tablespoon minced chives
    4 tablespoons extra-virgin olive oil
    6 tablespoons sour cream or crème fraîche *(see page 293)*
    4 heaping tablespoons domestic golden caviar
    1 heaping teaspoon black caviar

1. Before you are ready to bake the pizzas, preheat the oven with a pizza stone inside to 500 degrees F. for 30 minutes.
2. Cut the salmon into paper-thin slices. Reserve.
3. Knead 2 teaspoons of the minced chives into the pizza dough. Roll or stretch the dough into four 8-inch circles. Place the pizzas on a lightly floured wooden peel.
4. Brush the centers of the circles to within 1 inch of the edge with olive oil.
5. Slide the pizza crusts onto the stone and bake 8 to 10 minutes. When they are golden brown, transfer them from the oven to a serving plate. Spread with the sour cream or *crème fraîche.*
6. Arrange the slices of salmon decoratively over the cream.
7. Place a spoonful of golden caviar in the center of each pizza, then spoon a little of the black caviar into the center of the golden caviar. Sprinkle the salmon with the remaining chives.

PRESENTATION: Place the pizzas on heated dinner plates and serve immediately.

ANOTHER PIZZA WITH SMOKED SALMON AND CAVIAR

Makes 4 pizzas

1 recipe Pizza Dough (page 110)
3 to 4 ounces smoked salmon
¼ cup extra-virgin olive oil
½ medium red onion, cut into julienne strips
¼ bunch fresh dill, minced, plus 4 small sprigs for garnish
⅓ cup sour cream or créme fraîche *(page 293)*
*   freshly ground pepper*
4 heaping tablespoons domestic golden caviar
1 heaping teaspoon black caviar

1.   Before you are ready to bake the pizzas, preheat the oven with a pizza stone inside to 500 degrees F. for 30 minutes.

2.   Cut the salmon into paper-thin slices. Reserve.

3.   Roll or stretch the dough into four 8-inch circles. Place the pizzas on a lightly floured wooden peel.

4.   Brush the center of each pizza to within 1 inch of the edge with olive oil and sprinkle it with some of the red onion. Slide the pizza onto the stone and bake it for 8 to 12 minutes, or until the crust is golden brown.

5.   Mix the dill with the sour cream or *crème fraîche* and freshly ground pepper to taste. Transfer the pizzas to heated dinner plates and spread them with the sour cream mixture.

6.   Divide the salmon, arranging it decoratively, on top.

7.   Place 1 tablespoon golden caviar in the center of each pizza, then spoon a little of the black caviar in the center of the golden caviar.

PRESENTATION: Garnish each pizza with a small dill sprig, and serve from the heated dinner plates.

SPICY CHICKEN PIZZA

If you like your pizza spicier, use more jalapeño pepper and brush the dough with chili oil instead of olive oil.

Makes 4 pizzas

  1 recipe Pizza Dough (page 110), divided into 4 equal pieces
2 to 4 tablespoons extra-virgin olive oil
  1 chicken skinned and boned, cut into finger-size "stripes" (strips)
  1 jalapeño pepper, seeded and minced
  1 cup sliced shiitake mushrooms
  1 small red bell pepper, cut into ¼-inch "stripes" (strips)
  ¼ cup chopped fresh cilantro, plus a little additional for garnish
     salt
     freshly ground pepper
  2 tablespoons olive oil or Chili Oil (page 32)
  1 cup grated Italian fontina cheese
  2 cups grated mozzarella cheese or an equal amount sliced fresh mozzarella
  ½ cup sliced scallions

1.   Heat a large sauté pan and add half the olive oil. Add the chicken, jalapeño, *shiitake* and bell pepper and sauté over high heat, adding more oil as needed, until the chicken is still a little pink inside. (It will cook more in the oven.) Season with salt and pepper to taste. Stir in the cilantro. Pour off any excess oil and set aside to cool.

2.   Before you are ready to bake the pizzas, preheat the oven with a pizza stone inside to 500 degrees F. for 30 minutes.

3.   Roll or stretch the dough, a quarter at a time, into a 7- to 8-inch circle and place it on a lightly floured wooden peel.

4.   For each pizza, brush the dough with olive or chili oil, then top it with a quarter of each of the cheeses. Arrange a quarter of the cooled chicken mixture over the top, and top it with a quarter of the scallions. Assemble the 3 remaining pizzas in the same way.

5.   Slide the pizza onto the hot stone and bake for 10 to 12 minutes, or until the cheese is dancing.

PRESENTATION: Slide each pizza onto a warm plate. Garnish with a little cilantro. Cut into wedges to serve.

PIZZA WITH SHRIMP AND SUN-DRIED TOMATOES

Makes 4 pizzas

    1 recipe Pizza Dough (page 110), divided into 4 equal pieces
    2 tablespoons Chili Oil (page 32)
    1 cup grated Italian fontina cheese
    2 cups grated mozzarella or an equal amount sliced fresh mozzarella
 1/4 cup blanched garlic, chopped
    1 medium red onion, thinly sliced
 1/4 cup chopped fresh basil, plus 4 small sprigs for garnish
    8 ounces (20 to 24 medium) shrimp, peeled
 1/4 cup sun-dried tomatoes thinly sliced

1.   Before you are ready to bake the pizzas, preheat the oven with a pizza stone inside to 500 degrees F. for 30 minutes.

2.   Roll or stretch the dough, a quarter at a time, into a 7- to 8-inch circle and place it on a lightly floured wood peel.

3.   For each pizza, brush the dough with chili oil. Top it with a quarter of the fontina and mozzarella, leaving a ½-inch border along the edge. Top the cheese evenly with a quarter of the garlic, red onion, basil, shrimp and tomatoes. Assemble the 3 remaining pizzas in the same way.

4.   Slide the pizza onto the hot stone and bake it for 10 to 12 minutes, or until the cheese is bubbling.

PRESENTATION: Slide the pizzas on warm plates, garnish with basil sprigs and serve immediately. Cut into wedges to eat.

LAMB SAUSAGE PIZZA

Makes 4 pizzas

   1 recipe Pizza Dough (page 110), divided into 4 equal pieces
      about 2 tablespoons extra-virgin olive oil
   1 cup sliced shiitake *mushrooms*
      salt
      freshly ground pepper
   1 cup grated Italian fontina cheese
   2 cups grated mozzarella cheese or an equal amount fresh sliced mozzarella
 16 baby zucchinis, halved lengthwise, or 1 medium zucchini, cut into bâtonnets (see page 293)
   6 ounces Lamb Sausage Filling (recipe follows)
 ¼ cup chopped fresh coriander, plus a little additional for garnish

1.   Before you are ready to bake the pizzas, preheat the oven with a pizza stone inside to 500 degrees F. for at least 30 minutes.
2.   In a sauté pan, heat the olive oil and in it cook the mushrooms over high heat until *al dente*. Season to taste with salt and pepper.
3.   Roll or stretch the dough, a quarter at a time, into a 7- to 8-inch circle and place it on a lightly floured wooden peel.
4.   Using a quarter of the remaining ingredients for each pizza, spread the fontina and mozzarella to within ½ inch of the edge of the dough. Arrange the zucchini on top, then distribute the mushrooms over it and dot with the lamb sausage. Sprinkle with coriander.
5.   Slide the pizza onto the hot stone and bake 10 to 12 minutes, or until the cheese is bubbly and the sausage is cooked.

PRESENTATION: Serve the pizzas on warm plates and garnish with a little fresh coriander. Cut into wedges.

LAMB SAUSAGE FILLING

The sausage can be cooked slightly ahead of time so the pizzas will have less grease.

Makes about 1½ pounds

    1 pound lean lamb shoulder, cut into 1-ounce cubes
    4 ounces pork fatback, cubed
    ¼ cup chopped coriander
    1 teaspoon cuminseeds, ground to a powder
    6 cloves garlic, chopped
    1 small onion, chopped

½ cup dry white wine
   salt
   freshly ground pepper

1.   Mix all the ingredients together in a small bowl. Cover and refrigerate overnight.
2.   Put the sausage mixture through a food grinder with a fine disk (small holes) and add salt and pepper to taste.

Note: It is not necessary to put the ground lamb into sausage casings. I prefer to just sprinkle the meat loosely on top of the pizza.

PIZZA WITH CHANTERELLES, EGGPLANT AND LEEKS

Makes 4 pizzas

1 recipe Whole Wheat Pizza Dough (recipe follows), divided into 4 equal pieces
1 pound eggplant
8 ounces chanterelles
extra-virgin olive oil
salt
freshly ground pepper
4 plum tomatoes cut into thin slices
1 medium leek, white part only
4 teaspoons extra-virgin olive oil
dried red chili flakes
12 ounces grated mozzarella cheese
4 ounces fresh goat cheese, cubed,
8 blanched cloves garlic, chopped
fresh thyme sprigs for decoration
finely chopped fresh sage
chopped fresh oregano

1.   Cut the eggplant and chanterelles into ¼-inch slices.
2.   In a sauté pan, sauté the eggplant in a little olive oil over high heat. Season with salt and pepper. Remove the eggplant from the pan and set aside. Repeat with the chanterelles.
3.   Slice the tomatoes and the leeks.
4.   Before you are ready to bake the pizzas, preheat the oven with a pizza stone inside to 500 degrees F. for 30 minutes. It is important for the stone to be very hot.
5.   Roll or stretch the dough, a quarter at a time, into a 7 or 8-inch circle and place on a lightly floured wooden peel. Brush with olive oil and sprinkle with some chili flakes. For each pizza, top the dough with a quarter of the cheeses, dot with a quarter

of the eggplant and chanterelles, sprinkle with a quarter of the leeks and garlic, and finish with the tomato slices. Finally, top with the sage and oregano. Assemble the remaining 3 pizzas in the same way.

6.   Slide the pizza onto the hot stone and bake it for about 10 to 12 minutes, or until the crust is golden brown and the cheese has melted.

PRESENTATION: Serve the pizzas on warm plates and cut into wedges. Garnish with sprigs of fresh herbs.

WHOLE WHEAT PIZZA DOUGH

Makes four
7- to 8-inch pizzas

> *1 package fresh or dry yeast*
> *¼ cup warm water*
> *3¾ cups whole wheat flour*
> *1 cup cool water*
> *1 tablespoon olive oil*
> *1 tablespoon honey*
> *pinch salt*

1.   Dissolve the yeast in the ¼ cup warm water and let proof.
2.   Put the flour in a food processor.
3.   Mix the 1 cup cool water with the olive oil, honey and salt.
4.   With the motor running, pour the olive oil mixture and yeast slowly in through the feed tube. Process until the dough forms a ball on the blade. Transfer the dough to an oiled bowl, cover and let rise until double in bulk.

5.   Punch down the dough and knead it on a lightly floured surface for 1 minute. Divide the dough into 4 equal portions and roll them into tight balls. Place on a tray, cover with a damp towel and let rest for several hours or overnight in the refrigerator.

6.   Roll or stretch each ball of dough into a 7- to 8-inch circle. Place the circles, one at a time, on a wooden peel or on a baking sheet and build the pizzas as desired.

Notes: To make the dough in an electric mixer fitted with a dough hook, place the flour in the bowl and add the ingredients in the same order as when using the food processor. Knead the dough in the machine until it forms a smooth ball. Place the dough in an oiled bowl and let it rest, covered, until double in bulk.

To prepare by hand, place the flour on a work surface, make a well in the center and add the wet ingredients and proofed yeast. Slowly incorporate the flour into the wet ingredients working from the center outward. When a dough forms, knead it on a floured surface until smooth. Place in an oiled bowl to rest, covered, until double in bulk.

LOUIS BLANCO'S THREE CHEESE CALZONE WITH EGGPLANT AND BASIL

Makes 2 calzones

1 *recipe Pizza Dough (page 110), divided in half*
2 *baby Japanese eggplants*
  extra-virgin olive oil
  freshly ground pepper
6 *large fresh basil leaves*

¼ to ½ teaspoon dried red chili flakes
   2 *cups grated fresh buffalo mozzarella or substitute an-*
      other good mozzarella
   1 *cup grated fontina cheese*
   ½ *cup cubed fresh goat cheese*
   1 *tablespoon freshly grated Parmesan cheese*
   2 *sprigs fresh thyme or basil for garnish*

1. Before you are ready to bake the calzones, preheat the oven with a pizza stone inside to 500 degrees F. for 30 minutes.
2. Cut the eggplants into ¼-inch slices. Brush them on both sides with olive oil and season with freshly ground pepper. Grill them over a moderate fire until they are tender, only a minute or two on each side.
3. Chop the basil.
4. Roll or stretch half the dough into a 12-inch circle and place it on a lightly floured wooden peel or a heavily floured rimless baking sheet. Brush the dough lightly with olive oil to within 1 inch of the edge and sprinkle it with the dried chili flakes, according to your palate and tolerance. Working as quickly as possible, for each calzone spread half the mozzarella and fontina on one half of the dough, leaving a 1-inch border. Arrange half the eggplant slices over the cheese, then sprinkle it with half the chopped basil. Distribute half the goat cheese on top. Moisten the edges of the dough with water and fold the untopped dough over the filling, trapping as much air inside as possible. Press the edges together to seal the envelope and crimp them with the back of a fork.
5. Slide the calzones onto the hot stone and bake 12 to 15 minutes, or until they are golden brown. Remove from the oven and transfer to a warm platter.

PRESENTATION: Brush the calzones with olive oil, sprinkle with the Parmesan and decorate each with a sprig of thyme or basil. Serve immediately.

CALZONE WITH ARTICHOKES
AND PORCINI MUSHROOMS

Makes 4 calzones

1 *recipe Pizza Dough (page 110), divided into 4 equal pieces*
  about 2 tablespoons extra-virgin olive oil
2 *large artichoke hearts, very thinly sliced*
1½ *cups fresh porcini, sliced if large*
  salt
  freshly ground pepper
2 *tablespoons Chili Oil (page 32)*
1 *cup grated Italian fontina cheese*
2 *cups grated mozzarella cheese*
2 *tablespoons chopped garlic, blanched*
3 *teaspoons chopped fresh thyme, plus 4 sprigs for garnish*
2 *tablespoons unsalted butter, melted*
2 *tablespoons freshly grated Parmesan cheese*

1.   Before you are ready to bake the calzone, preheat the oven with a pizza stone inside to 500 degrees F. for 30 minutes.
2.   Place a large sauté pan over high heat. To it add the olive oil and when it is hot sauté the artichoke hearts and mushrooms. Season to taste with salt and pepper. Pour off any excess oil and let the vegetables cool.
3.   Roll or stretch the dough, a quarter at a time, into a 9-inch circle. Place the dough, one at a time, on a lightly floured wooden peel.
4.   Brush the circles to within 1 inch of the edge with chili oil. For each calzone, put a quarter of both cheeses on half the dough, still leaving the 1-inch border. Top with a quarter of the artichokes and mushrooms, the garlic and thyme. Assemble the remaining calzones in the same way.
5.   Moisten the edges of the circles with water. Fold the un-

topped half of dough, trapping as much air inside as possible, over the filling and press the edges together firmly to seal. With the backside of a fork press the edges of the dough to crimp them.

6.   Slide the calzones onto the stone and bake about 12 minutes, or until the crust is golden brown. Brush the calzones with melted butter and sprinkle them with Parmesan.

PRESENTATION: Slide the calzones onto an oval platter, place a sprig of fresh thyme on each and serve immediately.

Fish and Shellfish

I must confess that fishing has never been a great passion of mine, as it seems to require more patience than I normally have on hand. But cooking and eating fish . . . well, that's a different story. My appreciation did not come about until after my childhood; back then, ecstasy was a plate of fish sticks with tartar sauce! In a landlocked nation, exposure to the real thing is limited.

Americans, though, are lucky enough to have many seafood sources—oceans, bays, gulfs, rivers, lakes, streams—and even the inland states can have fish flown to their markets within hours. But nothing can beat a fish that has been swimming around earlier the same day, which you can get only if you live near the water. To bring such a prize home from the dockside vendor, or, of course, to hook your own, is to capture a taste you can find nowhere else.

Even before the birth of Christ, fish was held in high regard. According to Waverly Root, the ancient Egyptians, Chinese, and Assyrians all raised fish in manmade bodies of water. (Their palates obviously knew the importance of speeding the catch to the table.) In these health-conscious times, fish is acclaimed as a lean, easily digestible storehouse of complete protein, polyunsaturated fats, vitamins B and D, and the minerals iodine, fluorine and calcium. Grilling, the modern cooking method of choice, impregnates the flesh with a smoky taste, eliminating the need for heavy sauces. Something as basic as a little lemon butter or a tangy vinaigrette can be just the right finishing touch. But panfrying is a surer way to keep the less fatty types of fish from drying out, and I like to steam the delicate ones, such as sole, so that the flavor is better preserved.

Going to the fish market has always inspired me with new ideas for my restaurants. A perfect piece of fish really makes you eager to see what you can do with it. Look for bright, firm flesh, red gills and clear, prominent eyes. Dull-looking specimens sitting on ice are better left there. When buying a fillet, you have fewer signs to go by, so put your nose right up against it and sniff! But the benefits in flavor and moistness of a whole fish are tremendous.

You should, naturally, hunt around for fish that has been caught close by. Many of my recipes call for salmon, because just to the north of me is the Columbia River, which yields this superb fish. (Bass and snapper work particularly well as substitutes.) Local fish used in a dish is one of the best indicators of the true regional cuisine, which was established way before our modern transportation systems were. The Northwest is associated with salmon and oysters; while New England makes you think of lobsters, clams and haddock; the South, of crawfish and catfish; the Hawaiian Islands of tuna and mahi mahi. Out of thousands and thousands of species throughout the world, only a very small group exists in any given part of the country. You can almost tell where you are at dinnertime with your eyes closed!

I used to prepare fish in all sorts of elaborate ways, but now I favor simpler methods. If I were to name the most memorable fish I have ever had, it might very well be the applewood-barbecued salmon at a cookout I went to in Oregon. It was sauced with nothing more than drawn butter and a squeeze of lemon. It was heaven on earth!

Please don't overcook that lovely fish. In fact, don't hesitate to undercook it a bit at the thickest part, and you will see a great improvement in the overall result. Keep in mind that it will continue to cook a bit after it comes off the grill; medium to medium well will be well done by the time it is served.

When choosing a wine to complement fish, most people think white right away. But why not give red a chance? A light-bodied St. Emilion or Beaujolais goes extremely well with the pronounced flavor of trout, tuna, salmon, bass and swordfish, among others. Mesquite grilling further strengthens the character of those fish. If you've never tried red wine with fish before, you will be amazed at how nicely the two can get along.

I hope that by now you are ready to dash out the door with your rod and reel. Wherever you go to do your fishing, remember that the clear, cold water and a strong current are signs that the eating will be first-rate. Good luck . . . and let someone else buy those fish sticks!

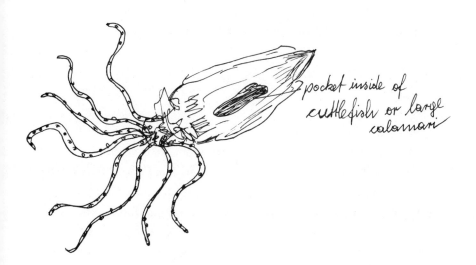

pocket inside of cuttlefish or large calamari

CRAB IN BLACK BEAN SAUCE

Lobster is an ideal substitute for crab in this recipe. Roast a whole lobster, split it in half and remove the stomach. Place the lobster on a hot serving plate and cover with the sauce.

Serves 1 or 2

   1 tablespoon Chinese black beans
⅓ cup sake
⅓ cup Chicken Stock (page 69)
  1 tablespoon soy sauce
  2 teaspoons minced fresh ginger
  1 tablespoon dark sesame oil
    one 2-pound crab
  2 scallions, thinly sliced
½ bunch Chinese garlic chives, thinly sliced
  4 tablespoons (2 ounces) unsalted butter

1. Soak the black beans in the sake, chicken stock, soy sauce and ginger for about 1 hour.
2. Preheat the oven to 400 degrees F.
3. Heat a heatproof sauté pan large enough to hold the crab until very hot. Add the sesame oil and in it, sauté the crab briefly on both sides to coat it with oil. Transfer the pan to the oven for 10 to 12 minutes, or until the crab is bright red.
4. Remove the crab from the sauté pan and set it aside to cool for a few minutes. When it is cool enough to handle, remove the top shell in one piece and reserve it in a warm spot. Remove the small tail and discard the gills. Cut the underside into quarters, leaving the legs attached.
5. Deglaze the pan with the sake mixture. Add the scallions, garlic chives and butter. Then add the quartered crab and toss

the mixture over moderate heat until the sauce thickens enough to adhere to the crab.

PRESENTATION: Reassemble the crab quarters on a large heated plate. Place the shell over the legs so that the crab is reformed. Spoon any remaining sauce over the top. Serve immediately.

GRILLED SALMON WITH GARLIC CREAM AND TOMATO BUTTER

Serves 4

Tomato Butter

 2 *large ripe tomatoes, quartered*
 1 *clove garlic*
 1 *branch fresh basil*
 4 *sprigs fresh parsley*
 2 *shallots, sliced*
½ *small carrot*
 1 *cup dry white wine*
 2 *tablespoons very good sherry or red wine vinegar*
 1 *teaspoon tomato paste (optional)*
12 *tablespoons (6 ounces) unsalted butter, softened slightly*

Garlic Cream

 1 *medium baking potato (about 8 ounces), peeled and sliced*
 6 *large cloves garlic, thinly sliced*
    about ½ cup milk
    about ½ cup heavy cream
    salt

Salmon

4 fillets of salmon, 6 ounces each
salt
freshly ground white pepper
4 nice basil leaves for garnish

1.   Prepare the tomato butter: Purée the tomatoes, garlic, basil, parsley, 1 of the shallots and the carrot in a food processor and reserve.

2.   Chop the remaining shallot and place it in a large saucepan with the wine and vinegar. Reduce the liquid over medium heat to 1 tablespoon. Pour in the reserved tomato purée and cook over medium heat until thick. (Most of the liquid should have evaporated and the flavor should be intense.) Reduce the purée more if necessary and stir in the tomato paste if needed.

3.   Whisk in the butter, a little at a time, over low heat. When all the butter is incorporated, strain the sauce through a very fine strainer into a clean saucepan. Be sure to press the purée firmly against the sides of the strainer to extract as much of the flavor as possible. Season to taste with salt, pepper and a little more vinegar if necessary. Keep warm.

4.   Prepare the garlic cream: While the tomato butter is cooking, cook the potato and sliced garlic in the equal parts milk and cream to cover until the potato is tender. The liquid will thicken and much of it will be absorbed. Pass the mixture through the finest disk of a food mill into a pan. Thin with a little warm cream if necessary. Add salt to taste and keep the cream warm.

5.   Prepare the salmon: Season both sides of the fillets with salt and pepper. Grill the fillets over a charcoal fire for 3 to 4 minutes per side, or until just cooked through.

PRESENTATION: Spoon the garlic cream into the centers of 4 warm dinner plates. Surround the garlic cream with tomato butter. Top the garlic cream with the grilled salmon and garnish each fillet with a basil leaf. Serve immediately.

GRILLED MAHI MAHI IN
RED ONION BUTTER

Serves 4

2 *pounds fresh boneless mahi mahi, cut into 4 equal pieces*
4 to 5 *tablespoons extra-virgin olive oil*
2 *medium red onions, sliced ⅛ inch thick*
   freshly ground white pepper
1 *sprig fresh thyme, leaves only, plus additional small*
   sprigs for garnish
½ *cup dry white wine*
½ *cup heavy cream*
   salt
4 *tablespoons (2 ounces) unsalted butter*

1.   Place the mahi mahi in a shallow dish, drizzle with 2 to 3 tablespoons of the olive oil and top with a few slices of onion and freshly ground pepper. Let marinate 2 to 3 hours in the refrigerator.

2.   Place a sauté pan over moderate heat and add the remaining oil. In it sauté the remaining onions rapidly until they are slightly golden, but still crisp. Stir in the thyme leaves.

3.   Deglaze the pan with the white wine and reduce it by half.

4.   Add the cream and continue to cook the mixture until slightly reduced. Season to taste with salt and pepper. Whisk in the butter, a little at a time. Set the onion butter aside and keep it warm.

5.   Remove the fish from the marinade and season both sides of it with salt. Grill the mahi mahi over mesquite until it feels slightly springy to the touch, or sauté it over high heat in a mixture of olive oil and butter.

PRESENTATION: Spoon the onion butter onto 4 warm dinner plates. Top with the grilled mahi mahi and garnish with small thyme sprigs if desired. Serve with a selection of freshly cooked vegetables.

Note: If mahi mahi is not available, pompano may be used instead.

GRILLED SALMON WITH LEEKS
AND PINOT NOIR BUTTER

Serves 4

4 *fillets of salmon, 6 to 8 ounces each*
2 to 3 *tablespoons extra-virgin olive oil*
   freshly ground white pepper
8 *baby leeks, cut into julienne strips*
½ *bottle Pinot Noir*
16 *tablespoons (eight ounces) unsalted butter, softened*
   salt
12 to 14 *ounces fresh chanterelles*
1 *tablespoon minced fresh Italian parsley, tarragon or chervil*

1.   Sprinkle the salmon with olive oil, pepper and a little of the leeks. Cover and let marinate for 5 to 6 hours in the refrigerator.
2.   In a saucepan, reduce the wine with ¼ cup of the leeks to 3 to 4 tablespoons. Whisk in 12 tablespoons (6 ounces) of the butter, a little at a time. Season to taste with salt and pepper. Strain the mixture into a clean saucepan and keep warm. If the sauce thickens too much, add a few drops water or cream to thin it.
3.   In a sauté pan, sauté the remaining leeks in 2 tablespoons of the butter until they are tender. Season to taste with salt and pepper. Reserve.

4. Clean the chanterelles with a dry, soft brush. If they are large, cut them in half or quarter them. Heat the remaining 2 tablespoons butter in a large sauté pan and in it cook the chanterelles over high heat until the liquid evaporates, Season with salt, pepper and chopped herbs. Reserve and keep warm.

5. Grill the salmon over hot mesquite until medium rare, approximately 4 minutes per side. Transfer to a warm plate.

PRESENTATION: Nap 4 warm dinner plates lightly with the Pinot Noir sauce. Divide all but 1 tablespoon of the leeks among them. Arrange the salmon fillets on the leeks and surround the salmon with bouquets of the sautéed chanterelles. Garnish the salmon with the 1 tablespoon reserved leeks. Serve immediately.

GRILLED TUNA WITH MINT VINAIGRETTE

Fresh salmon is also very good when used in place of the tuna.

Serves 4

1½ pounds fresh tuna, in 4 equal steaks
   freshly ground white pepper
2 to 3 tablespoons chopped fresh mint or basil, plus 4 sprigs
   for garnish
½ cup extra-virgin olive oil
1 tablespoon lime juice
1 tablespoon good red or white wine vinegar
1 tablespoon minced fresh parsley
2 medium shallots, minced
6 ripe plum tomatoes, peeled, seeded and diced
2 cloves garlic, blanched and cut into julienne strips
   salt

1.   Sprinkle the tuna with pepper, then let it marinate in 1 tablespoon of the mint or basil and 2 tablespoons of the olive oil for 2 to 3 hours in the refrigerator.
2.   In a bowl, combine the remaining ingredients. Taste carefully and correct the seasonings. Reserve.
3.   Sprinkle the tuna with salt. Grill it over charcoal, approximately 4 minutes per side, or until it is medium rare. If the slices of tuna are very thin, grill them only on one side. (Or you may broil or sauté them in a little oil and butter.)

PRESENTATION: Nap 4 plates with the vinaigrette and top it with one piece of the tuna. Garnish with the mint sprigs.

STRIPED BASS IN GINGER VINAIGRETTE

You could also use red snapper in this recipe.

Serves 4

> one *1-inch piece ginger, peeled and minced*
> 2 *large shallots, minced*
> ¼ *cup rice wine vinegar*
> 1 *cup extra-virgin olive oil*
> *juice of 2 limes*
> 2 *tablespoons soy sauce*
> 2 *tablespoons dark sesame oil*
> *salt*
> *freshly ground white pepper*
> 4 *striped bass fillets, 6 ounces each*
> 1 *bunch cilantro or Italian parsley, roughly chopped, plus a few whole leaves for garnish*
> ¼ *cup toasted sesame seeds for garnish*

1.   Combine the ginger, shallots, vinegar, olive oil, lime juice and soy sauce in a small bowl.

2. Whisking vigorously, add the sesame oil, salt and pepper to taste.

3. Season the striped bass on both sides with salt and pepper. Grill it over high heat until lightly done or sauté it in a little butter and oil. Striped bass fillets that are ½ inch thick take only 1 to 2 minutes on each side.

4. Just before serving, mix the cilantro or parsley into the vinaigrette. (This prevents the herbs from turning dark.)

PRESENTATION: Make a pool of the ginger vinaigrette on dinner plates at room temperature. Top with the grilled fish. Garnish with the toasted sesame seeds and a few cilantro or parsley leaves.

SIZZLING CATFISH

Any oily fish, such as trout or rock cod, can be used in this recipe.

Serves 2

> *peanut oil for deep frying*
> *one 6-inch catfish, gills and intestines removed*
> *eight ¼-inch slices fresh ginger*
> ¼ *cup sake*
> ¼ *cup soy sauce*
> *lemon juice*
> *salt*
> *freshly ground pepper*
> *cornstarch*
> 2 *scallions, sliced, for garnish*
> *lemongrass or garlic chives*

1.   Fill a wok or fryer large enough to hold the fish with peanut oil to cover the fish by 1 inch. Heat the oil until very hot. (A drop of water will dance on the oil when it is hot enough.)

2.   Make 4 deep, diagonal slashes (to the bone) on both sides of the fish. Insert the ginger in the slashes. Refrigerate.

3.   In a small saucepan, bring the sake and soy sauce to a boil, add lemon juice to taste and let the sauce cool.

4.   Season the fish lightly with salt and pepper, then dust it with cornstarch. Add the fish to the wok and let it swim into the hot peanut oil, head first (see illustration). Cook 5 minutes. To test for doneness, insert the tip of a knife next to the spine to see if the flesh is cooked through.

PRESENTATION: Pour a little sauce onto a platter. Remove the fish from the oil and let it drain briefly on several layers of paper towels. Then transfer it to the platter. Drizzle the fish with lemon juice and a little more of the sauce and sprinkle it with the sliced scallions. Garnish the plate with the lemongrass or garlic chives.

Note: Catfish has to be very fresh; if not, the flesh gets mushy. Many fish stores have tanks where they keep the fish alive and kill them when needed.

RED SNAPPER WITH FENNEL

Serves 4

4 *whole red snappers, 1 pound each, (heads on, please)*
   salt
   freshly ground pepper
4 *medium fennel branches*
2 *small fennel bulbs*

10 *tablespoons (5 ounces) unsalted butter*
 1 *tablespoon olive oil*
 4 *tablespoons or ¼ cup Fish Stock (page 70)*
 2 *tablespoons Pernod or anisette*
 1 *teaspoon minced fresh dill*
   juice of ½ lemon

1. Clean and scale the fish, then wash them thoroughly and pat dry. Season the insides with salt and pepper.
2. Preheat the oven to 450 degrees F.
3. Chop finely 1 tablespoon of the fennel branches and reserve it for the sauce. Place the remaining branches inside the fish, then arrange the fish on a rack in a large roasting pan.
4. Roast the fish in the oven for about 20 minutes, or until done. Test by placing the tip of a small knife near the spine to see if the flesh is cooked through. Do not overcook. The fish may also be grilled over a moderately slow fire. Mesquite imparts a very nice flavor.
5. Cut the fennel bulbs into ¼-inch slices and season them lightly with salt and pepper.
6. Heat a medium sauté pan and add 1 tablespoon of the butter and the olive oil. Add the fennel slices and sauté until tender-crisp. Keep warm.
7. In a saucepan, bring the stock and Pernod or anisette to a boil. Whisk in the remaining butter, a little at a time, over very low heat. Add the reserved chopped fennel, dill, lemon juice and salt and pepper to taste.

PRESENTATION: Place each fish on a hot oval dinner plate. Surround with some of the sautéed fennel, then spoon the butter sauce over the fish.

striped bass is an ideal substitute for red snapper.

MARINATED AND GLAZED SWORDFISH

Serves 4

4 slices swordfish, 6 ounces each
extra-virgin olive oil
freshly ground black pepper

Marinade

2 tablespoons orange or mandarin marmalade
1 teaspoon minced fresh ginger
1 teaspoon minced garlic (1 clove)
½ teaspoon freshly ground white pepper
salt
¼ cup fresh lemon juice
¼ cup white wine vinegar
¼ cup fresh orange juice
¼ cup extra-virgin olive oil or hazelnut oil

1.   Brush the swordfish with olive oil and grind a little pepper over the slices. Refrigerate until ready to use.

2.   Prepare the marinade: Combine all of the marinade ingredients, except the oil, in a non-reactive saucepan. Bring to a boil and reduce to ½ cup. Remove from the heat and let cool. Whisk in the oil. Store in the refrigerator until ready to use.

3.   Before you are ready to cook the fish, heat a grill, then brush it with oil to prevent the fish from sticking.

4.   Warm the marinade slightly.

5.   Brush the swordfish with a little of the marinade, then grill it quickly, until it feels springy to the touch. If the slices of fish are less than ½ inch thick, grill them only on one side.

PRESENTATION: Place the swordfish on warm plates and serve with a nice assortment of mixed greens.

Note: Leftover marinade can be used for steaks, ribs, or pork chops before grilling or barbecuing.

LOBSTER WITH SWEET GINGER

Serves 2

      1 piece fresh ginger, approximately 1 inch
      2 cloves garlic, minced
    ³/4 cup plum wine or port
      2 tablespoons rice wine vinegar
        one 2-pound lobster, split lengthwise
      2 tablespoons peanut oil
      2 tablespoons unsalted butter
      4 scallions, cut into ³/8-inch slices
1 to 2 teaspoons curry powder
    ¼ cup dry white wine
    ½ cup Fish Stock (page 70)
    ½ cup heavy cream
    ½ teaspoon dried hot chili flakes
      1 tablespoon Chinese black vinegar or balsamic vinegar
        salt
        freshly ground pepper

1.   Preheat the oven to 500 degrees F.
2.   Peel the ginger, reserving the peels, and cut it into fine julienne strips. Cut the peels into coarse julienne strips and set aside.
3.   In a small saucepan, cook the ginger and garlic with ½ cup of the plum wine and the rice wine vinegar until 1 tablespoon of liquid remains. Remove from the heat and reserve.
4.   Place a heavy heatproof 12-inch skillet over high heat until it is very hot. Add the oil and heat it almost to the smoking point. Carefully add the lobster halves, meat side down. Cook 3 minutes. Turn the lobster over and add 1 tablespoon of the butter. Continue to sauté until the lobster shells are getting red and the butter is nutty red. Transfer the lobster to the oven for about 10 minutes, or until the lobster is just cooked. Remove

from the oven, remove the lobster from the skillet and keep warm.

5.   Add the scallions, ginger peels and curry powder to the skillet. (Be careful, the handle might be hot.) Sauté the mixture lightly for 10 to 15 seconds, then whisk in the remaining plum wine and the white wine, stock, chili flakes and the vinegar. Reduce the liquid to ½ cup. Add the cream and reduce it by half. Add any liquid from the julienne of ginger, then whisk in the remaining tablespoon butter. Season the sauce to taste with salt and pepper.

6.   Crack the lobster claws with the back of a large chef's knife.

PRESENTATION: Arrange the lobster halves on a warm oval platter, meat side up. Strain the sauce over the lobster, then sprinkle the sweet ginger on top. Garnish with Fried Baby Spinach Leaves (recipe follows).

FRIED BABY SPINACH LEAVES

Wash large spinach leaves, cut off the stems and dry them well. Heat peanut oil to 375 degrees F. and in it fry the spinach until crisp and translucent. Be careful not to get splattered! Remove the leaves to paper towels to drain and salt them lightly (just like potato chips). The spinach should have a jade green color.

Meat and Poultry

*A*mericans have gotten themselves a reputation as a carnivorous people. The foods discussed in this chapter are consumed in the United States in greater quantities than almost anywhere else in the world. Although beef is ordered less and less in restaurants as clientele look to reduce their waistlines and cholesterol counts, it maintains its place as a staple in middle- and lower-income households.

This continued demand has brought about a reversion to old-fashioned farming methods that stress quality rather than quantity. The free-range chickens supplied by our friend Bart Ehman are as tasty as those from my parents' farm in Austria. And his lamb is exquisite—baby lamb that has never fed on anything but milk and is leaner and more delicate than corn-fed lamb. Immaturity also makes for finer pork; a suckling pig, with its melting flesh and crackling golden skin, is fare fit for a king.

Unlike fish, meat and poultry must hang for several days before being cooked, so that they tenderize through the action of their own enzymes. Veal, pork, and lamb usually take five days; birds about three. Beef requires at least three weeks of dry-aging in order to make that prime steak "cut like butter." When shopping for meat in a retail foodstore, you are buying a product that has already spent approximately three days in the refrigerator case. All meat and poultry should be used within six days of butchering (except beef, which keeps somewhat longer, depending on the thickness of the cut. A little arithmetic and taking transit time into account will tell you that your pan should be ready and waiting on the fire!

Each meat and each type of poultry has particular characteristics and therefore particular cooking methods that suit it. You will want beef that is bright red in color, with white fat that forms a lacy network of marbling throughout the meat. Prime grade has profuse marbling, which contributes to its tenderness and delicate flavor, while choice grade has less fat and a fuller flavor. Both grades have a relatively high fat content, making it ideal for grilling and barbecuing. Veal and baby lamb, by contrast, should be a clear, light pink, with no marbling and little fibrousness. This makes them good candidates for sautéeing and roasting. With their less assertive flavors, they fit in with many different modes of preparation. Gentle enough not to overpower refined seasoning, they can take on an altogether different personality under the influence of a zesty sauce.

I urge you to get into the "undercooking" habit, and see for yourself the magic it works. Although lamb, pork, and veal are still eaten well done in many parts of the world, I prefer veal and pork pink in the middle, and lamb medium rare. (Pork cooked to an internal temperature of 140 degrees F. destroys any trichinosis infestation.) Chicken ought to be slightly pink near the bone, otherwise parts will be dry and practically inedible (the breast in particular suffers terribly!). Quail and pigeon are most delectable medium rare. Preserving natural juices ties in logically with a cuisine that rejects thick, creamy sauces. In the classical era, meat was frequently cooked to death, then wetted down with those sauces to replace all the lost moisture. Today the meat must do its own work.

There are still challenges to be met in upgrading farm-raised animals. Game presents an especially frustrating problem, as it never develops its prized wild taste in a controlled environment; pigeon and quail fare best and are therefore the only wild fowl we have included here. Until that wrinkle is ironed out, you still have a lot of meat and poultry from which to choose. Go for top quality, and let the updated school of cooking show it off. You'll wonder how you became such a terrific cook over-night!

MEATS

NEW YORK STEAK WITH SHIITAKE AND ENOKI MUSHROOMS AND GRILLED NEW ONIONS

New onions are similar to scallions or green onions. They are slightly larger and the bulb end is rounder.

Serves 4

> *12 new onions or scallions*
> *4 New York steaks (8 to 10 ounces each), cut ½ inch thick*
> *salt*
> *freshly ground pepper*
> *4 tablespoons (2 ounces) unsalted butter*
> *1 pound fresh* shiitake *mushrooms, sliced ¼ inch thick*
> *⅓ cup Cognac*
> *1 cup* Demi-Glace *(page 33)*
> *1 package* enoki *mushrooms, stemmed*

1.   Heat a grill. When hot, grill the onions for about 2 minutes on each side, or until they are tender but crunchy. If you don't have a grill, blanch the onions in boiling salted water. Drain and keep warm.

2.   Season the steaks on both sides with salt and pepper. Reserve.

3.   In a heavy sauté pan, heat half the butter until bubbly. In it cook the *shiitakes* over high heat until they begin to brown slightly. Season lightly with salt and pepper. Remove from the pan and keep warm.

4.   Carefully pour the Cognac into the hot sauté pan and ignite. Let the flame die out naturally. Reduce the Cognac to 2 tablespoons, scraping any loose bits that cling to the bottom of the

pan. Stir in the *demi-glace*. Reduce the sauce until slightly thickened, but still very light. Return the mushrooms and their juice to the sauce and reduce more if necessary. Correct the seasonings.

5.   Stir in the remaining 2 tablespoons butter, a little at a time. Stir in the *enoki* mushrooms. Set the sauce aside and keep warm.

6.   Grill the steaks on the preheated grill for 1 to 2 minutes on each side, or sauté them in a very hot sauté pan with a little oil for 1 minute on each side, or until the meat is medium rare. Remove from the heat.

7.   If necessary, reheat the sauce very gently.

PRESENTATION: Divide the new onions equally among 4 warm dinner plates. Spoon the mushroom sauce over the onions. Place a steak in the middle of each plate. Serve immediately.

ROASTED NEW YORK STRIP
WITH TWO SAUCES

Serves 10 to 12

> *1 whole well trimmed New York strip, about 5 pounds*
> *salt*
> *freshly ground black pepper*
> *Foyot Sauce (recipe follows)*
> *Meaux Mustard Sauce (recipe follows)*

1.   Preheat the oven to 425 degrees F.

2.   Place the meat on a rack in a shallow pan. Roast it for about 45 minutes, or to an internal temperature of 120 degrees F.,

for medium rare. Remove from the oven and let rest in a warm
spot for 15 to 20 minutes.

3.   While the steak cooks, make the sauces and keep them warm.

PRESENTATION: Place the meat on a wooden carving board suitable for serving. Cut it into thin slices, allowing 3 or 4 per plate.
Spoon a little of each sauce beside the meat and decorate the
plates with freshly cooked baby vegetables in season.

FOYOT SAUCE

Makes about 2 cups

    2 *medium shallots, minced*
   1/4 *teaspoon freshly ground pepper*
   1/4 *cup dry white wine*
   1/4 *cup white wine vinegar*
    3 *egg yolks*
    4 *tablespoons water*
    2 *tablespoons defatted meat drippings*
       salt
   16 *tablespoons (8 ounces) clarified unsalted butter at room*
       temperature
    1 *tablespoon minced fresh tarragon*

1.   Combine the shallots, pepper, white wine and vinegar in a
small saucepan. Bring to a boil and reduce over moderate heat
to 1 tablespoon.

2.   In a stainless steel mixing bowl, combine the egg yolks,
water, meat drippings, a pinch of salt and the shallot reduction.
Whisk vigorously over simmering water until the mixture is
thick and light in both color and texture. (If you dip your fin-

gertip into this mixture, then blow on it, the egg yolks should remain on your finger as a thick coating.)

3.   Slowly whisk in the butter, a few drops at a time, until the sauce begins to emulsify. Then whisk in the remaining butter in a slow steady stream, until all of it is incorporated.

4.   Whisk in the tarragon. Season to taste with salt and pepper.

5.   The sauce can be kept warm over tepid water for up to 30 minutes. (Keep a little hot water handy and whisk in a few drops of it if the sauce begins to separate around the edges.)

MEAUX MUSTARD SAUCE

Makes 1½ cups

      1 *cup port*
      1 *tablespoon minced shallot*
      1 *cup Brown Stock (page 71)*
     ½ *cup heavy cream*
      4 *tablespoons (2 ounces) unsalted butter*
      2 *tablespoons Meaux mustard*
         salt
         freshly ground white pepper

1.   In a saucepan, reduce the Port with the shallot to ¼ cup. Add the stock and reduce it until thickened slightly. Add the cream and reduce it until thickened slightly.

2.   Whisk in the butter, a little at a time, until it is incorporated.

3.   Whisk in the mustard, to taste and season the sauce with salt and pepper.

4.   The sauce can be kept warm over tepid water for up to 30 minutes. Keep a little hot water handy and whisk in a few drops of it if the sauce begins to separate around the edges.)

SZECHUAN BEEF

To serve this dish for lunch, use half the amount of steak and less salad.

Serves 4

Ginger Vinaigrette

1 small shallot, minced
½-inch piece fresh ginger, peeled and minced
1 small clove garlic, minced
⅓ cup light salad oil or extra-virgin olive oil
1 tablespoon dark sesame oil
¼ cup rice wine vinegar or 3 tablespoons Chinese black vinegar
salt
freshly ground pepper

Szechuan Beef

4 well trimmed New York steaks, 1½ inches thick
light sesame oil
1 tablespoon Chinese or cracked black peppercorns
1 large shallot, chopped
1 cup dry red wine
1 cup Brown Stock (page 71)
½ teaspoon dried red chili flakes
1 large clove garlic, chopped
½-inch piece fresh ginger, peeled and chopped
4 tablespoons (2 ounces) unsalted butter
1 tablespoon mushroom soy or other soy sauce
2 tablespoons chopped fresh cilantro
salt
2 bunches watercress, stemmed and cleaned
1 bunch spinach, smaller leaves only
2 green onions, thinly sliced, for garnish

1.   Prepare the vinaigrette: Mix all the vinaigrette ingredients together. Taste and correct the seasonings.

2.   Prepare the beef: Drizzle the steaks with sesame oil and pat them with Chinese or black peppercorns on both sides. Place on a dish, cover with plastic wrap, refrigerate and let marinate several hours or overnight.

3.   Place the shallot and red wine in a saucepan. Bring to a boil and reduce by two thirds. Add the stock, chili flakes, garlic, and ginger. Continue to reduce the sauce until it is thickened slightly. Whisk in the butter, a little at a time, over low heat (or on the side of the stove). Add the soy sauce and cilantro. (Mushroom soy sauce is less salty, darker and thicker than regular soy sauce and is what we use at Chinois. It is available in Oriental markets. If you use regular soy sauce, add it slowly and taste frequently to prevent oversalting.) Correct the seasonings and keep the sauce warm.

4.   Preheat a grill until hot. Remove the steaks from the marinade and salt each side lightly. Grill the steaks about 5 minutes on each side, until medium rare. If a charcoal or gas grill is not available to you, sauté the steaks in a little butter and sesame oil. Transfer the steaks to a cutting board and let them rest.

5.   Toss the watercress and the smallest, tenderest of the spinach leaves with a little ginger vinaigrette. Divide among 4 dinner plates and set aside.

6.   Cut each steak diagonally into ⅜-inch slices. If the meat has gotten too cool, reheat slightly in the sauce.

PRESENTATION: Overlap slices of steak down the center of each salad. Reduce the sauce slightly if necessary and spoon it over the steak. Sprinkle green onions on top.

Variation: To make this a Southwestern dish, use extra-virgin olive oil in place of the sesame oil, omit the ginger and use a small piece of jalapeño pepper in the sauce reduction. Replace the ginger vinaigrette with Mustard Vinaigrette (page 46).

VEAL WITH JOHANNISBERG RIESLING, ALMONDS AND PINE NUTS

Serves 4

2 *tablespoons sliced almonds*

2 *tablespoons pine nuts*

8 *veal medallions, 3 ounces each, (2 per person)*

salt

freshly ground white pepper

1 *teaspoon flour*

2 *tablespoons oil*

½ *bottle Johannisberg Riesling, (approximately 6% residual sugar)*

½ *cup Brown Stock (page 71)*

4 *tablespoons (2 ounces) unsalted butter, softened*

1. Preheat the oven to 350 degrees F.

2. Toast the almonds and pine nuts in the oven in separate pans. The almonds will take 8 to 10 minutes; the pine nuts about 5 minutes. Remove from the oven and reserve.

3. Season both sides of the veal medallions with salt and pepper, then dust each side very lightly with flour. Pat off any excess.

4. Heat the oil in a heavy sauté pan large enough to hold the veal without crowding it. When the oil is hot, brown the medallions approximately 3 minutes per side, or until they are golden brown and just cooked through. Transfer the meat to a heated plate and keep warm. Pour off any excess fat from the pan.

5. Deglaze the pan with the wine, then reduce it to ¼ cup. Add the stock and continue to reduce the sauce until it is thickened slightly. Slowly whisk in the butter, a little at a time. Season the sauce to taste with salt and pepper and strain it into a small saucepan. Stir in the almonds and pine nuts, reserving a few for garnish. Also add any veal juice that has collected on the plate. Heat the sauce through.

PRESENTATION: Arrange the veal medallions on warm dinner plates and spoon the sauce over them. Garnish the veal with the reserved almonds and pine nuts.

GRILLED VEAL CHOP WITH VINEGAR BUTTER AND ARUGOLA

Serves 4

 4 *well trimmed veal chops, 10 ounces each*
   salt
   freshly ground black pepper
 1 *large shallot, minced*
 4 *tablespoons (2 ounces) unsalted butter*
 ¼ *cup Zinfandel vinegar or other strong vinegar*
 ½ *cup dry red wine*
 ¼ *cup veal* Demi-Glace *(page 33)*
 2 *bunches arugola*

1.   Preheat a grill.
2.   Season the chops with salt and pepper. Grill the chops for 5 to 7 minutes on each side, or until the veal is just cooked through.
3.   While the meat is grilling, make the sauce: Place the shallot in an enamel, stainless steel or other non-reactive saucepan with 1 tablespoon of the butter and sauté it for a few minutes over medium heat. Deglaze the pan with the vinegar, then reduce it to 2 tablespoons. Add the wine, reduce by half, then add the *demi-glace* and continue to reduce the sauce until it lightly coats the back of a spoon.

4.   Whisk the remaining butter into the sauce, a little at a time, over low heat. When all the butter has been incorporated, season the sauce with salt and pepper to taste. Strain the sauce into a clean saucepan and keep it warm.

5.   Wash and stem the arugola and pat it dry. Set aside.

PRESENTATION: Arrange a bed of arugola on each of 4 warm dinner plates. Place the veal chop on the greens and spoon the sauce over each. Serve with some crisp sautéed baby vegetables.

Note: The sauce should have a distinct flavor of vinegar. If, after it has been seasoned, it lacks character, reduce more vinegar in a separate pan and whisk it in, a little at a time, to taste.

GRILLED VEAL LIVER ON A BED OF ONION MARMALADE WITH MUSTARD SEEDS AND VINEGAR SAUCE

Serves 4

   4 *slices veal liver, 6 ounces each*
      olive oil
      coarsely ground fresh black pepper
2 or 3 *red onions, cut into eighths*
      salt
   1½ *cups Chicken Stock (page 69)*
      1 *tablespoon sherry wine vinegar*
      1 *cup heavy cream*
      1 *tablespoon yellow mustard seeds steeped in ¼ cup Port, plus additional mustard seeds for garnish*
      1 *large shallot, finely chopped*

> 5 tablespoons (2½ ounces) unsalted butter
> ¼ cup red wine vinegar
> 1 cup dry red wine
> ¼ cup veal Demi-Glace (page 33)

1. Trim away any membrane or nerves from the liver. Brush the liver with olive oil on both sides and season with pepper. Cover and refrigerate several hours.

2. Place the onions in a saucepan and season with salt and pepper. Add the stock and vinegar, bring to a boil, cover loosely and cook over moderate heat for about 15 minutes, or until the liquid has evaporated.

3. In a small saucepan, reduce the cream over low heat to 3 tablespoons. Add this to the onion mixture, bring to a boil, then set the marmalade aside in a warm spot. Bring the Port and mustard seeds to a boil in another small pan and reduce over low heat to 1 tablespoon.

4. While the onions are cooking, make the vinegar sauce: In a small saucepan, sauté the shallot with 1 tablespoon of the butter over medium heat for 2 or 3 minutes, or until glossy. Deglaze the pan with the red wine vinegar and reduce to a glaze, 2 tablespoons. Add the wine and reduce it by half. Add the *demi-glace* and continue to reduce it until the sauce lightly coats the back of a spoon.

5. Whisk in the remaining butter over low heat a little at a time. When all the butter has been incorporated, season the sauce to taste with salt and pepper. If it needs more tang, reduce a little more red wine vinegar in a separate saucepan by two thirds then add it to the sauce a little at a time until you obtain the desired flavor. Strain the sauce into a clean saucepan and keep it warm.

6. Preheat a grill. Season the liver with salt and grill it over moderate heat for 2 or 3 minutes on each side. The liver should still be pink inside; longer cooking will make the flavor very strong.

PRESENTATION: Make a bed of the onion marmalade in the center of each of 4 warm dinner plates. Place a liver slice on each and spoon a little vinegar sauce over them. Sprinkle with mustard seeds and decorate with colorful vegetables.

RACK OF LAMB WITH ROSEMARY AND ARTICHOKES

Letting the lamb rest after roasting distributes the juices evenly throughout the meat.

Serves 2

> *1 rack of baby lamb, about 1 pound*
> *freshly ground pepper*
> *1 small sprig rosemary, plus ½ teaspoon chopped rose-*
> *mary*
> *1 to 2 tablespoons extra-virgin olive oil*
> *1 cup Mirepoix (page 294)*
> *½ teaspoon whole black peppercorns*
> *½ bay leaf*
> *salt*
> *4 cooked fresh artichoke bottoms (see page 85)*
> *1 lemon, cut in half*
> *4 tablespoons (2 ounces) unsalted butter*
> *1 sprig fresh thyme, leaves only*
> *12 cloves garlic, peeled and blanched*

1. Trim all but a thin layer of fat from the lamb. Cut off the last 2 inches of the rib bones. Reserve all the trimmings. Rub the rack with pepper and the rosemary sprig, then rub it

with olive oil. Cover the rack with plastic wrap and let it stand in the refrigerator overnight.

2.   Make lamb stock: Brown the cut lamb bones and trimmings in a little olive oil. Add the *mirepoix* and brown for 2 to 3 minutes. Add the peppercorns and bay leaf. Add water to cover, bring it to a boil and simmer slowly until the stock is reduced to ½ cup. Strain and reserve.

3.   Preheat the oven to 450 degrees F. Place the lamb in a shallow roasting pan and season it with salt. Roast the rack for 10 to 12 minutes, or until the lamb is medium rare. Transfer the lamb to a carving board and let it rest in a warm spot for 10 minutes.

4.   Slice the artichoke bottoms into thin slices and toss them with lemon juice. In a sauté pan, sauté the artichoke slices slowly in 2 tablespoons of the butter, the thyme leaves, salt, pepper and 2 of the garlic cloves, cut into thin slices, until the artichokes are tender. Add more butter if necessary as they cook. Reserve.

5.   While the lamb is resting, discard any grease from the roasting pan. Deglaze the pan with the lamb stock. Add the chopped rosemary. When the sauce has reduced slightly, whisk in 1 tablespoon of the butter. Season the sauce to taste with salt and pepper and strain it. Keep the sauce warm.

6.   Heat a sauté pan, add the remaining butter and in it sauté the remaining garlic cloves until light golden brown.

PRESENTATION: Slice the lamb into chops. Arrange them attractively on warm dinner plates. Surround with the artichokes. Spoon the sauce over the lamb and scatter the cloves of garlic randomly over the artichoke slices.

RACK OF BABY LAMB
WITH WILD MUSHROOMS

Serves 4

> 2 *trimmed racks baby lamb, about 1 pound each*
> *extra-virgin olive oil*
> *coarsely ground fresh black pepper*
> *leaves of 1 branch of rosemary*
> *salt*
> 1 *shallot, minced*
> 12 *tablespoons (6 ounces) unsalted butter*
> ½ *pound fresh chanterelles, quartered if large*
> ½ *pound fresh* shiitake *mushrooms, quartered if large*
> ½ *pound fresh Japanese tree mushrooms, stemmed*
> *juice of ½ lemon*

1.   Brush all sides of the lamb with olive oil. Sprinkle generously with pepper and half the rosemary. Cover and let stand several hours or overnight.

2.   Preheat the oven to 400 degrees F. Heat a heatproof sauté pan until very hot and in it sauté the lamb quickly to brown it lightly on all sides. Salt the lamb and transfer it to the oven to roast for 12 to 15 minutes, until it is medium rare to medium. Remove the lamb and let it rest for 10 to 15 minutes in a warm spot.

3.   While the lamb is resting, sauté the shallot in half the butter for 2 to 3 minutes; do not brown. Add all the mushrooms and sauté them over moderate heat for about 5 minutes. Season with salt and pepper.

4.   At the last minute, melt the remaining butter in a small sauté pan with the remaining rosemary until the butter is foamy. Season the butter to taste with salt and pepper and add the lemon juice.

PRESENTATION: Divide the mushrooms among 4 warm dinner plates. Cut the lamb into chops and arrange 3 on each plate over the mushrooms. Spoon the foaming butter over the lamb and serve immediately. An assortment of tenderly crisp baby vegetables make a tasty accompaniment to this dish.

BABY PORK CHOPS WITH CRANBERRY SAUCE

Serves 4

> *4 tablespoons (2 ounces) unsalted butter*
> *12 ounces fresh or frozen cranberries*
> *3 to 4 tablespoons sugar*
> *1 cup dry red wine*
> *1 cup Veal Stock (page 71)*
>   *salt*
>   *freshly ground pepper*
> *12 baby pork chops, each ⅜ to ½ inch thick*

1.   Heat a sauté pan. Add 2 tablespoons of the butter. Stir in the cranberries and sugar. Cook the cranberries for several minutes over moderate heat until they begin to burst. Remove from the heat.

2.   In a separate saucepan, reduce the wine by two thirds. Add the stock and reduce until thickened slightly. Add to the cranberries and reduce a little to make a light sauce. Whisk in the remaining butter, bit by bit. Season the sauce to taste with salt and pepper and keep it warm.

3.   Preheat a grill. Season the pork chops on both sides with

salt and pepper and grill them over mesquite for 2 to 3 minutes on each side, or until they are cooked to medium. If a grill is not available to you, sauté them in a little butter. Keep warm.

PRESENTATION: Nap 4 warm dinner plates with the sauce. Pyramid 3 pork chops, by overlapping the bones, over the sauce. Serve immediately.

SPARERIBS CHINOIS

I like to drink beer or Champagne with these ribs because the bubbles clean the palate.

Serves 2 to 3

> 2 *pounds baby back ribs, in one or two racks*
> *freshly ground black pepper*
> *1 cup soy sauce (half mushroom soy is nice)*
> *1½ cups rice wine vinegar*
> *¼ cup chopped garlic*
> *¼ cup chopped fresh ginger*
> 2 *tablespoons chopped fresh cilantro or lemongrass*
> *1 small jalapeño pepper, minced*
> *1 large shallot, minced*

1.   Rub both sides of the ribs with the black pepper. Place them uncut in a roasting pan.
2.   Mix the soy sauce, vinegar, garlic, ginger, cilantro or lemongrass, jalapeño pepper and shallot and pour over the ribs. There should be enough liquid to barely cover the meat. Cover and marinate the ribs overnight in the refrigerator.

3. Preheat the oven to 325 degrees F. Drain the marinade from the ribs and roast the ribs in the oven for 40 to 45 minutes. Remove.

4. At serving time, grill the spareribs until they are really browned and hot through.

PRESENTATION: Cut the racks into individual ribs and arrange the ribs in an overlapping fashion on a warm platter. Serve with lots of napkins.

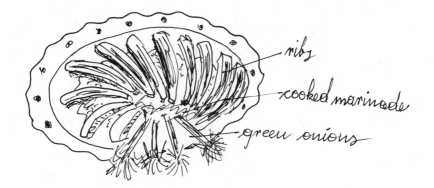

POULTRY

CHICKEN WITH GARLIC
AND PARSLEY

This entrée has been on the menu at Spago since we opened. It continues to be one of the favorites.

Serves 4

> 2 *whole chickens, about 2 pounds each*
> 2 *small heads garlic, separated into cloves and peeled*
> ¼ *cup Italian parsley leaves*
>   *salt*
>   *freshly ground white pepper*
> 2 *tablespoons (1 ounce) unsalted butter*
>   *juice of 1 large lemon*

1. Halve and bone the chickens completely, leaving the first wing joint intact.
2. In a small saucepan, blanch the garlic cloves in boiling water for 1 minute. Drain. Cut the garlic into paper-thin slices. Toss them in a small bowl with the parsley and a little salt and pepper.
3. Stuff a little of the garlic mixture into the pockets under the skin of the chicken breasts and thighs (about 2 teaspoons per chicken). Transfer the chicken to a large plate, cover with plastic wrap and chill until ready to use.
4. Heat a charcoal or gas grill until moderately hot. Grill the chickens 7 to 10 minutes per side, or just until the pinkness disappears. Do not overcook.
5. Heat the butter in a sauté pan and in it gently sauté the remaining garlic mixture. Add the lemon juice and season to taste with salt and pepper.

PRESENTATION: Divide the chicken halves among 4 large heated dinner plates. Top with the sautéed garlic and parsley. Serve with fresh vegetables cooked *al dente*.

Note: Make sure to get the charcoal very hot and let it get coated with gray ash before grilling the chicken. If you are using a gas or electric grill get it very hot, too, then turn the heat down to medium to cook the chickens.

GRILLED BABY CHICKENS WITH TRUFFLE VINAIGRETTE

Serves 4

      2 *baby chickens, approximately 1 to 1½ pounds each*
    ⅓ *cup walnut oil*
      1 *large whole black truffle*
      1 *tablespoon unsalted butter*
    ¼ *cup almond oil*
      2 *tablespoons sherry wine vinegar*
          salt
          freshly ground pepper
      2 *tablespoons minced fresh chervil*
      2 *tablespoons minced shallots*

1.   Halve and bone the chicken completely, leaving the first wing joint attached to the breast. Separate the breasts, legs and thighs of the chickens, leaving the first wing joints attached to the breasts. Brush the chickens with some of the walnut oil.

2.   Cut 4 nice slices from the center of the truffle. Melt the butter in a small sauté pan over low heat. In it cook the 4 truffle

slices lightly for several seconds, or until they begin to release their wonderful aroma and taste. Let them cool, then place 1 slice under the skin of each breast. Wrap the birds with plastic and refrigerate until ready to use. (The chicken and vinaigrette can be refrigerated overnight if necessary. Bring to room temperature before completing the recipe.)

3. Cut half the remaining truffle into very fine dice; reserve the remaining half for the vinaigrette.

4. Place the remaining walnut oil, the almond oil, 1 tablespoon of the vinegar, and salt and pepper to taste in a blender. Blend until creamy, add the remaining undiced truffle, and blend again. Taste carefully, adding vinegar as necessary to make a slightly tangy vinaigrette. (Vinegars vary greatly in intensity. The vinegar we use is very strong. This recipe can take anywhere from 1 to 4 tablespoons of vinegar, but it is better to err on the side of too little vinegar, for too much will overpower the flavor of the truffle.) Correct the seasonings. Set aside.

5. Preheat a grill until very hot. Season the chickens with salt and pepper. Grill over mesquite, or broil, about 10 minutes on each side, until the chicken feels springy when gently pressed with your finger.

PRESENTATION: Pool some of the vinaigrette in the center of 4 dinner plates. Sprinkle the chervil and shallots over the vinaigrette. Place half a chicken attractively on each plate and garnish with the diced truffle.

ROASTED CHICKEN BREASTS STUFFED WITH YELLOW AND RED BELL PEPPERS AND SWEET GREEN ONION SAUCE

Serves 4

4 large boneless chicken breasts, cut in half
salt
freshly ground white pepper
1 yellow bell pepper
1 red bell pepper
2 bunches green onions or scallions
1 tablespoon oil
3 tablespoons rice wine vinegar
4 tablespoons plum wine or sherry
½ cup heavy cream
4 tablespoons (2 ounces) unsalted butter at room temperature

1.   Flatten the chicken breasts with the help of a meat hammer and season them with salt and pepper.
2.   Char the yellow and red pepper over a gas flame or under a hot broiler until the skin is completely burned. Wipe off the skin. Quarter each pepper and remove the seeds.
3.   In a saucepan, blanch the green part of 4 of the green onions.
4.   Place 1 blanched green onion on the inside of chicken breast, then add a piece of the yellow pepper and a piece of the red pepper. Roll up the breast to enclose the peppers and secure with string. Season the outside with salt and pepper. Repeat with the remaining breasts.
5.   Preheat the oven to 400 degrees F.
6.   Heat a large heavy ovenproof skillet. Add the chicken breasts and brown them on all sides. Place the skillet in the hot oven and cook the breasts for 15 minutes. The chicken should be

slightly underdone. Remove from oven and keep the chicken warm on a plate.

7.   Halve the remaining green onions lengthwise, then cut them into 1-inch pieces.

8.   Heat a sauté pan. Add the oil and heat until hot. In it, sauté the green onion pieces for 1 minute. Add the vinegar and plum wine or sherry and reduce by two thirds. Add the cream and reduce it until the sauce lightly coats the back of a spoon. Whisk in the butter, a little at a time, over very low heat. Season the sauce to taste with salt and pepper.

PRESENTATION: Pool the sauce in the center of 4 warm dinner plates or one large platter. Cut each chicken breast into 6 slices and arrange the slices attractively on the sauce.

CHICKEN WITH ACACIA CHARDONNAY AND FRESH HERBS

Serves 4

4 *large boneless chicken breasts*

4 *ounces fresh goat cheese*
1 *tablespoon chopped fresh tarragon*
1 *tablespoon chopped fresh Italian parsley*
1 *tablespoon chopped fresh chervil*
   freshly ground white pepper
   salt
   about 4 teaspoons extra-virgin olive oil
1 *shallot, minced*
1 *cup Acacia Chardonnay*
1 *cup Chicken Stock (page 69)*

½ cup heavy cream

4 tablespoons (2 ounces) unsalted butter

1. Preheat the oven to 450 degrees F. or heat a grill until hot.
2. In a bowl, mix the goat cheese, half the herbs and white pepper to taste.
3. Loosen the skin of the chicken breasts. Divide the cheese mixture, place some of it under the skin of each breast and pat gently to distribute evenly.
4. Season the chicken lightly with salt and pepper. Sprinkle with olive oil. Roast in the oven for 15 to 20 minutes or cook on the hot grill for 8 to 10 minutes per side.
5. Combine the shallot and Chardonnay in a saucepan, bring to a boil and reduce to a glaze, about ¼ cup. Add the stock and reduce by half. Add the cream and continue to reduce until the sauce lightly coats the back of a spoon. Whisk in the butter in small pieces, making sure each piece is incorporated before adding the next. Season the sauce to taste with salt and pepper. Strain it into a clean saucepan and add the remaining chopped herbs.

PRESENTATION: Pool the sauce onto 4 warm dinner plates. Slice each chicken breast into scallops and place on the sauce. Serve immediately with the rest of the Acacia Chardonnay.

CHICKEN BREASTS STUFFED WITH GOAT CHEESE AND FRESH HERBS, WITH CHANTERELLE AND MAUI ONION VINAIGRETTE

Serves 4

6 ounces fresh goat cheese
½ bunch thyme leaves
1 bunch chives
½ bunch chervil or Italian parsley
  freshly ground pepper
2 whole chicken breasts, boned (use free range chickens if possible)

Vinaigrette

2 tablespoons (1 ounce) unsalted butter
6 tablespoons extra-virgin olive oil
12 ounces fresh chanterelles
  salt
  freshly ground pepper
1 medium Maui onion
1 bunch fresh chervil or Italian parsley
½ bunch thyme leaves
½ bunch fresh basil
⅓ cup walnut oil
¼ cup rice wine vinegar

1. Preheat the oven to 450 degrees F.
2. Crumble the goat cheese into a mixing bowl. Chop the fresh herbs, add to the cheese and season with pepper to taste.
3. Place the cheese mixture under the skin of the chicken breasts. Pat gently to distribute it evenly.
4. Place the chicken in a roasting pan and roast for 15 to 20 minutes, or until just barely done. Keep warm.

5.   While the chicken is roasting, prepare the vinaigrette: Heat a large skillet over high heat and add the butter and 2 table-spoons of the olive oil. Add the chanterelles and sauté them until *al dente*. Season to taste with salt and pepper. Turn into a large bowl to cool.

6.   Cut the onion into ¼-inch cubes. Add to the mushrooms. Chop the chervil, thyme and basil into ¼-inch pieces and add to the mushrooms.

7.   Toss the mushroom mixture with the remaining olive oil, the walnut oil and the rice wine vinegar. Season to taste with salt and pepper.

PRESENTATION: Make a pool of vinaigrette in the center of each of 4 dinner plates. Halve the chicken breasts and put a half over each serving of vinaigrette. Serve immediately.

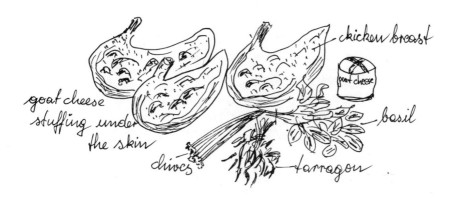

STIR-FRIED CHICKEN WITH GARLIC AND CILANTRO

Serves 2 for dinner
or 4 as an appetizer

Chinese Vinaigrette

3 tablespoons rice wine vinegar
1 tablespoon sesame oil
2 tablespoons peanut oil
2 tablespoons soy sauce
  juice of ½ lemon
  salt
  freshly ground pepper

Chicken

2 chicken legs
8 cloves garlic
1 bunch cilantro, leaves only
  green parts of 4 scallions
¼ cup plum wine
2 tablespoons sesame oil
2 tablespoons soy sauce
  salt
  freshly ground white pepper

1 small head iceberg lettuce or radicchio
2 tablespoons peanut oil
1 red bell pepper, cut into small cubes
12 snow peas or Chinese green beans, cut into small cubes

1.   Prepare the vinaigrette: In a small bowl, whisk together the vinegar, sesame oil, peanut oil, soy sauce and lemon juice. Season to taste with salt and pepper. Set aside.

2. Prepare the chicken: Bone the chicken legs and force the meat with the garlic, half the cilantro leaves, and the scallion greens through a meat grinder with a medium-fine blade. Add the plum wine, sesame oil, soy sauce, and salt and pepper and mix well. The mixture should be quite peppery.

3. Reserve 4 nice lettuce or *radicchio* leaves, as "nests." Slice the remaining lettuce into thin "stripes" (strips).

4. In a bowl, toss the lettuce with enough of the Chinese vinaigrette to coat lightly and half-fill the nests with it.

5. Heat a wok or heavy skillet over high heat until very hot and add the peanut oil. Add the chicken mixture and stir-fry it until almost done. Add the bell pepper and snow peas or green beans and cook for 30 seconds. Remove from the wok.

PRESENTATION: Fill each salad leaf with some of the chicken mixture and sprinkle with the remaining cilantro leaves.

I also like to use radicchio leaves instead of iceberg lettuce, not only is the color beautiful but I also like the slightly bitter taste of the radicchio leaves.

CHINESE DUCK WITH PLUM SAUCE
AND CHINOIS PANCAKES

The tartness of the sauce contrasts nicely with the richness of the duck.

Serves 6

Plum Purée

½ pound Elephant Heart plums, halved and pitted
½ cup plum wine
¼ cup raspberries, blueberries or fresh black currants

Ducks

3 Chinese ducks, preferably air-dried (about 4 pounds each)
¼ cup rice wine vinegar
1 teaspoon honey

Sauce

1 cup plum wine
2 sprigs fresh mint
2 strips orange peel, about 1 inch by 2 inches
1 cup rice wine vinegar
1 cup plum purée
½ cup veal Demi-Glace *or duck* Demi-Glace *(page 33)*
4 tablespoons (2 ounces) unsalted butter
salt
freshly ground pepper
Chinois pancakes (recipe follows)

1.   Prepare the plum purée: Place the plums, wine and berries in a small saucepan, bring to a boil and simmer until the plums are soft, about 15 minutes. Purée the mixture in a blender or

food processor and strain it through a fine sieve into a clean saucepan. Bring to a boil and reduce to 1 cup. Set aside.

2. Prepare the ducks: Preheat the oven to 325 degrees F. Mix ¼ cup of the rice vinegar with the honey and brush the duck all over with this mixture.

3. Place the ducks in a roasting pan and roast them about 30 minutes. Remove from the oven and pour off the accumulated fat. Give the ducks a quarter turn and return to the oven. Repeat this process for about an hour and a half, or until the ducks are dark golden brown on all sides. Remember to pour off the rendered fat each time you turn them. Transfer the ducks to another pan and let them rest so that the fat continues to drain from the insides.

4. Prepare the sauce: In a saucepan, reduce the plum wine with the mint sprigs and orange peel to a glaze. Add the vinegar and reduce it by two thirds. Add the plum purée and reduce it by half, until the flavor is quite intense. Add the *demi-glace* and continue to reduce the mixture by half, or until it is thickened slightly and tastes delicious. Over very low heat whisk in the butter, a little at a time. Season the sauce to taste with salt and pepper. Strain the sauce and keep it warm.

5. Remove the breasts and legs from the duck. Place them on a grill or under a broiler or salamander until the skin is crispy.

PRESENTATION: Slice the duck breasts into medallions. Separate the legs and thighs; arrange half a duck attractively on each plate. Sauce the duck with the plum sauce. Decorate each plate with a scallion-filled Chinois Pancake.

CHINOIS PANCAKES

Makes 6 pancakes

1/4 *cup flour*
   pinch salt
 1 *egg*
 1 *tablespoon sesame oil*
1/2 *cup milk*
 2 *teaspoons minced fresh ginger*
 1 *clove garlic, minced*
 1 *scallion, thinly sliced*
 1 *teaspoon unsalted butter*
 6 *small scallions, cut in half*

1.   In a small bowl, combine the flour, salt, egg and sesame oil. Whisk in the milk, then unless your batter is completely lump free, strain into another bowl. (The batter should be the consistency of heavy cream.) If the batter is too thick add water, 1 tablespoon at a time, until you get the desired consistency.

2.   Stir in the ginger, garlic and scallion.

3.   Heat the butter in a non-stick crepe pan over moderate heat. Add 2 tablespoons batter, then swirl the pan to coat the bottom with batter. Cook the pancake over high heat until golden brown. Turn it over and brown the other side. Remove from the pan and keep warm. Repeat the process until all the batter is used.

PRESENTATION: Cut each pancake in half, place a scallion on each and roll into a cone shape.

Note: The pancake may be made ahead and refrigerated. Before serving, wrap them in foil and reheat in a 350 degree F. oven for 7 to 8 minutes.

GRILLED PIGEON WITH SAUTÉED PEARS AND CRANBERRIES

Serves 6

6 *young pigeons (squabs)*
1¼ *cups Port*
3 *sprigs fresh thyme, leaves only*
freshly ground black pepper
1 *tablespoon almond, safflower or extra-virgin olive oil*
½ *cup* Mirepoix *(page 294)*
1 *cup fresh cranberries*
6 *tablespoons (3 ounces) unsalted butter, cut into small pieces*
salt
3 *small pears, peeled and cored*
1 to 2 *teaspoons sugar*

1.   Halve the pigeons and bone them, leaving in the leg and wing bones and reserving the removed bones.
2.   On a platter let the birds marinate in 1 cup of the Port, the thyme and the pepper for 3 to 4 hours.
3.   In a small saucepan, heat the oil over moderate heat. When it is hot, sauté the reserved pigeon bones until browned. Lower the heat, add the *mirepoix* and cook until it begins to sweat, about 5 minutes. Deglaze the pan with the remaining Port, then add water to cover by 1 to 2 inches (about 1½ cups). Bring the water to a boil and simmer it for 1½ to 2 hours. Strain the stock into a clean saucepan and reduce it by half. (There should be about ⅔ cup pigeon stock.)
4.   Strain the marinade from the pigeons into a small saucepan, bring it to a boil and reduce it to ¼ cup. Add the reduced stock and half the cranberries and reduce to ½ cup. Whisk in 3 tablespoons of the butter, a little at a time. Season to taste with salt and pepper. Strain and reserve the sauce in a warm place.

5.   Slice the pears ¼ inch thick. In a sauté pan, sauté them in 2 tablespoons of the butter for 3 to 4 minutes, or until they are tender. Reserve.

6.   Heat the remaining butter in another pan. When it is foamy, sauté the remaining cranberries with the sugar for 4 to 5 minutes.

7.   Preheat a grill. Sprinkle the pigeons with salt and pepper. Grill the birds for 3 to 4 minutes on each side, until medium rare. Or brown them quickly on all sides in a little hot oil, then roast them in a 400 degree F. oven for 8 to 10 minutes.

PRESENTATION: Divide the pears among 6 large warm dinner plates. Top with 1 pigeon half. Spoon a little sauce over the birds. Garnish with the sautéed cranberries.

PHEASANT BREAST WITH SAUTÉED DUCK LIVER

Serves 6

> *3 young pheasants*
> *oil*
> *1 teaspoon freshly cracked black peppercorns*
> *salt*
> *4 medium shallots, minced*
> *½ cup sherry vinegar*
> *½ cup dry red wine*
> *1 cup light duck or Chicken Stock (page 69)*
> *10 tablespoons (5 ounces) unsalted butter*
> *six 1-ounce slices duck liver, cut ¼ inch thick*

1. Preheat the oven to 450 degrees F.

2. Remove the wings and neck from each bird; set aside. Truss the pheasants with kitchen string.

3. Heat a heavy skillet over medium heat. Add a little oil to barely coat the bottom of the pan. Meanwhile, season the pheasants with salt and pepper. One at a time, brown the birds on all sides. Remove from the pan.

4. Place the reserved wings and necks in the bottom of a roasting pan large enough to hold the pheasants. Arrange the pheasants on top. Roast about 20 minutes, or until the meat is medium rare. Remove the birds from the pan and keep them warm. Discard the wings, necks and excess fat from the pan.

5. Sauté the shallots in the roasting pan for 1 to 2 minutes, adding a little butter if necessary.

6. Deglaze both the skillet and the roasting pan with the vinegar and combine the liquids in one pan. Add the wine and reduce it over high heat until the liquid becomes a little like syrup. Pour in the stock and reduce it by half. Whisk in 8 tablespoons of the butter, a little at a time. Season to taste with salt and pepper and strain the sauce into a clean saucepan. Keep warm.

7. Heat a non-stick skillet until very hot. Add the remaining butter and a little oil, then sauté the foie gras slices over very high heat for 30 seconds, or until golden brown.

PRESENTATION: Carve each pheasant breast half into 4 nice slices. Arrange the 4 slices on each dinner plate with a foie gras slice inserted in between. Spoon a little sauce over each serving.

I like to use only pheasant breasts because the legs are often tough when I cook the breasts medium rare. Legs can be used for Duck Sausage (page 113).

QUAIL ON CORN CAKES WITH ZINFANDEL SAUCE

Serves 4

> 8 *corn cakes, made with garlic (recipe follows)*
> 4 *quail, boned and halved*
>   *salt*
>   *freshly ground black pepper*
>   *all-purpose flour*
> 8 *tablespoons (4 ounces) unsalted butter, softened*
> 1 *tablespoon almond or safflower oil*
> 1 *cup Zinfandel*
> 2 to 3 *teaspoons fresh thyme leaves plus 4 small sprigs fresh thyme for garnish*

1.   Make the corn cakes and keep them warm.

2.   Season both sides of the quail with salt and pepper. Dust lightly with flour.

3.   Heat a large heavy sauté pan over moderate heat. Add 1 tablespoon of the butter and the oil. When it is very hot, add the quail and sauté them, skin side down, for 2 minutes. Turn and sauté an additional 2 minutes. If you like quail well done, cook for 4 minutes each side. The quail should be golden brown and medium rare. Transfer to a plate and keep warm.

4.   Pour off any fat in the pan and deglaze the pan with the Zinfandel. Add the thyme leaves and reduce the sauce to a glaze, 2 or 3 tablespoons.

5.   Whisk in the remaining butter over very low heat, a little at a time. If the sauce begins to separate around the edges, stir in a spoonful of stock or water to stabilize it. (This is a good remedy for any butter sauce or for a hollandaise-type sauce that has been left waiting over water that is just a little too hot.) Season to taste with salt and pepper.

PRESENTATION: On each of 4 warm dinner plates, place 2 cakes. Arrange one half quail on each cake. Spoon a little sauce over each bird and spoon the remaining sauce around the corn cakes. Garnish each dish with a sprig of fresh thyme.

CORN CAKES

Corn cakes are a good accompaniment to game birds, such as quail or squab.

Makes 8 to 10
corn cakes

  ¼ *cup yellow cornmeal*
   1 teaspoon brown sugar
   1 cup milk
   2 eggs, separated
   salt
   freshly ground white pepper
 2 or 3 cloves garlic, blanched, or 1 jalapeño pepper, minced
  ½ *cup fresh corn kernels (optional)*
   unsalted butter

1. Combine the cornmeal, sugar and milk in a saucepan. Bring to a boil over medium heat and cook, stirring constantly, until the mixture is thick and smooth, approximately 5 minutes. Remove from the heat and cool slightly.
2. Stir in the egg yolks and salt and pepper to taste. Add the garlic or jalapeño pepper and the corn kernels, if desired.
3. In a bowl, whip the egg whites with a pinch of salt until stiff. Stir a quarter of them into the cornmeal mixture, then fold in the rest.

4.   Heat a heavy non-stick skillet and to it add a little butter. Ladle batter into the skillet, using 1 tablespoon batter for each cake. Do not crowd cakes. Brown one side over medium heat, then turn and brown the other side. Remove from the pan and keep warm.

SQUAB WITH LEEKS AND POMEGRANATE SAUCE

Serves 4

 4 whole squab
 8 tablespoons (4 ounces) unsalted butter
 ¼ cup Mirepoix *(page 294)*
 ½ bay leaf
 ½ teaspoon black peppercorns
  pinch fresh thyme leaves
 2 pomegranates
 ¼ cup duck or veal Demi-Glace *(page 33)*
 4 small leeks, white part only, cut into julienne strips
  salt
  freshly ground pepper

1.   Bone the squab breasts, leaving the legs attached.
2.   Cut the bones into small pieces. Melt 1 tablespoon of the butter in a small saucepan. In it brown the bones, then add the *mirepoix* and cook over low heat for 10 minutes. Add the bay leaf, peppercorns and thyme. Cover with water and simmer until the mixture is reduced to ¾ to 1 cup. Strain the stock into a bowl and degrease it carefully. Reserve.

3.   While the squab stock reduces, squeeze the juice from the pomegranates through a strainer and reserve. Also reserve 1 to 2 tablespoons of the pomegranate seeds for decoration.

4.   Preheat the oven to 450 degrees F.

5.   Heat an ovenproof sauté pan, then add 1 tablespoon of the butter. In it sauté the squab breasts, skin side down, over high heat to brown them. Transfer the pan to the oven for about 15 minutes, or until the squab are medium rare. Remove from the oven, transfer the squab to a platter and keep warm.

6.   Throw away any fat remaining in the sauté pan. Return it to the heat, deglaze it with the pomegranate juice and reduce to a glaze. Pour in the reserved stock and the *demi-glace*, reduce by half, or until thickened slightly. Whisk in 4 tablespoons butter, a little at a time. Season the sauce to taste with salt and pepper.

7.   In a sauté pan, sauté the leeks gently in the remaining 2 tablespoons butter. Reserve.

8.   Slice the squab breasts into *aiguillettes*, leaving the leg attached to the last piece.

PRESENTATION: Make a bed of leeks in the center of each warm dinner plate. Arrange 1 squab breast nicely on the leeks. Sauce the squab and sprinkle with the reserved pomegranate seeds.

Note: Brown Stock (page 71) or Chicken Stock (page 69) may be used in place of the squab stock.

SAUTÉED SQUAB WITH
PANFRIED NOODLES

Serves 4

8 *whole shallots, unpeeled*
5 *tablespoons peanut oil*
4 *ounces Regular Pasta Dough (page 98)*
2 *tablespoons sesame oil*
2 *squab*
   salt
   freshly ground pepper
½ *cup dry red wine*
1 *cup Duck Stock (page 34) or Veal Stock (page 71)*
4 *tablespoons (2 ounces) unsalted butter, cut into small*
   pieces
3 *ounces* shiitake *mushrooms, sliced ⅜ inch thick*
16 *small snow peas, blanched*
10 *sprigs fresh chervil, 6 finely chopped*

1. Preheat the oven to 400 degrees F.
2. Rub the shallots with peanut oil, place in a small ovenproof dish, cover and roast for 1 hour, or until soft. Let the shallots cool slightly and gently squeeze them from their skins. Keep warm.
3. Cut the pasta dough into ¼-inch noodles and cook in a large pot of lightly salted boiling water until *al dente*. Rinse under cold water and drain well. Heat 2 tablespoons of the peanut oil and the sesame oil in a non-stick pan over moderate heat. Spread the noodles evenly in the pan and fry until crisp and golden brown. Turn and brown the other side. They should be crispy on the outside and still a little soft on the inside.
4. Pat the squab dry and season with salt and pepper. Heat the remaining peanut oil in an ovenproof sauté pan over moderate heat. Add the squab and brown quickly on all sides. Trans-

fer the pan to the oven and roast 10 to 12 minutes, or until the
squab are medium rare. Remove from the oven. Transfer the
birds to a plate and keep warm.

5.   Discard any fat from the pan, then deglaze it with the red
wine. Reduce to 1 tablespoon. Add the stock and reduce it until
the sauce is thickened slightly. Whisk in all but 1 tablespoon of
the butter, a little at a time. Reserve the sauce in a warm spot.
6.   Heat the remaining butter in a sauté pan over medium heat.
In it sauté the mushrooms until nearly done, add the snow peas
and chopped chervil, and toss to combine. Pour the reserved
sauce into the vegetables and correct the seasonings.
7.   Remove the breasts from the squab and slice them into
aiguillettes (page 293). Pour any accumulated squab juice into
the sauced vegetables and reheat them gently if necessary.

PRESENTATION: Place the fried noodles in the center of a large
platter. Arrange the squab *aiguillettes* attractively over the noodles. Spoon the vegetables and roasted shallots around the edge.
Decorate with the remaining sprigs of fresh chervil.

Vegetables

I love very fresh, very tender young vegetables done in a very simple manner. And I felt it would be better to include only a few recipes for them here. Just as important is my philosophy about the selection and treatment of vegetables.

At Spago and Chinois we use only the finest and freshest baby vegetables available to us at the peaks of their seasons. Baby vegetables have an exuberance of flavor more pronounced than in more mature vegetables.

It is true that vegetables of this quality are difficult to obtain in some areas. Most cities have produce markets that are worth a drive—take a friend along. And ask your local greengrocers if they are willing to special-order the produce you wish to have. You may be surprised at how happy they are to accommodate your needs.

Certainly, best of all is to grow your own vegetables in your own garden, along with fresh herbs. This can be done in quite a small space, and there are many good books that explain how to put small areas to creative use. If you don't have a green thumb, there are even people who will plant and maintain gardens for you in your own yard.

There are some things you should keep in mind as you cook the various vegetables I will discuss. Even baby vegetables come in different sizes, so cooking times may vary from those given in this book. High heat means different things to different people, as well as to their stoves. Some cooking equipment is capable of producing a much higher heat than others. So, as with many other recipes, your own sense of when something is "done" is your best guide. I can only tell you as a general rule that the vegetables at Spago and Chinois are cooked until they are just tender but still crunchy.

Beautifully cooked vegetables create an explosion of color on the plate as well as an explosion of taste on the palate.

All the vegetables included in this chapter can be stir-fried, so here are some things that I find useful to remember when stir-frying. Get your wok or skillet very hot, then add the oil around the edge and get it hot, too. Stir-fry the vegetables with a little seasoning, such as fresh herbs and pepper, and a little chicken stock or water. Finish the vegetables with some soy sauce instead of salt, but be sure to add the soy sauce off the heat; it will get very salty if it cooks for more than a few seconds.

For larger vegetables like eggplants, large zucchinis, onions, and so on, my preferred preparation is grilling. I generally cut the vegetables into ½-inch slices, let them marinate with a little olive oil or a squeeze of lemon juice, fresh herbs and a little salt and pepper, then I place them on a hot barbecue or grill.

Baby zucchini without blossoms should be finger-sized. They can either be blanched in salted boiling water for 30 to 45 seconds or sautéed in unsalted butter and a little oil with a little chicken stock for 1 minute to 1½ minutes. Season them with salt and freshly ground pepper. Fresh herbs may be used, but very sparingly, so as not to mask the flavor of this delicate vegetable.

Baby zucchini with blossoms may be treated in the same manner as baby zucchini without blossoms. (I also give a very tasty recipe for stuffed squash blossoms in *Wolfgang Puck's French Cooking for the Modern American Kitchen*.) The blossoms can be stuffed with a mixture of soft cheeses and deep fried, then dusted with Parmesan cheese and served as an hors d'oeuvre, or use them to garnish a pizza, as we do at Spago. They can be sautéed in a little butter with a little chicken stock, seasoned with salt and pepper and served with a medley of other vegetables.

Baby summer squash, approximately ½ inch in diameter, may be sautéed in a little unsalted butter and oil; for a unique, delicious flavor, use hazelnut oil.

Baby carrots should be peeled, with about ½ inch of the top left on. Preferably they should be no more than 2 to 3 inches long and ⅜ to ½ inch in diameter. If they are too long, you may pare the bottom (diagonally) to the desired length. If the only carrots available are larger in diameter, cut them in half lengthwise. Blanch the vegetables in a large quantity of boiling salted water for 2 to 3 minutes, then plunge them into ice water. Remove them when cold, dry and reheat at serving time in a little butter with salt and pepper and, if desired, with a sprinkling of herbs such as fresh dill or thyme. Occasionally some carrots are not very tasty; slice these thin and sauté them over low heat in a little butter and season with salt and pepper.

Large or medium asparagus spears should be peeled and trimmed, then tied into bunches with kitchen string, 6 or 7 to a bundle. Blanch them in a large quantity of boiling salted water for 5 to 8 minutes, remove and plunge into ice water to stop the cooking. Remove the string and reheat them either in boiling water for 1 minute or in unsalted butter until warm.

Baby asparagus should be about 3 inches long. They should be tied in small bundles (they need not be peeled). Blanch them in boiling salted water for 1 minute to 1½ minutes, then plunge them into ice water and reheat as above.

Broccoli flowerettes should be separated from the stalks and broken into small flowerettes about ½ inch in diameter. Blanch them in boiling salted water for 1 minute or sauté them in butter for 1 to 2 minutes, or until they are tender but still crunchy. Season with salt and pepper.

Broccoli stems should not be overlooked in your repertoire. Peel them and slice them ¼ inch thick. Sauté or stir-fry the slices for about 2 minutes, adding a little minced garlic. The cooking time for them will be slightly longer than for flowerettes. *Garlic* is very important to the kitchens of Spago and Chinois. It is good when rubbed with olive oil and roasted in a 400 degree F. oven until it is soft, about 1 hour. It can be blanched in boiling water for 1 minute, then caramelized and used as a garnish (especially good with lamb), or chopped and used on pizzas or in calzones. Blanched garlic has a much more subtle flavor than raw garlic and is more agreeable to eat in polite company.

Peas should be very young, so that the round succulent morsels are still sweet. Blanch them in boiling water for not more than 1 minute. Plunge into ice water, drain and reheat for a few seconds in butter before serving. Peas that are beginning to pass their prime are still preferable to the frozen or canned variety; they benefit from the addition of a spoonful of sugar to the cooking water. Old peas should be made into soup.

Snow peas may be cut into julienne strips and eaten raw in a salad. At Spago and Chinois they are blanched for 30 seconds, then plunged into ice water, drained and reheated at serving time in a little butter or hazelnut oil. Large or small julienne strips of snow peas are used in some pasta dishes and in the Twice Fried Rice at Chinois.

Corn on the cob is served at Spago in approximately 3-inch lengths rather than in whole ears. Blanch it in salted boiling water for about 1 minute. Corn that is overcooked will get caught between your teeth as well as stick to your teeth—rather an awkward situation!

Fiddlehead ferns have recently captured the imaginations of many. They are best cooked in chicken stock until tender, drained, cooled and later sautéed in butter or hazelnut oil, or stir-fried and seasoned with salt or soy sauce and freshly ground pepper.

Baby potatoes, with diameters of no more than ½ to ¾ inch, are best prepared simply. Place them in boiling salted water for 5 to 10 minutes, depending on their size. Drain and serve them as part of a melange of vegetables on your dinner plate; or serve them separately as a first course with a dollop of *crème fraîche* and caviar; or, with some gravlax on the side. Larger new potatoes can be "turned" (trimmed) to a size comparable to the other vegetables being served.

Baby red skinned potatoes may be boiled or roasted in olive oil and served as a vegetable, but they are marvelous when served on a plate of smoked salmon slices, with Caviar Dill Sauce (page 14) on the side.

Mushrooms come in so many varieties that it would be impossible to describe each one of them here. If you are lucky enough to have a supply and knowledgeable enough, you gather your own. If your knowledge is less than expert, gather your mushrooms at your local supermarket and produce markets. If they don't have what you want on hand, special order them or substitute another type. *White mushrooms* are the most common variety available in the United States. To clean them, rub them with a damp towel. If they are really dirty, use the tip of a small paring knife to peel them. You will find this quite easy.

Enoki mushrooms are Japanese mushrooms that are sold in plastic packages of about 3 ounces. They are a wonderful garnish but cannot be cooked for more than a few seconds or they disappear. After cutting off the root base, it is best to use them raw as a garnish or to mix them, uncooked, into the dish you are making.

Chanterelle, Shiitake, Oyster, Japanese Tree, and Elephant Ear (Wood Hue), Morels, Cêpes or (Porchini in Italian) are the other mushrooms most used at Spago and Chinois. Unless the mushrooms are dried they should never be soaked. Mushrooms should be cooked at a very high heat in either olive oil or another oil that has a high burning temperature. A small piece of butter improves the flavor, as do a few minced shallots or garlic, salt and pepper. If desired, finish the mushrooms with a little more butter and a sprinkling of minced fine herbs.

Baby turnips are another culinary delight. They should be peeled and blanched for 5 to 7 minutes, depending on their size, then heated in butter or olive oil and seasoned with salt and pepper. *Japanese eggplant* can be sliced or halved, brushed with olive oil and grilled for 1 to 2 minutes per side until cooked through.

Onions can be blanched (small ones) or caramelized in butter and a little stock. They can be sliced and turned into a marmalade (page 161) or simply brushed with olive oil and grilled (mesquite imparts an especially good flavor).

Green Beans and haricots verts are best when simply prepared. Blanch them in a large pot of boiling salted water until tender but still crispy, then plunge them into ice water (to stop the cooking) and drain. Reheat them either in boiling water for a few seconds or in butter. Season them simply with salt and freshly ground pepper.

Pepper should be freshly ground or it has all the flavor of sand!

Red, yellow and green bell peppers can be blanched in boiling salted water, cut into strips and sautéed in olive oil or peeled (char the skin over an open flame or under a hot broiler, then steam the peppers in a paper sack for 10 minutes, peel and rinse). Use in a pasta dish or on a pizza. They can also be puréed and used in a butter sauce or cut into little cubes and used in a vinaigrette.

Chili peppers are used peeled as above or left unpeeled—How hot do you like them?—in the fresh *salsa* that accompanies the sautéed oysters we serve at Spago and in many of the other sauces. They are responsible for a number of the wonderfully spicy dishes we serve at Chinois, too, such as the blackened redfish (or salmon).

Okra is a much overlooked vegetable in many parts of the United States. It is good when blanched simply in boiling salted water until just tender. Drain and serve immediately.

GRATIN OF SALSIFY

Serves 4

    4 salsify
    1 lemon, halved
        milk
        water
        salt
    ⅔ cup heavy cream
        freshly ground white pepper
    1 clove garlic, peeled
    ¼ cup finely grated Swiss cheese

1.   Peel the salsify. Cut it in half lengthwise, then into 1½-inch lengths. Rub the cut surfaces with lemon.

2.   Place the salsify in a saucepan with equal parts milk and water to cover. Add a pinch of salt. Bring to a boil, reduce the heat and simmer until tender, about 15 minutes.

3.   While the salsify is cooking, reduce the cream with a little salt, pepper, and the garlic clove by a third to a half. Set aside.

4.   Preheat the oven to 400 degrees F.

5.   When the salsify is tender, drain it and rinse it under cold water, and drain again. Place it in a shallow, ovenproof baking dish in a single layer. Remove the garlic clove from the cream and pour the cream over the salsify. Correct the seasonings and sprinkle with the cheese.

6.   Place the gratin dish in a *bain-marie* (see page 293). Bake in the hot oven until the cream is bubbly and the cheese is golden brown.

PRESENTATION: Serve directly from the gratin dish as a side dish to accompany beef, lamb, pork or chicken.

ARTICHOKE MOUSSE

Serves 4

4 or 5 very large artichokes
2 lemons, halved
4 tablespoons (2 ounces) unsalted butter, at room temperature
about 2 tablespoons heavy cream
salt
freshly ground pepper

1.   Trim away the leaves from the artichokes to expose the bottoms. Rub the cut surfaces with lemon to prevent oxidation.
2.   Bring a large pot of salted water to a boil. Add the juice of half a lemon and the artichoke bottoms, cover with a linen towel or several thicknesses of paper towels and cook until the artichokes are tender, 40 to 50 minutes.
3.   Remove the artichokes and drain. Remove and discard the fiber from the center of the chokes.
4.   Purée the artichoke bottoms in a food processor with the butter. Pass the purée through a *tamis* or fine strainer into a heavy saucepan and heat through. Stir in the cream and correct the seasonings with salt, pepper and lemon juice.

PRESENTATION: Serve as a side dish to accompany lamb or chicken or use as a bed for sliced meats and poultry.

Note: To reheat, place the mousse in a heavy saucepan, add 1 tablespoon each of unsalted butter and heavy cream. Heat slowly, stirring constantly.

VEGETABLE FRIED RICE

Serves 4

2 tablespoons peanut oil

½ cup broccoli flowerettes

½ cup chopped red bell pepper

½ cup snow peas

½ cup diced into small pieces lobster, duck, chicken meat (optional)

2 cups cooked rice (can be cooked the day before; the grains should be separate)

1 egg, slightly beaten

2 tablespoons soy sauce

1.   Heat a wok or heavy skillet.

2.   Add the peanut oil and heat until hot. Then add all the vegetables and the fish or fowl, if used, and stir-fry for 2 minutes.

3.   Add the rice and stir-fry for another 2 minutes, or until the rice is jumping in the wok.

4.   Pour the beaten egg around the rim of the wok so that the egg scrambles before it touches the rice. Mix the scrambled egg into the rice, add the soy sauce and stir well. Season to taste with salt and pepper.

PRESENTATION: Turn into a heated serving dish. Serve immediately.

Bread

*S*ome of my very earliest recollections involve bread. Back in Austria, we had a neighbor next door who delighted in baking bread for his household, and the wonderful aroma drifting in through our window let us know when he was again performing his ritual. He always made the same massive brown rye loaves, which he would store in his cellar for up to two weeks. (Refrigeration was not yet in widespread use, and the heavy crust of this bread was all that retained its moisture.) Sometimes that wonderful smell comes back to me as if our neighbor still lived eight hundred yards away.

Bread has, since antiquity, been the "staff of life." Man first made unleavened bread during the late Stone Age. Sometime further on, a batch of dough unexpectedly fermented, and raised bread was born; yeast eventually was found to be a more reliable leavening. All of these breads were baked on hot stones or metal plates before the Egyptians invented the oven. It was not until the 1800's that baking powder was introduced and quick breads came into existence.

American history shows that corn was the only grain used for bread until the coming of the Europeans, when wheat and other grains crossed the Atlantic. Today we see an incredible assortment of breads that tell stories about local customs and products. Boston brown bread, buckwheat cakes, blueberry muffins, sourdough bread and beaten biscuits are elements of this nation's folklore. And corn, with its patriotic significance, wears many different faces, in johnnycakes, spoonbread, cornsticks, hush puppies and tortillas.

While many aspects of cooking change with time, bread baking is a comforting link with the past, something done very much as it has always been. Yet it is also a status symbol of the 1980's. Even those with seven-figure incomes brag that they make their own bread. And it doesn't have to be all that time-consuming. If your schedule won't permit you to stay home while the yeast does its work, you can finish a batch of quick bread in one-third the time. But do try a yeast bread when you have several hours to spare. Yeast breads normally require kneading, which is great for releasing tension after a rough day (as many corporate executives are finding out!). As you take out your aggressions on the dough, you are developing the gluten and laying the groundwork for an excellent loaf.

While good bread should have a distinctiveness that sets it apart from the rest, it should not compete with the other foods with which it shares the table. A plain bread, crusty and fragrant, is the perfect means for picking up every drop of a complex sauce without overwhelming it. However, an ordinary meal can come to life with the help of an unusual bread. Experiment with the many varieties at home. Go pound some dough in your kitchen after work, and find out what tasty therapy it can be!

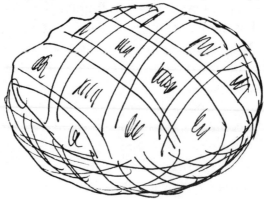

CORN MUFFINS WITH JALAPEÑO PEPPERS AND FRESH ROSEMARY

Makes 12 muffins

>   *1 medium ear of corn*
> *16 tablespoons (8 ounces) unsalted butter*
>   *3 small jalapeño peppers, finely chopped*
>   *2 teaspoons chopped fresh rosemary*
>   *2 packed tablespoons light brown sugar*
>   *1 egg*
>   *1 teaspoon salt*
>   *1 teaspoon baking soda*
>   *1 cup all-purpose flour*
>   *1 cup stoneground cornmeal*
> *1¼ cups buttermilk*

1.   Preheat the oven to 425 degrees F.

2.   Cut the kernels from the ear of corn. Set aside.

3.   In a saucepan, melt 1½ tablespoons of the butter. Brush medium-size muffin tins with some of the butter and set aside. Add the jalapeño peppers to the remaining butter in the pan and cook slowly for 1 minute. Remove from the heat. Add the corn and rosemary to the pan with the peppers and set aside.

4.   In the bowl of an electric mixer, cream the remaining butter with the sugar, then add the egg and mix well. Scrape down the sides of the mixer as necessary. The mixture should be light and fluffy.

5.   Mix together the salt, baking soda, flour and cornmeal. Add to the mixer a quarter of the flour mixture, then a quarter of the buttermilk, mixing well after each addition. Continue with alternate additions of flour and buttermilk until all has been used.

6.   Stir in the jalapeño and corn mixture.

7.   Spoon the batter into the muffin tins until they are three-

quarters full and bake for 18 to 20 minutes. A toothpick inserted in the center will come out clean.

8. Let the muffins rest in the tins for about 5 minutes, then remove them from the pan.

PRESENTATION: Place in a napkin-lined basket or bowl. Serve hot with fresh unsalted butter.

SPAGO'S BRIOCHE LOAF

Long, slow rising develops a much better flavor as well as a lighter loaf. If the dough is allowed to rise too rapidly at too warm a temperature, it will take on a very unpleasant "sourish" taste.

Makes 3 large loaves;
or 3½ pounds brioche dough

> ½ *cup milk*
> *approximately 1 package fresh or dry yeast*
> 5½ *cups (1⅓ pounds) all-purpose flour*
> 6 *eggs*
> ¼ *cup sugar*
> 1 *teaspoon salt*
> 1 *pound unsalted butter, softened*
> ¼ *cup chopped fresh dill (optional)*
> 1 *egg, beaten lightly, for egg wash*

1. Heat the milk until tepid (90 to 100 degrees F.). Pour it into the bowl of an electric mixer. Add the yeast and stir until dissolved. (If the weather is cold, use a little more yeast; if it is very warm, use a little less.) Stir in ¾ cup of the flour to form a sticky dough. This is called a "sponge."

2. Pour the rest of the flour over the top of the sponge. Cover loosely with a cloth and let the sponge proof for 1 to 2 hours,

or until the sponge begins to bubble up through the top of the flour or around the edge of the bowl.

3.   Fit the mixer with a dough hook, and at slow speed add the eggs, one at a time, then the sugar and salt. Knead until the dough is very elastic and shiny. It will wrap itself around the dough hook when it is ready.

4.   Knead the butter briefly by hand to make certain that it is malleable and has no lumps. With the mixer on low speed add 1 to 2 tablespoons butter at a time until it is all incorporated. Continue kneading with the dough hook until the dough again masses around the dough hook. The brioche will be very shiny and elastic and will pull cleanly away from the sides of the bowl.

5.   Cover the mixing bowl with a large cloth or towel and let the brioche rise in a cool place for 2½ to 3 hours, or until triple in bulk.

6.   After the dough has risen, turn on the mixer at very slow speed to "punch down" the brioche. This takes only 1 or 2 turns.

7.   Turn the brioche into a buttered bowl. Cover with plastic wrap and refrigerate overnight.

8.   When the brioche is ready to use, remove it from the refrigerator and form it into loaves or the desired shapes on a baking sheet. Add the optional dill when shaping the dough. Cover loosely and let rise again until double in size.

9.   Preheat the oven to 350 degrees F. When ready to bake the brioche, brush it lightly with the egg wash, then place it in the oven and bake 35 to 45 minutes, or until the top is dark golden brown and the bottom of the loaf sounds hollow when you knock on it with your knuckles.

10.   Remove from the pans and from the oven and let them cool on racks at room temperature. Slice and toast the brioche for Cured Fresh Salmon (page 15) or use as desired.

Note: The brioche dough may be made up to 3 days in advance and kept in the refrigerator until ready to use. The baked loaves may be frozen, well wrapped, for 1 to 2 weeks.

MAIDA HEATTER'S BREADSTICKS

Makes 16–20 breadsticks

1 cup sesame seeds
1 recipe pizza dough (page 110)
1 egg, beaten
   coarse salt

1.   Toast the sesame seeds in a frying pan over medium heat for a few minutes, until they are lightly browned.

2.   To shape the breadsticks, break off small handfuls of the dough and roll them into long, skinny cylinders—about ½ inch wide and 12 inches long—with your hands, working on a lightly floured surface. Place the breadsticks on parchment paper, brush them with the beaten egg, and sprinkle them lightly with a bit of coarse salt and the toasted sesame seeds. Let them rise uncovered at room temperature for about 20 minutes.

3.   Preheat the oven to 400 degrees F. with a pizza stone inside.

4.   Slide the parchment onto the hot stone and bake for about 20 minutes, until the breadsticks are toasted dry and golden. Or bake them for about 15 minutes, until they are nicely colored, then turn off the heat and leave them in the oven until they are fully dry—5 to 10 minutes, depending on their thickness. (If you don't have a pizza stone, you can place the parchment directly on baking sheets.)

MY NOT KOSHER MATZOH

This matzoh is by no means kosher, but it tastes fantastic! I like it best when it's served still warm. If you can't get semolina flour, you can substitute an equal amount of all-purpose flour.

Makes about 6 sheets of matzoh

  1 ½ *cups semolina flour, finest grind*
  1 ½ *cups all-purpose flour*
  2 *teaspoons salt*
  4 *eggs*
  ½ *cup extra virgin olive oil*
  2 *tablespoons kosher salt*
  2 *tablespoons fresh thyme leaves, or 2 teaspoons dried*
  ½ *cup finely chopped onion*

1.   Place the flours, salt, eggs, and half the olive oil in the bowl of a food processor fitted with a steel blade or an electric mixer fitted with a dough hook. Mix or process until the dough forms a ball.

2.   Turn the dough into a clean bowl and cover with a damp towel. Let it rest at room temperature for at least 2 hours.

3.   Preheat the oven to 400 degrees F.

4   Using a pasta machine or a rolling pin, roll out the dough until it is very thin, like lasagna (number 1 on the pasta machine, or as thin as possible without tearing). You should have approximately 6 sheets, about 6 by 10 inches each.

5.   Place the dough on baking sheets and brush very lightly with the remaining olive oil. Sprinkle lightly with the salt, thyme, and onion. Bake the matzoh for about 10 minutes, or until golden brown and crispy.

PECAN AND WALNUT BREAD

Makes three 10–inch loaves

This bread is fantastic toasted, with butter and marmalade for breakfast, or just grilled and served with ripe cheese and wine. The recipe works best in the large quantity given. It freezes well.

> 1⅓ *packages (1 tablespoon plus 1 teaspoon) active dry yeast*
>   3 *cups lukewarm water*
>   5 *cups all-purpose flour*
>   3 *cups rye flour*
> 4½ *tablespoons salt*
>   1 *tablespoon honey*
>   1 *teaspoon chopped fresh rosemary or thyme leaves, or ½ teaspoon dried*
>   7 *tablespoons (3½ ounces) unsalted butter*
> 1½ *cups chopped walnuts*
> 1½ *cups chopped pecans*

1.   Dissolve the yeast in ½ cup of the lukewarm water.

2.   Place the remaining water, both flours, and the salt, honey, rosemary or thyme, and butter in a mixer fitted with a dough hook. Mix for about 5 minutes. Add the dissolved yeast and continue to knead in the mixer for about 15 minutes. Add the walnuts and pecans and continue to knead until the nuts are well mixed into the dough. The dough should come together neatly in a ball.

3.   Cover the mixing bowl with a damp towel and let the dough rise for about 45 minutes at room temperature, or until it approximately doubles in volume.

4.   Knead the dough briefly by hand to remove any large air pockets.

5.   Butter and flour three 10- by 4-inch loaf pans. Divide the dough in three parts, shape each into a 10-inch cylinder, and place them in the prepared pans. Let the loaves rise in the pans for about an hour, or until they at least double in volume.

6.   Preheat the oven to 375 degrees F.

7.   Bake the loaves for about 20 minutes, or until they are nicely browned, then reduce the heat to 325 degrees F. and continue baking for another 25 minutes. Remove from pans and let cool.

SIMPLE SOURDOUGH FARMER'S BREAD

Makes three 10-inch loaves

I bake this bread in a rather hot oven to give the loaves a nice thick crust. The sourdough starter must be prepared at least a day ahead.

> 7 *cups rye flour*
> 4 *cups lukewarm water*
> 1⅓ *packages (1 tablespoon plus 1 teaspoon) active dry yeast*
> 3¼ *cups whole wheat flour*
> 4½ *tablespoons salt*
> 2 *teaspoons cumin*

1.   To prepare the sourdough starter: Place 1½ cups of the rye flour and ⅔ cup of the lukewarm water in a large bowl and mix well. Cover with a damp towel and let sit at room temperature for at least 24 hours. The mixture will become a little bubbly and give off a slightly fermented smell. (If the room is cool, this may take a little longer.)

2.   Dissolve the yeast in ½ cup of the lukewarm water.

3.   Place the remaining water, the sourdough starter, the remaining rye flour and the whole wheat flour, the salt, and the cumin in the bowl of an electric mixer fitted with a dough hook. Mix for about 5 minutes. Add the dissolved yeast and knead the dough in the mixer for another 20 minutes. The dough should come together neatly in a ball.

4.   Cover the mixing bowl with a damp towel and let the dough rise at room temperature for about 45 minutes, or until it doubles in volume.

5.   Knead the dough briefly by hand to remove any large air pockets.

6.   Butter and flour three 10- by 4-inch loaf pans. Divide the dough in three parts, shape each into a 10-inch cylinder, and

place them in the prepared pans. Let the loaves rise for 1 hour or so, or until they at least double in volume. With a sharp knife, cut three diagonal slashes, about ½-inch deep, on the tops of the loaves. (This allows the dough to expand as it bakes.)

7.   Preheat the oven to 375 degrees F.

8.   Bake the loaves for about 25 minutes, or until they are golden brown. Reduce the heat to 325 degrees F. and continue baking for about 20 minutes. Remove the loaves from the pans and let cool. (If you have some wooden bread molds, flour them well and let the dough rise in them. Unmold the loaves onto a floured surface, brush with warm water, and slide onto a preheated pizza stone. Bake as directed.)

Desserts

With all my heart, I had always wanted as a boy to be a pastry chef. At the age of fourteen I set out for a promising interview I had in a well-known pastry shop in Klagenfurt, my home town. I went down the stairs to the work area, looking all around for the chef. As nervous as I was, I didn't watch where my feet were going, until I came to the realization I'd walked through all the *gènoise* cakes that had been put on the floor to cool. The bakers all looked at me. I looked at them. Fortunately, they had the consideration to find someone else to scream at. But it was about then that I had second thoughts about my choice of career, and shortly afterwards I got my first job doing kitchen work.

One of the goldenest of the golden rules in making up a menu, whether professionally or at home, is to pay special attention to the dessert course. Though so many of our restaurant regulars talk about dieting, our pastries just disappear! The guests' strategy is often to eat very little for the main part of the meal, and then to go for that big piece of cake at the end. I don't know how well that diet works, but the point is that nobody seems able to resist a delicious dessert.

Another reason to give careful thought to this part of the meal is that the ending is equal to the beginning in importance—especially if things get off to a bad start for any reason. A splendid chocolate torte is one of the surest ways to soothe an upset customer; without question, chocolate is still number one in popularity. But the finest dessert is not necessarily the fanciest. My personal preference is for a simple tart or sherbet that captures the essence of fruit at its peak. Whether the theme is berries, peaches or mangoes in summer, or apples, pears or grapes in winter, such a dessert treats nature's best in an uncomplicated, respectful manner. This, in my belief, is the principle behind all good cooking.

If you are planning to entertain, many desserts can be prepared in the morning, well before everyone arrives. This gives you freedom from tight time restrictions (and from guests sticking their fingers in your icing), and you can put greater precision into the rest of your work. Don't assume you can make dessert the day before, though, or your masterpiece may taste like your refrigerator. Desserts that can be prepared earlier in the week and frozen include many chocolate desserts, buttercream cakes, and of course ice creams. But some desserts are such prima donnas that they must be left at room temperature and eaten within hours; pie, tarts, and anything based on puff pastry are such temperamental ones.

Even if you've already served so much food that you doubt anyone has room for dessert, try setting out a *petit four* tray of truffles and cookies with the coffee. That tray should empty out pretty quickly. A sweet tooth cannot be denied!

SPAGO'S INDIVIDUAL APPLE PIES

The puff pastry that tops these apple tartlettes can be replaced with sugar dough.

Makes eight 4-inch tarts

⅔ *recipe Sugar Dough (recipe follows)*
  8 *small cooking apples (Pippin, Granny Smith or Golden Delicious)*
  6 *tablespoons (3 ounces) unsalted butter*
½ *cup sugar*
  4 *tablespoons Calvados*
½ *pound Puff Pastry Baumanière (page 228)*
  1 *egg, beaten lightly, for egg wash*
    Caramel Ice Cream (page 255)
    Caramel Sauce (page 256)

1.   Roll the sugar dough into two 11-inch squares. Put each on a parchment paper-lined tray and chill for 20 minutes. Cut eight 5-inch circles and fit them into eight 4- by ½-inch tartlette tins or flan rings. Trim away any extra dough and chill the tins in the refrigerator.

2.   Peel, core and slice the apples ¼ inch thick.

3.   Melt 4 tablespoons of the butter in a sauté pan over moderate heat, add the apples and sprinkle with the sugar. Cook quickly so that the sugar caramelizes, but the apples remain slightly crunchy.

4.   Pour the Calvados over the apples and let it heat for a few seconds. Ignite. Remove the pan from the heat and let the flame die out naturally. Set aside.

5.   Preheat the oven to 325 degrees F.

6.   On a floured surface, roll the puff pastry very thin. Cut 8 circles, 4 inches in diameter. With the tip of a small sharp knife, then draw a design in the center of the puff pastry circles. Take care not to cut all the way through. Refrigerate until needed.

7.   Divide the apples equally among the tart shells. Place half a teaspoon of butter in the center of each. Top each with a puff pastry circle, leaving the sides unsealed.

8.   Bake for 40 to 45 minutes, or until the pastry is golden brown. Let them rest for about 10 minutes before serving. Remove the pies from the tins or rings.

PRESENTATION: Nap each dessert plate with caramel sauce. Place a tart in the center and a scoop of caramel ice cream on the side.

SUGAR DOUGH

Makes 2½ pounds

1 pound unsalted butter, slightly softened
3⅓ cups (12 ounces) pastry flour
3⅓ cups (12 ounces) all-purpose flour
*   pinch salt*
¾ cup (6 ounces) sugar
3 egg yolks
2 tablespoons heavy cream

1.   Cut the butter into large pieces and place the pieces in the bowl of an electric mixer fitted with a paddle or dough hook.

2.   Add the pastry and all-purpose flour, salt and sugar. Mix on low speed until the butter is evenly distributed throughout the flour.

3.   Add the egg yolks and cream. Continue to mix on low speed until the dough pulls away from the sides of the bowl.

4. Remove the dough and divide it into 2 pieces. Flatten each piece into a 6-inch round. Wrap in plastic and chill for at least 2 hours or overnight. Use as needed. The dough will remain fresh for 2 or 3 days in the refrigerator; or wrap securely in plastic, then in foil, and it will keep frozen for 2 to 3 months.

Note: The dough may also be made in a food processor using the same technique, but make half a batch at a time for best results.

To prepare the dough by hand, place the flours, sugar and salt in a large bowl or on a work surface. Mix together. Cut in the butter with your fingertips. Make a well in the center of the flour mixture. Pour in the egg yolks and cream. Using your fingertips, quickly work in the flour until the dough holds together. Form the dough into rounds, wrap it in plastic wrap and chill.

egg yolks   butter   cream   flour

when you make the dough by hand form a crater with the flour and place all ingredients in the center before you start to knead.

PASTRY CREAM

An all-purpose pastry cream that can be used to fill pastries such as cream puffs, *feuilletées*, and napoleons. To lighten, fold in whipped cream.

Makes 5 cups

4 cups milk
1 vanilla bean, split lengthwise
12 egg yolks
1⅓ cups sugar
¾ cup unsifted flour
1 teaspoon unsalted butter

1.   In a large saucepan, bring the milk and vanilla bean to a simmer. Turn off the flame, cover the pan, and let steep for 20 minutes. Remove the vanilla bean.

2.   In a large mixing bowl, using a wire whisk, whip the egg yolks and sugar until pale lemon in color. Sift in the flour and stir with the whisk.

3.   Slowly pour the hot milk into the egg yolk mixture, whisking all the while. Return contents of the bowl to the saucepan and, over medium heat, bring to a boil. Continue to beat with the whisk until the mixture thickens and boils for 1 minute.

4.   Transfer the pastry cream to a bowl and dot with butter to avoid crust formation. Chill and use as needed. Pastry cream will keep three to four days, refrigerated.

PLUM TART

This is a popular dessert at Chinois; it complements the food we serve there.

Makes one 10-inch tart

⅓ recipe Sugar Dough (page 222)

Brown butter filling

1 egg
⅓ cup sugar
¼ cup all-purpose or pastry flour
4 tablespoons (2 ounces) unsalted butter
1 vanilla bean, split
⅓ cup Pastry Cream (see page 224)
1 to 2 teaspoons almond extract
6 tablespoons ground almonds
*1¾ pounds Elephant Heart plums (8 to 10 large plums)
 or other plums that are red on the inside*

Garnish

2 tablespoons red currant jelly
1 tablespoon brandy
*½ cup sliced almonds, toasted in a 350 degree F. oven
 for 8 to 10 minutes*
*2 tablespoons powdered sugar
 plum leaves for decoration*

1.   Preheat the oven to 350 degrees F. On a floured surface, roll the sugar dough ⅜ inch thick and with it line a 10-inch flan ring or tart pan with a removable bottom. Line the pastry with coffee filters or parchment paper and fill the shell with pie weights. Bake the shell for 20 to 25 minutes, or until it is slightly browned. Remove and set aside to cool.

2.   Prepare the filling: Whisk together the egg, sugar and flour and set aside. In a small saucepan, heat the butter and vanilla bean over moderate heat until the butter is dark brown and gives off a nutty aroma. Whisk the hot butter thoroughly into the egg mixture. Whisk in the pastry cream. Remove the vanilla bean. Stir in the almond extract to taste and the ground almonds.

3.   Pit the plums and quarter them, leaving the skins on.

4.   Spread the brown butter mixture in the bottom of the cooled tart shell. Beginning at the outside of the tart shell, arrange the plum quarters on their sides in 3 tight concentric circles on top of the filling. Pack in as many plums as possible, making certain that the surface is completely covered.

5.   Bake the tart for 50 to 60 minutes, until the crust is light brown. Remove and let cool in the flan ring.

6.   At serving time, remove the ring and slip a 10-inch cardboard round, covered with foil, under the tart.

7.   Prepare the garnish: In a small saucepan, melt the currant jelly with the brandy and reduce the mixture over low heat to a thick syrup. Brush the top of the tart with the glaze to make the fruit shine. Just before serving, center an 8-inch lid or cardboard round over the tart. Make a border of almonds around it on the top of the tart, then sprinkle the almonds with powdered sugar. Carefully remove the lid or round, taking care not to spill any powdered sugar in the center of the tart. Remove the flan ring.

PRESENTATION: Cut the tart into wedges and serve it on nice dessert plates with a scoop of Plum Sherbet (page 266). Decorate with plum leaves.

Note: Ground almonds can be purchased in gourmet and health-food markets. It is also possible to grind your own in a food processor; add 1 tablespoon sugar or flour to prevent the almonds from becoming a paste.

CRÈME BRÛLÉE TART

¼ recipe (½ pound) Puff Pastry Baumanière (recipe follows)

½ to ¾ cup fresh fruit, such as sliced strawberries, apricots, or ripe pears, or raspberries, or blueberries (a mixture is nice)

1 recipe Crème Brûlée *(prepare as for Ginger Crème Brûlée, page 269, but omit the ginger)*

¼ cup sugar

1.   Roll the puff pastry ¼ inch thick and pierce it all over with the tines of a fork. Line a flan ring with the pastry and chill the ring for 20 minutes.

2.   Preheat the oven to 350 degrees F.

3.   Line the flan ring with parchment paper or coffee filters and fill the shell with pie weights. Bake the pastry shell for about 25 minutes, or until the pastry is golden brown. Remove the shell from the oven and let cool to room temperature. Remove the pie weights.

4.   Distribute the fruit evenly over the bottom of the shell, then pour in the *crème brûlée*. Smooth the top with a long-bladed spatula.

5.   Just before serving, sprinkle the sugar evenly over the top and place the tart under a hot broiler, near the heat, for 1 or 2 minutes, or until the sugar caramelizes. Or use a small blow torch to do the same thing.

PRESENTATION: Cut the tart into wedges and serve on dessert plates with Raspberry Sauce (page 263).

PUFF PASTRY BAUMANIÈRE

This recipe is used at L'Oustau de Baumanière, as well as at many other of the finest restaurants in France. Because of the difference in available ingredients—all of them—American-made pastry never attains the same "lighter than air" quality that is the trademark of the French *feuilleté*, but this is close!

Makes about 2 pounds

Détrempe (Flour Mixture)

2 *tablespoons salt*
2¼ to 2½ *pounds pastry flour*
1 to 1¼ *cups ice water*
14 *tablespoons (7 ounces) unsalted butter*

Butter block

21 *ounces unsalted butter*

1.   Place all the ingredients for the *détrempe* in the bowl of an electric mixer fitted with a dough hook. Turn at slow speed until the *détrempe* is elastic, adding a little more pastry flour if necessary. Patience—this takes a while because there is less gluten in pastry flour than in other flours.

2.   For the butter block, place the butter on a work surface and knead the water out of it with your hands. Again this requires patience. Wipe up the excess water on your work surface as you go. Shape the butter into a rough square, about 8 inches.

3.   Flour the work surface lightly. Roll the *détrempe* into a rough square large enough to enclose the butter block. Place the butter block in the center of the *détrempe*. Fold the sides of the *détrempe* over the ends of the butter. Tap lightly to seal the butter inside and pinch to seal any gaps.

4.   Roll the rough pastry into a long rectangle approximately ¾ inch thick, 12 inches wide and approximately 20 to 24 inches

long. Roll evenly and in *one* direction as much as possible. Brush off any excess flour with a large pastry brush and fold the dough into thirds. Give the dough a quarter turn and repeat the rolling and folding. Cover the dough with a towel and let it rest in the refrigerator for at least 20 minutes. (Longer if the day or your kitchen is very hot.)

5. Complete 2 more "turns" and again let it rest, covered, in the refrigerator. Then complete the last 2 "turns." The dough is now ready to use as you wish.

Notes: If it is a very cold day, it will be possible to complete more than 2 turns at a time; if you are an experienced pastrymaker, it will be possible to complete all 6 turns at once.

If kneading the water out of the butter is the least favorite part of this recipe, then break the 21 ounces butter into pieces and process it in a food processor with ¾ cup flour. The result will be slightly different, but delicious nonetheless.

Some pastry chefs substitute half milk and half water as the liquid for the *détrempe*.

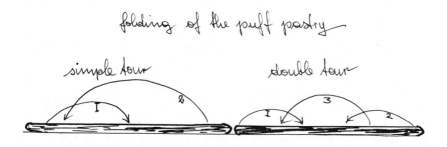

folding of the puff pastry

simple tour   double tour

RICE TART WITH FRESH FRUIT

Serves six to eight 4-inch tartlettes;
or, one 8-inch tart

⅔ *recipe Sugar Dough (page 222)*

½ *cup Arborio (Italian short-grain) rice*

2 *cups milk*

 zest of 2 oranges

1 *vanilla bean, split and scraped*

½ *cup sugar*

7 *tablespoons (3½ ounces) unsalted butter, softened*

4 *egg yolks*

½ *cup Grand Marnier*

2 *cups heavy cream, lightly whipped*

 about 1 cup poached sliced fruit, such as pears, peaches or apricots; or fresh raspberries, blueberries, blackberries or sliced strawberries—whatever is in season (a mixture is nice)

1.   Preheat the oven to 350 degrees F.

2.   On a floured surface, roll the sugar dough about ⅜ inch thick and with it line six or eight 4- by ½-inch flan rings or one 8-inch pie tin or flan ring. Place the ring(s) on a parchment-lined baking sheet. Line the ring(s) with coffee filters or parchment paper and fill them with pie weights. Bake for about 20 to 25 minutes, or until the tart shells are golden brown. Remove from the oven and let cool. Remove the pie weights.

3.   Put the rice in a saucepan and add water just to cover. Bring to a boil and cook over moderate heat for 2 minutes. Drain. Put the milk, orange zest, vanilla bean and sugar in an ovenproof saucepan. Add the rice and bring to a boil. Cover the pan and place in the oven for about 30 minutes, or until the rice is cooked and the liquid is absorbed.

4.   While the rice is cooking, cream the soft butter and add the yolks, one by one, mixing well until they are all incorporated. The mixture should be smooth and satiny.

5.   When the rice has cooked, whisk in the egg-butter mixture over low heat until the whole mixture has thickened. Mix in the Grand Marnier and let cool.

6.   Fold in the lightly whipped cream and chill until nearly set.

7.   Line the bottoms of the chilled tart shell(s) with the fruit. Pour the rice mixture into the shells, smooth the tops and chill until set, about 30 minutes.

PRESENTATION: Before serving, caramelize the tops of the tarts by sprinkling a tablespoon of sugar on each tart (use about ¼ cup sugar for a single large tart). Place under a hot broiler or use a small blow torch. Take care to only brown the sugar, not burn it. Remove the ring(s). Serve the tarts on individual plates or cut the large tart into wedges and serve with a sauce made from a purée of the same fruit in the tart.

If you use domestic rice be careful to keep the rice al dente. I prefer the rice from Italy (like Arborio) which makes excellent risotto.

STRAWBERRY MARZIPAN TART

Makes one 10-inch tart

⅓ recipe Sugar Dough (page 222)
¾ pound unsalted butter, slightly softened
½ cup sugar
* 3 eggs*
* 2 tablespoons orange liqueur*
*   finely grated zest of 2 oranges*
* 1 teaspoon almond extract*
* 2 cups ground almonds*
¼ cup currant jelly, melted
* 2 baskets strawberries, sliced ¼ inch thick*

1.   Preheat the oven to 350 degrees F.
2.   On a floured surface, roll the pastry ⅜ inch thick and line a 10-inch flan ring with it. Place the ring on a parchment paper-lined baking sheet and chill it until needed.
3.   Cream the butter and sugar lightly in an electric mixer; don't let the butter get too soft. Add the eggs and mix lightly.
4.   Stir in the liqueur, zest and almond extract, then mix in the ground almonds.
5.   Pour into the chilled pastry shell and bake for 1 hour to 1 hour 15 minutes, or until the pastry and marzipan are a deep golden brown.
6.   Remove the tart from the oven and let cool to room temperature.
7.   Brush the top of the tart with the currant jelly. Cover the top of the tart with sliced strawberries arranged in concentric circles or in a flower petal design, making certain the whole top of the tart is covered.

PRESENTATION: Remove the flan ring and transfer the tart to a flat serving platter. Cut into wedges.

WALNUT TART

Makes one 9-inch tart,
serving 8 to 10

¹/₃ recipe Sugar Dough (page 222)
2¹/₂ cups sugar
1¹/₄ cups water
1 teaspoon fresh lemon juice
¹/₂ cup heavy cream
12 ounces walnut halves
14 tablespoons (7 ounces) unsalted butter
1 egg, lightly beaten, for egg wash
1 recipe Ganache (recipe follows)

1.   On a floured surface, roll half the sugar dough ⅜ inch thick and line a 9- by 1½-inch flan ring or cake pan with it. Roll the rest of the pastry into a circle 10 inches in diameter and ⅜ inch thick. Place the pastry on baking sheets and chill while preparing the filling.

2.   Combine the sugar, water and lemon juice in a large saucepan and stir gently to mix. Bring to a boil and cook until the mixture turns a rich caramel color, or reaches 334 degrees F. on a candy thermometer. (If the caramel should crystallize as it cooks, let it continue cooking until the crystals melt again. The caramel will become quite dark and it will be necessary to add 2 to 3 tablespoons additional cream.)

3.   Remove the pan from the heat and pour in the cream. It will bubble a lot. Swirl gently until the bubbles subside. Reserve 9 walnut halves for decoration and mix in the rest gently. Add the butter. When the butter has melted, stir the filling gently until the mixture is smooth.

4.   Transfer the mixture to a large metal bowl and let it cool to lukewarm.

5.   Turn the filling into the prepared flan ring. Brush the edges

of the shell with egg wash and top with chilled pastry circle. Pinch the edges to seal them well, then trim away the excess dough. Cut several small slashes in the top pastry to allow the steam to escape. Chill until ready to bake.

6.   Preheat the oven to 400 degrees F.

7.   Bake the tart in the bottom third of the oven until the crust is golden brown, about 40 to 50 minutes. Remove the tart and let cool to room temperature. Invert the tart onto a 9-inch cardboard. (If the tart sticks to the flan ring, gently heat it over low heat or use a small blow torch to loosen the caramel.)

8.   Heat the ganache in a double boiler or very low heat to a nice spreading consistency. Pour it over the top of the tart, smoothing the top and sides nicely with a large, narrow spatula.

PRESENTATION: Decorate the top of the tart with the reserved walnut halves and place it on a lovely serving plate. Serve with unsweetened lightly whipped cream if desired.

Note: The components of the tart may be made in advance and assembled when you have time.

PECAN PIE

Makes one 10-inch tart, to serve 6–8

1½ cups light corn syrup
¾ cup sugar
¾ cup brown sugar
4 eggs
2 egg yolks
3 tablespoons unsalted butter

⅓ recipe Sugar Dough (page 222)
1½ cups pecan halves

1.   Preheat the oven to 375 degrees F.

2.   Place the corn syrup, sugars, eggs, and egg yolks in a mixing bowl. Beat well.

3.   Heat the butter in a small sauté pan over medium heat until it turns brown and has a nutty aroma. Mix it into the corn syrup mixture.

4.   Line a 10-inch tart pan with the Sugar Dough. Arrange the pecan halves in the bottom of the shell. Ladle the filling over the pecans.

5.   Bake the tart for 40 to 45 minutes, or until a skewer inserted near the center comes out clean. Remove and let cool at room temperature.

PRESENTATION: Cut into wedges and serve with caramel sauce or rum-flavored whipped cream.

GANACHE (CHOCOLATE CREAM)

Makes 1 quart

1 pound bittersweet or semisweet chocolate
2 cups heavy cream
4 tablespoons (2 ounces) unsalted butter at room tem-
perature

1.   Cut the chocolate into small pieces and place in a metal mixing bowl.
2.   In a saucepan, bring the cream to a boil and pour it over the chocolate. Stir until the chocolate has melted.
3.   Stir in the butter until incorporated.
4.   Store the ganache in the refrigerator until you are ready to use it. It will keep for 2 to 3 weeks under refrigeration.
5.   Reheat the ganache over hot but not boiling water until it reaches the consistency desired. (It is important that the ganache not get too hot or the butter will separate from the base.)

LEMON PIE

Makes one 11-inch pie

⅓ recipe Sugar Dough (page 222)
4 lemons
2 limes
4 eggs
1 cup sugar
¼ cup heavy cream
8 tablespoons (4 ounces) unsalted butter, cut into small
pieces

Candied Lemon Slices (optional; recipe follows)
¼ *cup water*

1. Preheat the oven to 375 degrees F.
2. With the sugar dough, line an 11-inch fluted tart tin with a removable bottom. Line the shell with coffee filters or parchment paper, then fill with pie weights or dry beans. Bake the shell for 20 minutes, or until golden brown around the edges.
3. As the shell bakes, prepare the filling: Zest the lemons and juice them and the limes. You should have about 1 cup of juice. Combine the zest, juice, eggs, ¾ cup of the sugar, cream and butter in a heavy saucepan. Cook over medium heat, stirring constantly, until the filling coats the back of a spoon. Do not let it boil. Pour the filling into a heatproof bowl and let it cool until the crust is ready.
4. When the crust is done, remove it from the oven. Combine the remaining ¼ cup sugar and the ¼ cup water in a small saucepan. Place over medium heat (the flame should not come up the side of the saucepan) until it caramelizes. Do not stir the caramel while it cooks; brush down the sides of the pan with water if necessary to prevent crystals from forming. When the caramel begins to color, swirl the pan gently to ensure even coloring. Drizzle the caramel over the bottom of the prebaked shell, then pour in the filling and return the pie to the oven for another 15 to 20 minutes, or until the crust is a rich golden brown and the filling is set.
5. Remove the pie from the oven and let it cool to room temperature. If desired, chill until 1 hour before serving.

PRESENTATION: If you are using them, overlap the candied lemon slices in a circular pattern on top of the pie. Transfer the pie to a flat serving dish, removing the rim and the metal bottom in the process. Cut the pie into wedges and serve with Strawberry Sauce (page 264) and a dollop of lightly sweetened whipped cream.

CANDIED LEMON SLICES

2 or 3 lemons
1 cup sugar
½ cup water

Slice the lemons paper thin. Bring the sugar and water to a boil in a saucepan over medium heat and cook until the bubbles are thick and clear. Add the lemon slices. Cook them in the syrup for 1 minute. Remove the pan from the heat and let the fruit steep in the syrup for 5 minutes. Remove the lemons from the sugar syrup and drain on a rack. Dip the edges of the lemons in crystallized sugar if desired.

KEY LIME PIE

Makes one 9-inch pie

⅓ recipe Sugar Dough (page 222)
4 eggs
4 egg yolks
⅔ cup sugar
1 cup Key lime juice
6 tablespoons (3 ounces) unsalted butter, cut into small pieces
1 to 2 tablespoons sugar for caramelizing

1.   Preheat the oven to 375 degrees F.
2.   With the sugar dough, line a 9-inch fluted tart tin with a removable bottom. Line the shell with coffee filters or parchment paper, then fill with pie weights or dry beans. Bake the

shell for 20 minutes, or until golden brown around the edges. Cool the shell and remove pie weights or beans and papers.

3.   Combine the eggs and egg yolks in a large stainless steel bowl. Whisk in the sugar thoroughly, then whisk in the lime juice.

4.   Place the bowl over hot but not boiling water. Whisk vigorously until the mixture is light and thick. It should mound on itself when a little of it is dropped from the whisk.

5.   Remove the bowl from the heat and distribute the butter over the top of the filling. When the butter has melted, fold it into the filling.

6.   Turn the mousse into the tart shell and smooth the top with a long metal spatula. Chill.

PRESENTATION: Sprinkle the additional sugar over the top of the pie and caramelize the pie under a very hot broiler or with a small blow torch. Remove the pie from its ring and transfer it to a flat serving dish, removing the metal bottom. Cut into wedges and serve with Strawberry Sauce (page 264).

It is very important to cook the eggs with the lime juice and sugar until the mixture is very thick, but be careful that the eggs do not curdle.

ALMOND CAKE WITH GINGER

Makes one 8-inch cake

⅓ *recipe Sugar Dough (page 222)*
10 ounces almond paste (recipe follows)
10 tablespoons (5 ounces) unsalted butter
⅔ *cup sugar*
4 eggs
½ *cup pastry flour*
¼ *cup ground almonds*
⅓ *teaspoon baking powder*
   finely grated zest of 2 lemons
2 tablespoons dark rum
¼ *teaspoon almond extract*
4 to 6 ounces candied ginger, chopped

1.   On a floured surface, roll the sugar dough ⅜ inch thick and line an 8-inch wide by 2-inch deep round springform pan or flan ring with it. Chill.

2.   Preheat the oven to 350 degrees F.

3.   In a bowl, mix together the almond paste, butter and sugar. Add the eggs, one at a time. Then add the flour, ground almonds, baking powder and lemon zest. Mix in the rum and the almond extract.

4.   Turn the batter into the chilled pastry shell and bake for 1 hour. Sprinkle the chopped ginger on top of the cake and continue to bake for another 45 to 55 minutes, or until the top of the cake and the pastry are dark golden brown. Remove the cake from the oven and let it cool in the pan.

PRESENTATION: Cut the cake into wedges and serve on individual dessert plates with an assortment of ice creams or sherbets.

ALMOND PASTE

Makes 2 cups

Combine ⅔ cup finely ground almonds and 1¾ cups powdered sugar in a food processor. Process briefly to mix together. Add enough of a small egg white, slightly beaten, and ½ teaspoon almond extract and process to form a ball of paste on the blade.

CHEESECAKE WITH CARAMELIZED APPLES

This is a different, delicious variation on a traditional cheese-cake. It makes a light, satisfying end to a summer meal.

Makes one 9-inch cheesecake

⅓ recipe Sugar Dough (page 222)
1 large Granny Smith or Pippin apple
1½ tablespoons unsalted butter
3 tablespoons sugar
2 tablespoons heavy cream
3 medium lemons
9 ounces cream cheese, softened
½ cup sugar
2 eggs
1½ cups sour cream

1. Preheat the oven to 350 degrees F.
2. On a floured surface, roll the pastry ¼ inch thick. Cut a 9-inch circle and fit it into the bottom of a 9-inch springform pan.

Prick the dough with a fork to prevent it from rising, then bake it for 20 minutes, or until the pastry is slightly colored. Remove from oven and let cool.

3.   Peel, halve and core the apple and cut it into ¼-inch slices. In a saucepan, sauté the slices over moderate heat in the butter and the 3 tablespoons sugar until the apple is lightly caramelized but still tender. Add the cream and cook until it has been absorbed. Remove from the heat and reserve.

4.   Finely grate the zest from the lemons and reserve. Juice the lemons to render 6 tablespoons juice and set aside.

5.   In a large mixing bowl, combine the cream cheese and the remaining ½ cup sugar. Whisk in the eggs, one at a time, then add 1 cup of the sour cream and the lemon juice.

6.   Pour the mixture through a fine strainer into a clean bowl and stir in the lemon zest.

7.   Arrange the apple slices over the bottom of the crust in a single layer.

8.   Pour the cheese mixture over the apples. Tap the pan gently against the counter to settle the batter.

9.   Bake the cake for 15 to 18 minutes. The cake is done when the sides are set but the center moves slightly when the pan is shaken gently. There should not be any cracks in the top.

10.   Stir the remaining ½ cup sour cream until it is quite liquid. Drizzle it over the top of the hot cheesecake and spread it as evenly and smoothly as possible. Let cool to room temperature, then chill the cake for several hours.

PRESENTATION: Remove the cheesecake from the pan. Smooth the top with a hot knife if necessary. Cut into wedges and serve immediately.

CHOCOLATE MOUSSELINE CAKES

Makes 10 individual cakes; or
10 individual one-cup molds

slightly melted butter
sifted cocoa powder
1/2 cup *Simple Syrup (recipe follows)*
1/4 cup *dark rum*
   1 cup *Spago's Brioche Loaf cubes, cut about 3/4-inch square,*
      (page 208)
   7 ounces *bittersweet chocolate, cut into small pieces*
   1 ounce *unsweetened chocolate, cut into small pieces*
   3 *eggs*
1/4 cup *sugar*
1/4 cup *heavy cream*
1/4 cup Crème Fraîche *(page 293)*
   2 *tablespoons* Cognac
   2 *teaspoons powdered espresso dissolved in 1 teaspoon hot*
      water

1. Preheat the oven to 350 degrees F.
2. Prepare ten 1-cup soufflé molds or a square 9-inch cake tin by brushing them generously with butter and dusting them with sifted cocoa powder, tapping out the excess. Set aside.
3. In a saucepan, reduce the simple syrup with the rum by half. Gently toss the brioche cubes in the syrup, then drain them on a rack until needed.
4. Melt the bittersweet and the unsweetened chocolate in a metal bowl set over a *bain-marie*. Let cool slightly.
5. Beat the eggs and sugar together in the bowl of an electric mixer until triple in volume.
6. As the eggs are beating, whip the heavy cream to soft peaks, then whisk in the *crème fraîche*. Whip together until quite stiff, but take care not to make butter. Fold in the Cognac and espresso.

7. Fold the chocolate into the egg-sugar mixture, then fold in the whipped cream; then gently fold in the brioche cubes.
8. Spoon the batter into the prepared molds, filling each ⅔ full.
9. Place the molds in a *bain-marie* and bake for 35 minutes. Turn off the oven and let the cakes sit in the oven for another 15 minutes. Remove the cakes from the oven and let them cool, out of the water, to room temperature.

PRESENTATION: Invert the cakes onto dessert plates. Serve with Vanilla Ice Cream, or with a dollop of *crème fraîche* (page 293) or unsweetened whipped cream.

SIMPLE SYRUP

Makes 1 cup

2 *cups sugar*
1 *cup water*

Combine the sugar and water in a saucepan. Bring to a boil and boil 1 to 2 minutes, or until the liquid is clear. Remove from the heat. Let cool and store in a container, covered, in the refrigerator until ready to use.

GINGER CAKE

Makes one 12 × 18-inch sheet cake

2 to 3	*tablespoons unsalted butter, melted*
	flour
10	*tablespoons (5 ounces) unsalted butter, softened*
10	*tablespoons (5 ounces) brown sugar*
4	*egg yolks*
2/3	*cup dark molasses*
1 1/2	*tablespoons baking soda*
2	*tablespoons boiling water*
5	*teaspoons ground ginger*
1/2	*teaspoon freshly ground nutmeg*
1/2	*teaspoon cinnamon*
1/2	*teaspoon salt*
1/2	*teaspoon ground allspice or ground cloves*
1/2	*cup sour cream*
6	*egg whites*
1/3	*cup sugar*

1.   Preheat the oven to 350 degrees F. Line a 12 by 18 inch baking sheet with sides with parchment paper or waxed paper. Brush the paper with the melted butter and flour the paper lightly.

2.   In a bowl, cream the butter and brown sugar. Beat in the egg yolks, 1 at a time, then mix in the molasses.

3.   Activate the baking soda by dissolving it in the boiling water, then mix it into the batter.

4.   Sift in the ginger, nutmeg, cinnamon, salt, allspice or cloves. Mix in the sour cream.

5.   In a clean bowl, whip the egg whites until they hold soft peaks. Slowly beat in the sugar and continue to beat to stiff, shiny peaks.

6.   Fold ⅓ of the whites into the cake batter to lighten it, then fold in the remaining whites. Turn the batter onto the prepared baking sheet and spread it as evenly as possible.

7.   Bake about 15 minutes, or until the cake tests done when pressed with your finger or until a toothpick inserted in the center of the cake comes out clean. Let cool.

8.   Cut the cake into small rounds and use them as the bottoms of individual *crème Brûlées*; or use in place of puff pastry or sugar dough for Apple Tartlettes (page 221). Freeze any unused cake, well wrapped, for up to 2 weeks.

HAZELNUT MARJOLAINE WITH COFFEE BUTTERCREAM

Serves 12 or more

Meringue Layers

    8 ounces hazelnuts
    2 tablespoons all-purpose flour
1¾ cups sugar
       about 3 tablespoons unsalted butter, melted
    8 egg whites
 ½ teaspoon fresh lemon juice

Coffee Buttercream

    1 cup sugar
 ¾ cup water
    3 egg yolks
    1 egg
 ½ pound unsalted butter, softened
 ¼ cup espresso

Ganache (Chocolate Cream)

¾ pound bittersweet or semisweet chocolate
1 cup heavy cream or crème fraîche

Cream filling

1½ cups crème fraîche *or ¾ cup heavy cream plus 2*
tablespoons sour cream.

1.   Prepare the meringue layers: Preheat the oven to 350 degrees F.

2.   Place the hazelnuts on a tray in the oven for about 15 minutes, or until they are dark golden brown. Remove and let cool, then rub them with a clean, dry towel to remove the skins. Increase the oven to 400 degrees F.

3.   Grind the hazelnuts in a food processor or blender with the flour and all but 2 tablespoons of the sugar until the mixture resembles cornmeal or coarse flour. Set aside.

4.   Line two 12- by 18-inch baking sheets with parchment paper. Brush generously with the melted butter.

5.   Using an electric mixer, whip the egg whites and lemon juice to soft peaks. Add the reserved 2 tablespoons sugar slowly and continue to beat to stiff, shiny peaks. Fold in the ground hazelnuts. Divide the mixture between the baking sheets and spread over the entire surface, as evenly as possible. The layers should be about ⅜ inch thick.

6.   Bake for 10 to 12 minutes, or until golden brown. Turn the pans as necessary so that the meringues brown evenly. Remove the pans to racks and let them cool. When the meringues are cool enough to handle, turn them onto a work surface lined with waxed paper or parchment and carefully remove the paper from the back.

7.   Prepare the buttercream: Combine the sugar and water in a small saucepan. Bring to a boil and cook until the bubbles are clear and large; the syrup will be thick but without color.

8.   In the bowl of an electric mixer, whip the egg yolks and whole egg until thick, light and fluffy. With the mixer turning, slowly pour the sugar syrup down the side of the mixing bowl. Continue to beat on high speed until the mixture is cool.

9.   Beat in the butter, about 1 tablespoon at a time, making sure each piece has been incorporated before adding the next. When all the butter has been incorporated, beat in the espresso. Chill until needed.

10.   Prepare the ganache: Cut the chocolate into small pieces and place in a metal mixing bowl. Stir in the cream or *crème fraîche*, then place the pan over hot but not boiling water, stirring until smooth. Remove from the *bain-marie* and cool until thick enough to spread.

11.   Prepare the cream filling: If you are using *crème fraîche*, whisk until stiff. If you are using heavy cream, whip until stiff, then fold in the sour cream. Chill.

12.   To assemble the marjolaine: Cut each meringue layer in half lengthwise. Trim the 4 halves so that they are all the same size, about 5 by 15 inches. Place a piece of foil-covered cardboard slightly smaller than the meringue layers on an inverted baking sheet. Place a meringue layer on it and spread with ⅔ of the *ganache*. Top with another layer of meringue and spread it with the cream filling. (If at any time the marjolaine begins to get warm, chill for a few minutes in the refrigerator or freezer.) Put the third layer of meringue over the cream filling and spread with the coffee buttercream. Top with the last layer of meringue.

13.   Stir the remaining *ganache* over hot water until it is thin enough to use as a glaze (about the consistency of very heavy cream). Pour over the top of the cake and spread quickly with a long-bladed spatula to smooth. Place the cake in the freezer until it has set up, (about 1 hour), then remove it from the freezer and trim away the sides and ends with a sharp, serrated knife or with an electric knife.

PRESENTATION: Decorate the top of the marjolaine with cocoa powder or powdered sugar dusted through a fine sieve. Cut into slices. Pool the dessert plates with *Crème Anglaise* (page 263) or with Raspberry Sauce (page 263) or Strawberry Sauce (page 264). Center the slices on the sauce. The *marjolaine* can also be placed on a long, flat serving platter or silver tray, or it can be cut into bite-size pieces and served in *petit-four* cups with coffee or as part of a tray of assorted *petit fours*.

CHOCOLATE BREAD PUDDING
WITH HAZELNUTS

Makes twelve ½-cup servings

8 slices (5 ounces) Spago's Brioche Loaf (page 208) or challah
2¾ cups heavy cream
6 ounces bittersweet chocolate, cut into small pieces
11 tablespoons (5½ ounces) unsalted butter, at room temperature
5 eggs, separated
¾ cup toasted and skinned ground hazelnuts (see page 247)
1 cup almonds
1 cup sugar
Frangelico to taste

1.   Preheat the oven to 350 degrees F. Butter twelve ½-cup molds.
2.   Cut the bread into cubes, place it in a mixing bowl, then

combine with ¾ cup of the cream. Let stand about 30 minutes, or until the cream has been absorbed.

3.   Melt the chocolate in a mixing bowl set over a *bain-marie*. When the chocolate is smooth, remove the bowl from the *bain-marie*.

4.   Cream the butter in a large mixing bowl, then add the egg yolks, hazelnuts, ¾ cup of the sugar, the bread and melted chocolate. Mix well. (The mixture should be free of large lumps.)

5.   Whip the egg whites to soft peaks, then gradually whip in the remaining ¼ cup sugar and continue to whip to stiff, shiny peaks. Stir ¼ of the whites into the chocolate mixture, then gently fold in the remaining egg whites. (It is better to have a little of the whites showing than to overfold.)

6.   Divide the pudding mixture among the molds and place the molds in a *bain-marie*. Cover loosely with buttered foil, buttered side down. Bake for about 45 minutes, or until the puddings are set.

7.   Whip the remaining 2 cups cream until it mounds softly on itself, as for *crème chantilly*, then perfume it with Frangelico to taste.

PRESENTATION: Unmold the puddings on individual dessert plates or a large platter and decorate with a little of the cream on top. Pass the remaining cream in a pretty bowl.

CHOCOLATE SOUFFLÉ

Serves 6

2 *tablespoons (1 ounce) unsalted butter*
4 *tablespoons sugar*
4 *ounces bittersweet chocolate, cut into small pieces*
4 *eggs, separated*
2 *tablespoons Grand Marnier*
3 *egg whites*
  juice of ½ lemon
  powdered sugar for garnish
  unsweetened whipped cream

1. Preheat the oven to 400 degrees F.
2. Butter and dust with about 2 tablespoons of the sugar six 1-cup soufflé dishes. Chill until needed.
3. Melt the chocolate in a metal bowl set over a *bain-marie*. Remove from the heat and stir in the egg yolks and the Grand Marnier.
4. Whip all 7 egg whites until they form soft peaks. Whip in the lemon juice and the remaining 2 tablespoons sugar. Continue to whip the whites until they are stiff but still very shiny. Stir a quarter of them into the chocolate mixture, then gently fold in the remaining whites.
5. Fill the molds with the soufflé mixture. Run your thumb around the inside edge of each dish so that the soufflés will form a hat. Bake for 8 to 10 minutes, or until the edges are set but the middle is still just a little soft.

PRESENTATION: Serve on napkin-lined dessert plates. Dust the tops with powdered sugar, if desired, and spoon a dollop of whipped cream into the center of each soufflé. Serve immediately.

THREE CHOCOLATE TERRINE

1 loaf, 6-cup size

Whipped Cream Filling

2¼ cups heavy cream
½ cup sour cream or Crème Fraîche *(page 293)*

White Chocolate Filling

4 egg yolks
¼ cup sugar
½ cup heavy cream
½ cup half-and-half
1 vanilla bean, scraped
1 tablespoon espresso or very strong coffee
2 ounces white chocolate, cut into small pieces

Milk Chocolate Layer

4 egg yolks
¼ cup sugar
½ cup heavy cream
½ cup half-and-half
1 vanilla bean, scraped
1 tablespoon malt
2 ounces milk chocolate, cut into small pieces

Dark Chocolate Layer

4 egg yolks
¼ cup sugar
½ cup heavy cream
½ cup half-and-half
1 vanilla bean, scraped
2 ounces bittersweet chocolate, cut into small pieces
1 tablespoon espresso or very strong coffee

1.   Prepare the cream filling: Whip the cream until it has thickened slightly and then whip in the sour cream or *crème fraîche* and continue to whip it to soft peaks. Reserve, covered, in the refrigerator.

2.   Butter and line with waxed paper the bottom, sides and ends of a standard 6-cup loaf pan.

3.   Prepare the white chocolate layer: Whip the egg yolks and sugar until they make a ribbon.

4.   Combine the cream, half-and-half, vanilla bean and espresso in a saucepan and bring to a boil. Remove from the heat and add the white chocolate. Stir until melted, then turn into the bowl of an electric mixer and whip until cool and mousselike, about 10 minutes.

5.   Refrigerate until cold, then fold in 1½ cups of the reserved whipped cream filling.

6.   Pour into the bottom of the loaf pan and freeze.

7.   Prepare the milk chocolate layer: Whip egg yolks and sugar until they make a ribbon.

8.   Combine the cream, half-and-half, vanilla bean and malt in a small saucepan and bring to a boil, stirring continuously. Remove from the heat and stir in the chocolate until melted. Strain into the bowl of an electric mixer and whip on low speed until the mixture is cool and mousselike, about 10 minutes.

9.   Refrigerate until cold, then fold in 1½ cups of the reserved whipped cream filling. Pour over the frozen white chocolate layer. Return the pan to the freezer.

10.   Prepare the dark chocolate layer: Whip the egg yolks and sugar until they make a ribbon.

11.   Combine the cream, half-and-half and vanilla bean in a small saucepan and bring to a boil. Remove from the heat and stir in the chocolate until melted. Then turn into the bowl of an electric mixer, add the espresso and whip on low speed until the mixture is cool and mousselike, about 10 minutes.

12.   Refrigerate until cold, then fold in 1½ cups of the reserved whipped cream filling. Pour over the frozen milk chocolate.

13.   Cover the terrine and freeze for several hours or overnight.

PRESENTATION: Unmold the terrine onto a nice serving platter.
Cut into slices with a hot knife. Decorate with mint leaves and
berries or serve with a chocolate sauce or *Crème Anglaise* (page
263).

BANANA ICE CREAM

Makes about 1½ quarts

> 8 *egg yolks*
> ½ *cup sugar*
> 2 *cups milk*
> 2 *cups heavy cream*
> 1 *vanilla bean, split*
> 4 *over-ripe bananas (the skins should be brown)*
> ¼ *cup sour cream*
> 2 *tablespoons mild honey*
> 1 *teaspoon walnut extract, or to taste (optional)*

1.   Whisk the egg yolks and sugar together in a large mixing
bowl.
2.   In a saucepan, bring the milk, cream and vanilla bean to a
boil. Slowly whisk one third of the hot cream into the egg-yolk
mixture, then stir in the remaining liquid.
3.   Return the hot cream mixture to the saucepan and place
over low heat. Cook gently, stirring constantly, until the mixture
coats the back of a spoon. Strain through a fine sieve into a
large, cold bowl.

4. Purée the bananas, sour cream, honey and walnut extract in a food processor; add some of the cream mixture to liquefy. Stir the banana mixture into the bowl. Chill.

5. Place the mixture in an ice-cream freezer and freeze according to the manufacturer's instructions.

CARAMEL ICE CREAM

Makes about 1 quart

8 *egg yolks*
⅔ *cup sugar*
2 *cups milk*
2 *cups heavy cream*
1 *vanilla bean, split*
1 *cup Caramel Sauce (recipe follows)*

1. In a mixing bowl, whisk the egg yolks and sugar together thoroughly. In a saucepan, bring the milk, cream and vanilla bean to a boil.

2. Slowly whisk one third of the hot liquid into the egg-yolk mixture, then whisk in the remaining liquid.

3. Return the mixture to the saucepan and place over low heat, stirring constantly, until it thickens enough to coat the back of a spoon. Remove from the heat and stir in the caramel sauce.

4. Strain the custard into a bowl that has been placed over ice. Stir occasionally as the custard cools.

5. Place the custard in an ice-cream freezer and freeze according to the manufacturer's instructions.

CARAMEL SAUCE

If you want a still richer sauce, add 4 tablespoons unsalted butter after adding the cream.

Makes about 1½ cups

1 *cup sugar*
½ *cup water*
⅓ *cup heavy cream*

1.   Combine the sugar and water in a small saucepan. Wash down any crystals on the sides of the pan with a pastry brush dipped in water and bring to a boil.
2.   Cook gently until the liquid is a deep golden brown. Remove the pan from the heat and carefully whisk in the cream, a little at a time.
3.   If the caramel is not quite smooth, heat gently, stirring until smooth.

JACK DANIEL'S CHOCOLATE CHOCOLATE CHIP ICE CREAM

Makes 2 quarts

1 *vanilla bean, split*
2 *cups milk*
2 *cups heavy cream*
8 *egg yolks*
¾ *cup sugar*
1 *cup bittersweet chocolate, cut into small pieces*

¼ cup Jack Daniel's, or to taste
½ cup bittersweet chocolate, melted

1.   Heat the vanilla bean with the milk and cream in a large saucepan until the liquid comes to a boil. Remove from the heat.
2.   In a bowl, whisk the egg yolks and sugar together until foamy.
3.   Whisk half of the hot milk mixture into the sugar and egg yolks, then return to the saucepan. Cook over low heat, stirring constantly, until the custard coats the back of a spoon. Do not let it boil. (If the custard comes to a boil, it will curdle and you have to do it over.) Strain the custard into a large cold bowl.
4.   Stir the chocolate pieces into the hot mixture until melted and the mixture is smooth. Refrigerate until chilled.
5.   Stir in the Jack Daniel's to taste, then pour the custard into an ice-cream freezer and freeze according to the manufacturer's directions.
6.   While the ice cream is freezing, prepare the chocolate chips: Heat a heavy baking sheet in a preheated 350 degree F. oven. Spread the melted chocolate over the bottom of the baking sheet, making a thin, even layer. Chill until hard. Score the chocolate with a sharp knife into small squares, approximately ¼ inch in size. (It is sometimes easier to score the chocolate with a hot, dry knife.) Using a metal pastry scraper or a palette knife, scrape "chips" from the baking sheet. Freeze the chips until needed.
7.   When the ice cream is ready, transfer it to a cold freezer-proof bowl. Fold in the chocolate chips. Keep frozen until ready to use.

PRESENTATION: Dip an ice-cream scoop into hot water and ar-range 2 or 3 scoops on chilled dessert plates. Serve with small cookies.

CHOCOLATE MANDARIN ICE CREAM

Makes 2 quarts

> 2 *cups milk*
> 2 *cups heavy cream*
> 1 *vanilla bean, split and scraped*
>   *zest of 3 tangerines, grated or finely chopped*
> 1 *pound semisweet chocolate*
> 8 *egg yolks*
> ½ *cup sugar*
>   *juice of 3 tangerines*
> ¼ *cup Mandarine Napoleon liqueur*

1. In a sauce pan, scald the milk and cream with the vanilla bean and tangerine zest. Remove from the heat, cover and let the mixture steep for 30 minutes.

2. Melt the chocolate in a metal bowl over a *bain-marie* and remove from the heat when smooth.

3. Whisk the egg yolks and sugar together in a large mixing bowl. Slowly whisk the cream mixture into the egg yolks, then return the mixture to the saucepan.

4. Cook the custard over low heat until it coats the back of a spoon. Strain the custard back into the mixing bowl and whisk in the melted chocolate, tangerine juice and liqueur.

5. Let the custard cool, then chill it in the refrigerator.

6. Freeze it in an ice-cream freezer according to the manufacturer's directions.

WHITE CHOCOLATE ICE CREAM WITH WILD STRAWBERRIES OR RASPBERRIES

If you put whole berries in the ice cream, they are not so nice to eat because they get very hard and lose their flavor.

Makes about 3 quarts

> *1 quart cream or milk*
> *1 vanilla bean, split*
> *1 pound white chocolate, cut into small pieces (see Note below)*
> *12 egg yolks*
> *2 boxes fresh raspberries or wild strawberries (see Note below)*

1.   In a saucepan, heat the cream or milk over low heat with the vanilla bean and the chocolate, stirring frequently. Remove the pan from the heat when the chocolate has melted.

2.   In a mixing bowl, whisk the egg yolks until they are lemon-colored.

3.   Slowly whisk the milk into the yolks, then return the mixture to the saucepan.

4.   Cook the mixture over low heat until the custard coats the back of a spoon.

5.   Strain the custard into a bowl and chill it in the refrigerator, stirring once in a while to keep a skin from forming.

6.   Remove the vanilla bean, then freeze in an ice-cream freezer according to the manufacturer's directions. The ice cream should be very soft when it is removed from the freezer.

PRESENTATION: Scoop into chilled dessert bowls or dishes. Garnish with the fresh berries and serve with a cookie.

Note: Different brands of white chocolate vary in their "choco-latey" taste. Some have a stronger chocolate flavor, while others have a pronounced vanilla flavor. Therefore the amount of chocolate used in the ice cream can vary greatly, and it is wise to taste your chocolate carefully.

Wild strawberries are preferable as a garnish for this ice cream, but difficult to obtain. There are some being grown commercially in the United States and they are sold as *"Fraises du Bois."*

EGG NOG ICE CREAM

Makes 1½ quarts

8 *egg yolks*
⅔ *cup sugar*
2 *cups heavy cream*
2 *cups half-and-half*
1 *teaspoon freshly ground nutmeg*
¼ *teaspoon ground cloves*
¼ *cup bourbon*
¼ *cup dark rum*

1.   In a mixing bowl, whisk the egg yolks and sugar together. Set aside.
2.   Heat the cream, half-and-half, nutmeg and cloves together in a saucepan. When it comes to a boil, whisk the mixture into the egg yolk mixture. Return the mixture to the saucepan and cook it over low heat until the custard coats the back of a spoon. Strain the custard back into the mixing bowl.

3. Add the bourbon and rum and chill the custard in the refrigerator.

4. Freeze it in an ice-cream freezer according to the manufacturer's directions.

HONEY ALMOND ICE CREAM

Makes 1 1/2 quarts

1 cup (4 ounces) whole almonds, skins on
8 egg yolks
1/3 cup sugar
1/3 cup honey
2 cups milk
2 cups heavy cream
1 vanilla bean, split

1. Preheat the oven to 350 degrees F. On a baking sheet, toast the almonds for 15 minutes. Set aside.

2. Whisk the egg yolks, sugar and honey together in a mixing bowl.

3. In a saucepan, bring the milk, cream and vanilla bean to a boil.

4. Whisk the hot milk mixture into the egg yolks, then return to the saucepan. Cook over low heat until the custard coats the back of a spoon.

5. Strain the custard into the mixing bowl, let cool and chill. Remove the vanilla bean.

6. Stir in the toasted almonds and freeze the mixture in an ice-cream freezer according to the manufacturer's directions.

MAPLE WALNUT ICE CREAM

Makes 1½ quarts

2 *cups Vermont maple syrup*
8 *egg yolks*
2 *cups milk*
2 *cups heavy cream*
1 *cup lightly toasted walnuts (toast in a preheated 350 degree oven for 5 minutes)*

1.   Place the syrup in a good-size saucepan. Bring the syrup to a boil (it will boil up like cream), lower the heat and reduce the syrup by half. (It is best to measure it.)

2.   Whisk the egg yolks in a mixing bowl. Set aside.

3.   When the syrup is reduced, add the milk and cream to the pan. Place over low heat and stir until the mixture is smooth.

4.   Whisk the hot liquid into the egg yolks, then return the mixture to the saucepan. Cook until the custard coats the back of a spoon.

5.   Strain the custard into the mixing bowl and let cool slightly. Chill in the refrigerator.

6.   Grate the walnuts with a Mouli grater or in a food processor fitted with the fine shredding disk. Using the metal blade releases the oil in the nuts and gives the ice cream a gray color.

7.   Stir the grated nuts into the cold custard and freeze it in an ice-cream freezer according to the manufacturer's directions.

RASPBERRY ICE CREAM
WITH RASPBERRY SAUCE

Makes 2 quarts

8 *egg yolks*
1 *cup sugar*
1 *quart heavy cream*
1 *vanilla bean, split lengthwise*
1 *basket raspberries*

Raspberry Sauce

1 *basket raspberries*
   sugar
   Framboise *(raspberry liqueur) to taste (optional)*
   sprigs of fresh mint for garnish

1.   In a bowl, whisk together the egg yolks and sugar thoroughly.
2.   In a heavy saucepan, heat the cream with the vanilla bean until the cream comes to a boil.
3.   When the cream is hot, whisk half of it into the egg-yolk mixture, then return it to the saucepan. Cook, but do not let it boil, stirring constantly, over low heat until the custard coats the back of a spoon. (This sauce is known as *crème anglaise*.)
4.   Strain the custard sauce into a bowl and stir it, set over ice, until cool. Chill.
5.   Crush 1 box of the raspberries with a fork and stir them into the custard mixture. Place in an ice-cream freezer and freeze according to the manufacturer's directions.
6.   Prepare the sauce: Purée the raspberries, then put them through a fine sieve to remove the seeds. Sweeten the purée with sugar to taste and, if desired, add *framboise* to taste.

PRESENTATION: Pool the sauce on chilled dessert plates. Place a scoop of ice cream in the center and garnish with the mint sprigs. Serve with some nice cookies.

Note: This sauce can also be made with strawberries.

CONCORD GRAPE SHERBET

The Concord grape season is only a few weeks long, but this sherbet is worth the wait. Look for very ripe juicy fruit to use in this dessert.

Makes 5 to 6 cups

> *1³/₄ pounds Concord grapes, stemmed*
> *2 cups Beaujolais*
> *¹/₄ level teaspoon cracked peppercorns*
> *¹/₂ cup sugar*

1. Combine all the ingredients in a non-reactive saucepan.
2. Bring to a full boil. Remove the pan from the heat, cover, and let steep for 20 minutes.
3. Purée the mixture in a food processor in 2 or 3 batches. Strain through a fine strainer into a bowl and chill.
4. Freeze in an ice-cream freezer according to the manufacturer's directions.

GRAPEFRUIT TEQUILA SHERBET

Makes 1 quart

2½ *cups fresh grapefruit juice*
1 *cup Simple Syrup (page 244)*
⅓ to ½ *cup fresh lemon or lime juice*
⅓ *cup tequila*

1. In a mixing bowl, mix the grapefruit juice with the simple syrup. Add ⅓ cup of the lemon juice and the tequila. Taste carefully and add more lemon juice if the mixture is too sweet.
2. Freeze in an ice-cream freezer according to the manufacturer's directions.

PRESENTATION: Serve alone or with pecan pies and garnish with Candied Grapefruit Peel (page 238).

I love the sweet pink grapefruits from Texas. This Sherbet is also excellent as a palate refresher, but reduce the sugar to one half cup.

PLUM SHERBET

Makes 1 quart

> 6 *plums (about 1½ pounds), Elephant Heart if possible*
> 2 *cups Port*
> ½ *cup sugar*
> 1 *teaspoon freshly cracked black peppercorns*
> 1 or 2 *lemons*
> ¼ *cup fresh raspberries or fresh* cassis *(black currants, optional)*
> *plum leaves for garnish*

1.   Pit the plums and cut them into quarters. Place in a saucepan with the Port, sugar, half the cracked peppercorns and a ½-inch strip of lemon zest. If you are unable to get Elephant Heart plums or other plums with purple flesh, add the raspberries or *cassis* for color. Bring to a boil, reduce the heat and cook gently for 15 to 20 minutes, or until the plums are soft. Remove from the heat and let cool to room temperature.

2.   Purée the plum mixture in a food processor or a blender. Strain into a clean bowl.

3.   Juice the lemon(s) and add ¼ cup of the juice and the remaining peppercorns. Taste carefully and add more lemon juice to taste. Chill.

4.   Place in an ice-cream freezer and freeze according to the manufacturer's directions.

PRESENTATION: Scoop the sherbet into dessert bowls and garnish with the plum leaves. Serve with your favorite cookies.

TANGERINE SHERBET

Makes 1½ quarts

3 cups tangerine juice (about 18 tangerines)
zest of 10 tangerines, grated or minced
¾ cup fresh lemon juice (5 to 6 lemons)
zest of 4 lemons
1½ cups Simple Sugar Syrup (page 244)
¼ cup Mandarine Napoleon liqueur

1. In a bowl, mix together all the ingredients.
2. Strain through a fine mesh sieve into a bowl. Chill.
3. Freeze in an ice-cream freezer according to the manufacturer's directions.

TEA SHERBET

Makes 1 quart

3 cups strong-brewed mint tea
2 to 3 sprigs fresh mint, chopped
Simple Syrup (page 244)
fresh lemon juice

1. Let the mint steep in the brewed tea for 30 minutes.
2. Add the sugar syrup to make it very sweet. Then add lemon juice to taste to bring back the tea flavor and to reduce the sweetness.
3. Freeze the mixture in an ice-cream freezer according to the manufacturer's directions.

CHINOIS SAKE FRUIT

This is an easy dessert to make. I got the inspiration from the Italian *zabaglione*.

Serves 6

Sauce

1½ cups fresh orange juice
1¼ cups mirin (sweet sake)
1 cup sake
½ cup plum wine
5 egg yolks
   juice of 1 orange
3 tablespoons sugar
4 tablespoons (2 ounces) unsalted butter
1½ cups heavy cream

1 basket strawberries
1 basket raspberries
1 ripe papaya
2 large oranges
   sugar

1.   Prepare the sauce: Combine the orange juice, mirin, sake and plum wine in a saucepan. Bring to a boil and reduce to 1 to 1¼ cups. The reduction will be slightly thick. Set aside to cool.

2.   Whisk the egg yolks with the juice of 1 orange and the sugar over a *bain-marie* until they are thick and foamy. Remove from the heat and whisk in the reduced sauce.

3.   In a small pan, heat the butter until it is brown and add it to the sauce. Whisk the sauce over ice until it has cooled.

4.   In a separate bowl, whip the cream until stiff, then fold it into the cooled sauce.

PRESENTATION: Slice the fruits and arrange them on plates. Spoon the sauce over the top. Sprinkle with a little sugar and caramelize with a small blow torch or under a very hot broiler. Serve immediately. To give added flavor, sprinkle a little sake over the top.

GINGER CRÈME BRÛLÉE

Serves 8 to 10

6 *egg yolks*
½ *cup sugar*
3 *cups heavy cream*
1 *vanilla bean, split*
3 *dime-size pieces fresh ginger*
7 *tablespoons (3½ ounces) unsalted butter, softened*
½ *cup brown sugar*

1. In a large metal bowl set over a *bain-marie*, whisk the egg yolks and sugar together until the mixture is light and thick enough to form a ribbon. This takes quite a long time; be strong and be patient. Remove from the heat.
2. Carefully whisk in the cream. Add the vanilla bean and ginger. Place the bowl back over the *bain-marie* and cook slowly for about 45 minutes, stirring frequently. Take care the water does not boil. The custard will be done when the mixture adheres to your finger without dripping.
3. When the custard is done, remove from the heat and whisk in the butter, a little at a time, until all of it has been incorporated. Strain through a fine strainer into a bowl, then ladle into eight one-cup serving ramekins or into a shallow 1 to 1½-quart serving dish. Chill at least 6 hours or overnight.

4. Sieve an even layer of brown sugar (or regular sugar) over the custards approximately ¼ inch thick. With the rack up as far as it will go, run the ramekins under a hot broiler for 2 or 3 minutes, or until the sugar caramelizes. (You can use a small blow torch to accomplish the same task.) Chill until serving time.

PRESENTATION: Place the individual ramekins on dessert saucers or spoon the *crème brûlée* from the larger serving dish onto dessert plates.

PEARS POACHED IN ZINFANDEL

Serves 4

4 *ripe pears*
1 *lemon*
1 *bottle Zinfandel*
1 *whole vanilla bean, split in half*
½ *teaspoon black peppercorns*
½ *cinnamon stick*
⅓ *cup sugar*
1 *box fresh raspberries*
   fresh mint sprigs for garnish

1. Peel, halve and core the pears. Rub each half with lemon juice.
2. In a heavy non-reactive saucepan, bring the Zinfandel, vanilla bean, peppercorns, cinnamon stick and sugar to a boil.
3. Reduce the heat, add the pears and poach them until tender, approximately 20 minutes. (The time will vary depending upon the ripeness of the fruit.)

4.   Remove the pears and drain them thoroughly, reserving the poaching liquid. Arrange 2 pear halves per serving on warm plates.

5.   Toss the raspberries in the poaching liquid, then drain them immediately so that they are warm but not mushy.

PRESENTATION: Sprinkle the warm berries over the pears. Garnish with the mint sprigs. Serve immediately.

CHOCOLATE CHIP COOKIES

It is the pastry flour that makes these cookies tender.

Makes about 36

      8 *tablespoons (4 ounces) unsalted butter*
      6 *tablespoons (3 ounces) sugar*
      6 *tablespoons packed (3 ounces) brown sugar*
      1 *teaspoon vanilla*
    ½ *teaspoon salt*
      1 *egg*
  2⅔ *cups (10 ounces) sifted pastry (or all-purpose) flour*
    ¼ *teaspoon baking soda dissolved in 2 teaspoons hot water*
      1 *cup (4 ounces) chopped nuts*
      1 *cup (6 ounces) chocolate chips*

1.   Cream the butter in an electric mixer until light.

2.   With the mixer running slowly, add the sugar, brown sugar, vanilla, salt, egg, flour and dissolved baking soda. Mix until just blended.

3.   Stir in the chopped nuts and chocolate chips.

4.   Preheat the oven to 350 degrees F. If the dough is too soft, chill it until it stiffens a little. Then, shape balls of the dough 1 inch in diameter and place them on a baking sheet, leaving 2 inches in between.

5.   Bake the cookies for 15 to 17 minutes. They should be golden brown and only very slightly soft. Let the cookies cool on the sheet, then transfer them to a rack.

6.   Store the cookies in an airtight container.

CHOCOLATE TRUFFLES WITH BRANDIED APRICOTS

I like truffles that have been dipped in chocolate, rolled in cocoa, then frozen. I eat them right out of the freezer.

*Makes about 90
bite-size truffles*

2 *ounces dried apricots*
¾ *cup apricot brandy*
2½ *pounds bittersweet or semisweet chocolate*
1½ *cups heavy cream*
8 *tablespoons (4 ounces) soft unsalted butter*
½ *cup cocoa powder*

1.   Cut the apricots into very small cubes and put them into a small saucepan. Add ½ cup of the apricot brandy, place the pan over medium heat and bring to a boil. Remove from the heat and place the apricots in a small bowl and let them sit overnight or until most of the brandy has been absorbed.

2.   Cut 1 pound of the chocolate into small pieces and place it

in a metal mixing bowl. Bring the cream to a boil and stir it into the chocolate until the chocolate is melted. Stir in the butter until it is completely incorporated, then stir in the remaining apricot brandy. Then thoroughly mix in the brandied apricots. Chill several hours or overnight in the refrigerator.

3.   Cut the remaining 1½ pounds chocolate into small pieces and melt it in a *bain-marie* over hot but not boiling water.

4.   Sift the cocoa powder onto a large plate.

5.   Using the small end of a melon baller, shape small bite-size truffles, put them on a tray lined with waxed paper and place the tray in the freezer.

6.   Using a fork, dip each truffle into the melted chocolate, letting the excess drop off, then put them on the plate of sifted cocoa powder. Let the chocolate set for 20 to 30 seconds, then roll the truffles in the cocoa. Roll 2 or 3 truffles at a time around in the bottom of a sieve to remove the excess cocoa, then place in small paper or foil bonbon cups.

PRESENTATION: Use as part of a tray of *petits fours* or serve 1 or 2 with coffee at the end of dinner. These can be frozen and eaten thawed or straight from the freezer, as is.

. . . . *if the chocolate gets too thick while you are coating the truffles, reheat chocolate again over hot water.*

BOURBON TRUFFLES

Makes 150 small truffles

 2 *cups heavy cream*
1 1/3 *pounds bittersweet chocolate, cut into small pieces*
 5 *tablespoons (2 1/2 ounces) unsalted butter, at room temperature*
 1/3 *cup bourbon*
1 1/2 *pounds bittersweet chocolate*
 1 *cup cocoa powder, 1 pound ground bittersweet chocolate or 2 cups powdered sugar*

1.   Bring the cream to a boil in a large saucepan. Place the chocolate pieces in a large mixing bowl, pour the boiling cream over them, and let stand until the chocolate is melted. Stir in the soft butter, then stir in the bourbon. (If you wish to vary the tastes of the truffles, divide the truffle mixture into portions and flavor each with a different liqueur—Grand Marnier, kirsch, and so on.) Chill overnight in the refrigerator or cool over a large bowl of ice water.

2.   Using a small melon baller, scoop out small truffles and place them on a tray lined with waxed paper. Chill several hours or overnight.

3.   Melt the 1 1/2 pounds chocolate in a metal bowl set over a *bain-marie*. Sift the cocoa powder or powdered sugar onto a large plate; or, place the ground chocolate on a large plate.

4.   Using a fork, dip each truffle into the melted chocolate, letting the excess drip off; then place them in the cocoa powder, ground chocolate or powdered sugar. Let set for 20 or 30 seconds, then roll them in the coating. Transfer the truffles to a plate.

PRESENTATION: Place in small bonbon cups or serve on a doily-lined tray.

FRESH MINT TRUFFLES

Makes 90 to 100 small truffles

1 *pound white chocolate, cut into small pieces*
1/2 *cup heavy cream, heated*
8 *tablespoons (4 ounces) unsalted butter, cut into small pieces and softened*
1 *tablespoon green* crème de menthe
1/4 *cup white* crème de menthe
1/4 *cup packed fresh mint leaves, very finely chopped*

1 *pound bittersweet chocolate, cut into small pieces*
2 *cups powdered sugar, 1 cup cocoa powder or 1 pound ground bittersweet chocolate*

1.   Melt the white chocolate in a metal bowl set over a *bain-marie*. Remove from the heat and whisk in the hot cream, butter, green and white *crème de menthe* and fresh mint. Turn the mixture into a cake tin and chill it for several hours or overnight.
2.   Using a small melon baller, scoop out small balls of the truffle mixture. Dip the scoop in hot water frequently to keep the mixture from sticking. Place the balls on a tray lined with waxed paper and freeze them.
3.   Melt the bittersweet chocolate in a metal bowl set over a *bain-marie* and sift the powdered sugar or cocoa powder onto a large plate; or, place the ground chocolate on a large plate.
4.   Using a fork dip each truffle into the melted chocolate, letting the excess drip back into the pan. Place the truffles on the cocoa, sugar or chocolate and let them sit for 20 to 30 seconds. Then roll the truffles to coat on all sides. Repeat until all the truffles are dipped and coated.

PRESENTATION: Place the truffles on a doily-lined platter or in paper or foil bonbon cups. Serve with coffee.

CASSIS TRUFFLES

Makes 90 to 100
small truffles

> *1 pound white chocolate, cut into small pieces*
> *1 cup fresh* cassis *(black currants)*
> *2 tablespoons sugar*
> *¼ cup water*
> *¼ cup heavy cream, heated*
> *8 tablespoons (4 ounces) unsalted butter, cut into small*
> *pieces and softened*
> *¼ cup* crème de cocoa
>
> *1 pound bittersweet chocolate, cut into small pieces*
> *1 pound ground bittersweet or unsweetened chocolate or*
> *2 cups powdered sugar*

1.   Melt the white chocolate in a metal bowl set over a *bain-marie*.

2.   In a saucepan, cook the *cassis*, sugar and water over low heat until all the liquid has evaporated.

3.   Stir the *cassis* and hot cream into the chocolate, then stir in the butter and *crème de cocoa* and stir until the mixture is smooth. Turn the mixture into a cake tin and chill for several hours or overnight.

4.   Using a small melon baller, scoop out small balls of the truffle mixture. Dip the scoop into hot water frequently to keep the mixture from sticking. Place the truffles on a tray lined with waxed paper as they are formed, then place the tray in the freezer until the truffles become very firm.

5.   Melt the bittersweet or unsweetened chocolate in a metal bowl set over a *bain-marie*. Sift the powdered sugar onto a large plate. If you prefer to use ground chocolate, the easiest procedure is to break it into small pieces, place them in a food

processor and process to a fine grind. Place the ground chocolate on a large plate. Chill.

6.   Using a fork, dip each truffle into the chocolate, letting the
excess drip off, then place in the powdered sugar or ground
chocolate. Let the truffles sit for 20 to 30 seconds and roll them
in the sugar or chocolate. Transfer the truffles to a plate. Repeat
until all the truffles are dipped and rolled.

PRESENTATION: Serve the truffles on a doily-lined platter garnished with fresh *cassis*; or place them in bonbon cups to serve
with coffee or as part of a platter of *petits fours*.

Menus

DINNER

American Caviar
Sally Lunn Melba Toast

Roast Rack of Lamb Salad
with Greens Vinaigrette

Boneless Quail
with Wild Rice Stuffing
Cream Sauce
Fresh Asparagus

Baked California Goat Cheese
with Native Olive Oil Dressing

Florida Citrus Sherbets

St. Clement
Chardonnay 1981

Freemark Abbey
Cabernet Bosché 1975

Schramsberg
Crémant Demi-Sec 1980

1983 SUMMIT OF INDUSTRIALIZED NATIONS

THE WILLIAMSBURG INN
Colonial Williamsburg, Virginia
Monday, May 30, 1983

*T*his is the menu served to the Heads of State at the Economic Summit in Williamsburg, Virginia. Among the Heads of State attending the dinner were Ronald Reagan, Pierre Elliot Trudeau, François Mitterand, Margaret Thatcher, Helmut Kohl, Yasuhiro Nakasone and Alessandro Pertini. Certainly, the most important participant was Barbara Lazaroff, my wife, who gave so generously of her time and talent by personally bathing the gritty lettuce three times so that not a grain of the offending dirt would become lodged between the dentures and gums of this distinguished group. Hooray for Barbara!!!

BLACK CAVIAR ON WARM POTATO SLICES WITH
CRÈME FRAÎCHE
WARM LAMB SALAD
STEAMED QUAIL WITH WILD RICE AND MORELS
ASPARAGUS
FRESH AMERICAN GOAT CHEESE ON CROUTONS
THREE CITRUS SHERBETS
CHOCOLATE CHIP COOKIES

Prior to the opening of Chinois on Main, I presented this dinner at a private party in the patio of Spago. It was a preview menu representative of the food that would be served when the restaurant opened in September of 1983.

SALMON SOUP WITH LEMONGRASS
MINTED SQUAB SALAD
CRAB WITH BLACK BEAN SAUCE
STEAMED GREY SOLE
CHINESE DUCK WITH PLUM SAUCE
CHINOIS PANCAKES
GREEN TEA SHERBET
MELON BALLS IN LICHEE WINE
GINGER CRÈME BRÛLÉE
GINGER COOKIES

This menu suggests the flavor of the American Southwest. I served it to the President of West Germany at a gala party given in his honor at a large ranch in Texas.

BAY SCALLOPS AND SHRIMP SEVICHE
IN TORTILLA CUPS
CREAM OF AVOCADO SOUP
ROASTED QUAIL ON CORN CAKES WITH GARLIC
GRAPEFRUIT TEQUILA SHERBET
INDIVIDUAL PECAN PIES

This menu is typical of food served at Spago for large birthday or anniversary celebrations. It could also be prepared at home (with help) for a large gathering.

KIR ROYALS
VARIETY OF PIZZAS:
VEGETARIAN PIZZA, DUCK SAUSAGE PIZZA, AND
LAMB SAUSAGE PIZZA
SALAD OF ARUGOLA, MÂCHE, AND RADICCHIO
WITH SMOKED SALMON
ROAST VEAL WITH ONION AND
MUSHROOM BUTTER SAUCE
PLATTER OF ASSORTED PASTRIES AND ICE CREAMS

The American Wine and Food Festival

Spago's Annual American Wine and Food Festival has been a big success since it began. In fact, it has gotten so popular that it has been moved to the Pacific Design Center in Los Angeles. The proceeds go to Meals on Wheels, a charity that I like a lot because it helps the senior citizens of our area.

Contributing to the festival's success are about seventy wineries from California's wine-growing regions, as well as Washington State and New York State. Each winery brings a Chardonnay, a Cabernet Sauvignon and a third wine of its choice.

Many great restaurateurs and chefs from the Los Angeles area and from as far away as San Francisco, New Orleans and New York come to fix their specialties. Specialty food purveyors from around the country bring such delicacies as pâté, smoked fish, caviar and cheese.

I thought you might enjoy seeing a menu from this event.

CALIFORNIA SUNSHINE
California
Assorted Domestic Caviars

K-PAUL'S
New Orleans
Jambalaya
Blackened Redfish
Blackened Pork Chops
Cajun Popcorn
Crayfish Bisque

LE DOME
Los Angeles
Navarin of Lamb
Rabbit in Mustard Sauce
Escargots in Puff Pastry
Oysters

SHAMROCK SMOKED FISH
California
Smoked Salmon
Smoked Sturgeon
Smoked Monkfish

TROIS PETITS COCHONS
New York
Fifteen Assorted Pâtés

VALENTINO
Santa Monica
Grilled Marinated Eggplant with Caprini
Green Tortellini with Duck
Capellaci Stuffed with Ricotta, Spinach, Tomato
and Gorgonzola

SPAGO AND CHINOIS
Los Angeles and Santa Monica
Curried Oysters
Fresh Goat Cheese Croutons
Baby Roasted Lamb with Thyme
Duck Sausage Pizza
Grilled Scallops with Tomato Basil Vinaigrette
Assorted Cookies
Fresh Mint Truffles

This is a menu we prepared for a party given by Victoria Principal and her husband, Dr. Harry Glassman at Chinois on New Year's Eve.

CURRIED OYSTERS WITH CUCUMBER SAUCE
AND SALMON PEARLS
SPICY DUCK SOUP
LOBSTER WITH FIVE SPICES
CHINESE DUCK WITH PLUM SAUCE
AND CHINOIS PANCAKES
SZECHUAN BEEF
HOT SIZZLING FISH
ASSORTED DESSERTS

Here is the dinner menu that I created for students and friends at Mondavi Winery's Great Chefs of America class. I especially enjoyed their Cabernet 1978.

CURRIED OYSTERS
ROBERT MONDAVI SPARKLING WINE

LOBSTER RAVIOLI
ROBERT MONDAVI 1981 CHARDONNAY RESERVE

WARM LAMB SALAD
ROBERT MONDAVI 1980 PINOT NOIR RESERVE

PIGEON WITH FOIE GRAS
ROBERT MONDAVI PRIVATE RESERVE CABERNET
1978

APPLE TART WITH CARAMEL ICE CREAM
ROBERT MONDAVI 1981 JOHANNISBERG RIESLING
BOTRYTIS

This is the menu that we prepared for Sunday lunch at the Great Chefs of America classes at the Mondavi Winery.

PIZZA WITH SMOKED SALMON
ROBERT MONDAVI 1981 FUMÉ BLANC RESERVE

ASPARAGUS WITH DUCK PROSCIUTTO

RACK OF LAMB WITH SAUTÉED ARTICHOKES
ROBERT MONDAVI 1978 CABERNET SAUVIGNON
RESERVE

GRAPEFRUIT TEQUILA SHERBET
TUILES
ROBERT MONDAVI 1982 MUSCATO D'ORO

This is the very elegant menu created by Jean Andre Charial and his very capable staff on the occasion of our marriage May 20, 1984. The dinner was at the enchanting medieval L'OU-STAU DE BAUMANIÈRE, the three-star restaurant in Les Baux de Provence, France, owned by Monsieur Raymond Thuilier, under whom I did my apprenticeship and whose guidance has been a lasting influence on my philosophy as a chef.

BARBARA ELLEN LAZAROFF
et
WOLFGANG JOHANN PUCK
le menu cree par R. Thuilier
à l'occasion de leur Mariage medieval
le 20 Mai 1984

AMUSE BOUCHE
Assorted Hors d'Oeuvres
CHAMPAGNE BAUMANIÈRE
Blanc de Blanc 1978

FOIE GRAS FRAIS
Fresh Goose Liver
CHÂTEAUNEUF DU PAPE
Blanc, Domaine de Mont Redon 1982

FRICASSÉE DE HOMARDS ET DE LANGOUSTES
Fricassee of Lobster and Langoustines
ACACIA CHARDONNAY WINERY LAKE 1982

GIGOT D'AGNEAU EN CROÛTE
Leg of Baby Lamb in Pastry
MOUSSELINE D'ARTICHAUTS
Mousseline of Artichokes
GRATIN D'AUBERGINES
Gratin of Eggplant
CHÂTEAUNEUF DU PAPE
Domaine de Beaucastel 1972

FROMAGES
Assorted Cheeses

GÂTEAU AU DESSUS DES NUAGES
Wedding Cake
FRIANDISES
Assorted Sweets
CAFÉ
Coffee
Don Ruinart
Rosé 1976, en Magnum

COMTE DE CHAMPAGNE 1976
jusqu'à l'aube

L'OUSTAU DE BAUMANIÈRE
13520 LES BAUX DE PROVENCE
FRANCE

I always like to give people a choice of dishes so that every palate can be a happy one.

NEW YEAR'S EVE MENU

FIRST COURSE
BAKED POTATOES WITH BLACK
AND GOLDEN CAVIAR
OR
SALAD ST. SYLVESTRE WITH SAUTÉED GOOSE LIVER
OR
OYSTERS AND CLAMS ON THE HALF SHELL
WITH MIGNONNETTE SAUCE

SECOND COURSE
RAVIOLI WITH BLACK TRUFFLES
OR
GRILLED SALMON WITH DILL AND LEEKS

THIRD COURSE
CRISPY ROASTED DUCK BREAST
WITH CASSIS AND PEARS
OR
GRILLED VEAL CHOP WITH WILD MUSHROOMS
OR
MEDALLION OF VENISON WITH CABERNET SAUCE
AND GLAZED CHESTNUTS
OR
JOHN DORY WITH THREE CAVIARS

ASSORTMENT OF NEW YEAR'S DESSERTS
COFFEE

This is the menu that I created for the wedding of Lynda Carter and Robert Altman. The setting was the romantic outdoor patio-dining area of the Bel Air Bay Club.

This is an elegant buffet menu that could be used on the most formal occasion. The hors d'oeuvres were passed at the reception with Champagne.

HORS D'OEUVRES

SMALL BAKED POTATOES
WITH
RED AND BLACK CAVIAR AND CRÈME FRAÎCHE

SCOTCH SMOKED SALMON ON TOASTED BRIOCHE

DINNER
COLD LOBSTER WITH CAVIAR SAUCE

FRESH SAUTÉED GOOSE LIVER
WITH
APPLES AND GREEN PEPPERCORNS

BABY LAMB CHOPS WITH FRESH HERB BUTTER
LOBSTER RAVIOLI

SALMON IN PUFF PASTRY
WITH
FRESH HERB BUTTER SAUCE

CHINESE OYSTERS

SALAD OF MIXED GREENS AND GOAT CHEESE

SIRLOIN STEAK ROASTED WITH CRACKED PEPPERS
BEARNAISE SAUCE
MEAUX MUSTARD SAUCE
STIR-FRIED FRESH BABY VEGETABLES

WEDDING CAKE

When Mary and Irving "Swifty" Lazar held an Oscar Night Party at Spago, this is the menu they selected.

APPETIZERS
ASSORTED PIZZAS
INCLUDING
SMOKED SALMON WITH GOLDEN
AND SEVRUGA CAVIAR
SAUTÉED PACIFIC OYSTERS WITH SPICY SALSA
MARINATED SALMON WITH DILL CREAM
AND TOASTED FRESH BRIOCHE
BABY NEW POTATOES WITH GOLDEN
AND SEVRUGA CAVIAR

DINNER
CHOICE OF
GRILLED FRESH TUNA WITH TOMATO
MINT VINAIGRETTE
ROASTED VEAL LOIN WITH PORT WINE SAUCE

SALAD
AMERICAN FIELD SALAD WITH GOAT CHEESE

DESSERTS
ASSORTED PASTRIES AND ICE CREAMS

WINE SELECTION
POMMERY BRUT CHAMPAGNE
MOËT WHITE STAR IMPERIAL BRUT CHAMPAGNE
DOM RUINART BLANC DE BLANCS '75 CHAMPAGNE

PINOT GRIGIO SANTA MARGHERITA '83
CHATEAU BELAIR LUSSAC ST. EMILION '82

A wonderful occasion to mix tradition with inventiveness.

PASSOVER SEDER MENU

FRESH MATZOH

CHICKEN SOUP WITH JULIENNED SHIITAKE
MUSHROOMS
AND MATZOH BALLS

GEFILTE FISH

POTATO LATKE WITH SAUTÉED DUCK LIVER AND
KOSHER PORT WINE SAUCE

WHOLE BAKED SALMON WITH ALMONDS AND DILL

STUFFED BABY LAMB MESOPOTAMIA WITH
CHOPPED PRUNES AND NUTS
SPICY RATATOUILLE

APRICOT CAKE

Jason Epstein, Random House's editor extraordinaire, came to Spago for dinner one night when this book was overdue for at least one year. I thought I should make him a special dinner so he wouldn't be too mad with me.

DUCK LIVER SALAD

PASTA WITH WHITE TRUFFLES

GRILLED JOHN DORY WITH TOMATO BASIL
VINAIGRETTE

ROASTED BABY LAMB WITH CARAMELIZED GARLIC

PLATTER OF ASSORTED DESSERTS

Glossary

AL DENTE: Italian for "almost cooked"; used to describe the almost firm stage to which vegetables or pasta should be cooked.

AIGUILLETTES: the breast meat of fowl such as duck, chicken, squab, quail, and so on, cut with the grain and with the knife at about a 20-degree angle, resulting in long, thin slices.

BAIN-MARIE: a device for cooking food over simmering water in stacked pots on top of the stove, or in a dish set in a larger pan of hot water in the oven.

BÂTONNETS: strips of meat or vegetables about 2 inches by ⅜ inch.

BEURRE MANIÉ: equal parts soft butter and flour mixed well and used at the last minute to thicken sauces.

BLANCHING: cooking vegetables or other foods briefly in a large pot of boiling water in order to wilt them, to set their color or to partially cook them. After blanching, the item should be quickly immersed in ice water to stop the cooking process.

BOUQUET GARNI: a bundle of aromatic herbs, usually consisting of parsley, thyme, peppercorns and a bay leaf tied together and used to flavor stocks, soups, stews, and so on.

BRUNOISE: finely diced vegetables, generally cut ¼ inch or smaller, used in fillings, soups and sauces.

CAPER: small pickled buds from the caper bush that grows wild in the south of France, Algeria, Turkey, and elsewhere; not to be confused with nasturtium seeds.

CHIFFONNADE: finely shredded vegetables.

CONCASSÉ: chopped.

CRÈME FRAÎCHE: naturally fermented cream, used in the preparation of many French dishes and sold here in the United States in specialty food stores. A suitable substitute can be made at home by mixing in a small saucepan 1 cup heavy cream (preferably "raw" or unpasteurized) with ½ cup sour cream or 2 teaspoons buttermilk. Stir over low heat until lukewarm. Pour into a clean jar and let sit at room temperature until it thickens, which will take a few hours or overnight, depending on the kitchen temperature. Cover and refrigerate. It will keep up to 10 days.

CROQUANT: French for "crisp or crunchy"—should be akin to *al dente* in texture.

DEGLAZE: to add liquid to a hot pan after the sautéed or roasted ingredients have been removed and the fat discarded. The resulting GLAZE is an important part of many sauces. Reduced by half, a *glace* is a completed stock reduced to a syrup. Both are best and most flavorful when reduced over low heat.

EMULSION: a stable mixture of two liquids that normally separate from each other, like butter sauces, which are liquid plus butter.

FISH FUMÉ: fish stock.

JULIENNE STRIPS: food cut into matchlike strips.

MIREPOIX: equal parts of coarsely chopped onions, carrots and celery.

MISE EN PLACE: assembly of all the ingredients necessary to complete a recipe.

MOUSSE or MOUSSELINE: a purée of vegetables, meat or fish lightened by the addition of whipped cream. The terms also apply to desserts and sauces lightened in the same manner.

NAP: to lightly cover food or a plate with sauce.

PURÉE: mashing or sieving food, made tender by cooking, to a smooth pulp.

REDUCE: to cook a liquid, decreasing its volume by evaporation, in order to intensify its flavor and thicken its consistency.

ROUX: equal parts butter and flour cooked together for several minutes and used to make white sauces *(béchamel* or Mornay as examples) or as a thickening agent in some sauces.

SAUTÉ: to brown food in a hot skillet or sauté pan in a small amount of fat.

SIMMER: to cook a liquid barely at the boiling point, with only a few bubbles breaking the surface.

STOCK: a liquid in which meat, poultry, fish bones or vegetables and their appropriate seasonings have been cooked; used as the basis of soups, stews and sauces.

STRIPES: strips.

SWEAT: to cook food over low heat, releasing its flavor without affecting its color, until it is translucent and glossy.

Index

Acacia Chardonnay and fresh herbs, chicken with, 172–73
Aiguillettes, 293
Al dente, 293
Almond(s)
  cake with ginger, 240
  honey, ice cream, 261
  marzipan tart, strawberry, 232
  paste, 241
  veal with Johannisberg Riesling, pine nuts and, 158
Altman, Robert, 289
American Wine and Food Festival, 283
Angel hair pasta
  with goat cheese and broccoli, 77–78
  with smoked salmon and golden caviar, 78–79
Appetizers, 3–53
  asparagus with duck prosciutto, 50–51
  bay scallops with sautéed apples, 16–17
  bay scallops and shrimp seviche in tortilla cups, 9–10
  chicken salad Chinois, 52–53
  chili oil, 32
  Chinois sea scallops with spicy vinegar, 26–27
  Chinois special scallops, 6–7
  cured fresh salmon, 15–16
    with golden caviar sauce on toasted brioche, 14–15
  curried oysters with cucumber sauce and salmon pearls, 18–20
  foie gras with sautéed apples, 4–5
  garlic lamb in lettuce leaves, 31
  goat cheese croutons, 20–21
  goat cheese salad with arugola and *radicchio*, 40–41
  lamb salad Mondavi, 29–30

  mandarin steak salad, 27–29
  marinated tuna with Maui onions and avocado, 12
  rack of lamb Chinois, 43–44
  roasted duck legs with Napa cabbage and pancetta, 38–39
  roast saddle of lamb salad, 45
  salad of grilled chanterelles or *cêpes*, 42
  scrambled eggs with fresh truffles, 23–24
  smoked salmon and caviar on buckwheat cakes, 13–14
  Sonoma lamb salad, 39–40
  spicy honey-glazed baby pork ribs, 24–25
  spinach salad with duck liver on croutons, 34–36
  squab salad rolls, 32–34
  stir-fried scallop salad, 8–9
  sweetbreads with vinegar butter and *mâche*, 36–37
  Swiss chard and goat cheese ramekin, 21–22
  tortillas, 11
  twice fried rice, 17–18
  warm lobster salad with white truffles, 48–49
  watercress salad with barbecued chicken breast, 46–47
  See also Pasta; Pizza
Apple(s)
  caramelized, cheesecake with, 241–42
  pies, Spago's individual, 221–22
  sautéed
    bay scallops with, 16–17
    foie gras with, 4–5
Apricots, brandied, chocolate truffles with, 272–73

Artichoke(s)
  calzone with, and porcini mushrooms, 126–27
  mousse, 200
  pasta with sweetbreads and, 84–85
  rack of lamb with rosemary and, 162–63
Arugola
  goat cheese salad with, and *radicchio*, 40–41
  grilled veal chops with vinegar butter and, 159–60
Asparagus
  baby, 195
  with duck prosciutto, 50–51
  spears, large or medium, 195
Avocado, marinated tuna with Maui onions and, 12

Baby lamb, 149, 150
Baby spinach leaves, fried, 146
Baby vegetables, 193–98
Bain-marie, 293
Banana ice cream, 254–55
Barbecued chicken breast, watercress salad with, 46–47
Basil, Louis Blanco's three cheese calzone with eggplant and, 124–25
Bass, *see* Striped bass
Bâtonnets, 293
Bay scallops
  with sautéed apples, 16–17
  and shrimp seviche in tortilla cups, 9–10
  smoked, black pasta with, 95–96
Beard, James, xi
Beef, 149, 150
  New York steak(s)
    salad, mandarin, 27–29
    with *shiitake* and *enoki* mushrooms and grilled new onions, 152–53
    Szechuan beef, 156–57
  New York strip, roasted, with two sauces, 153–54
Beer with pizza, 109
Bell peppers, 198
  yellow and red, roasted chicken breasts stuffed with, and sweet green onion sauce, 171–72
Beurre manié, 293
Bisque, crayfish, 60–62
Black bean sauce, 134–35
Black Forest ham and goat cheese pizza, 112–13
Black pasta
  dough, 102–3
  with smoked scallops, 95–96
Black truffle(s), 49

ravioli with foie gras and, 91–93
vinaigrette, 169–70
Blanching, 293
Bouillon, court, 50
Bouquet garni, 293
Bourbon truffles, 274
Brandied apricots, chocolate truffles with, 272–73
Bread, 205–15
  corn muffins with jalapeño peppers and fresh rosemary, 207–8
  Maida Heatter's breadsticks, 210
  my not kosher matzoh, 211
  pecan and walnut bread, 212–13
  simple sourdough farmer's bread, 214–15
  Spago's brioche loaf, 208–9
    toasted, cured fresh salmon with golden caviar sauce on, 14–15
Bread pudding, chocolate, with hazelnuts, 249–50
Brioche loaf, Spago's, 208–9
  toasted, cured fresh salmon with golden caviar sauce on, 14–15
Broccoli
  angel hair pasta with goat cheese and, 77–78
  flowerettes and stems, 195–96
Brunoise, 293
Buckwheat cakes, smoked salmon and caviar on, 13–14
Butter
  Pinot Noir, 138–39
  red onion, 137
  tomato, 135–36
  vinegar, 36–37, 159–60
Buttercream, coffee, hazelnut marjolaine with, 246–49

Cabbage, Napa, roasted duck legs with, and pancetta, 38–39
Cake(s)
  almond, with ginger, 240
  buckwheat, smoked salmon and caviar on, 13–14
  cheesecake with caramelized apples, 241–42
  chocolate mousseline, 243–44
  corn, 185–86
    quail on, with Zinfandel sauce, 184–85
  ginger, 245–46
Calzone
  with artichokes and porcini mushrooms, 126–27
  three cheese, with eggplant and basil, Louis Blanco's, 124–25
Caper, 293

Caramel (caramelized)
  apples, cheesecake with, 241–42
  ice cream, 255
  sauce, 256
Carrots, baby, 195
Carter, Lynda, 289
Cassis truffles, 276–77
Catfish, 132
  sizzling, 141–42
Caviar
  golden
    angel hair pasta with smoked
      salmon and, 78–79
    pizza with smoked salmon and,
      115–16
    sauce, 14–15
    smoked salmon and, on buckwheat
      cakes, 13–14
  salmon, curried oysters with cucumber
    sauce and, 18–20
Cêpes, 197
  grilled, salad of, 42
Chanterelle(s), 197
  grilled
    chanterelle ravioli with, 82–83
    salad of, 42
    and Maui onion vinaigrette, 174–75
    pizza with, eggplant and leeks, 122–
      23
  ravioli with grilled chanterelles, 82–83
Charial, Jean Andre, 287
Cheese(s)
  for pizza, 108
  three, calzone with eggplant and basil,
    Louis Blanco's, 124–25
  See also Goat cheese
Cheesecake with caramelized apples,
  241–42
Chervil, cream of leek and, soup with
  white truffles, 56–57
Chez Gu, 107–8
Chiffonade, 293
Chicken(s), 149
  baby, grilled, with truffle vinaigrette,
    169–70
  benefits of "undercooking," 150
  breast(s)
    with Acacia Chardonnay and fresh
      herbs, 172–73
    barbecued, watercress salad with,
      46–47
    roasted, stuffed with yellow and red
      bell peppers and sweet green on-
      ion sauce, 171–72
    stuffed with goat cheese and fresh
      herbs, with chanterelle and Maui
      onion vinaigrette, 174–75
  with garlic and parsley, 168–69

legs, stir-fried, with garlic and cilantro,
  176–77
salad, Chinois, 52–53
spicy, pizza, 117–18
stock, 69
Chili oil, 32
Chili peppers, 198
Chinese duck with plum sauce and Chinois pancakes, 178–79
Chinese vinaigrette, 176–77
Chinois
  chicken salad, 52–53
  pancakes, 180
    Chinese duck with plum sauce and,
      178–79
  pigeon breasts, 80–81
  rack of lamb, 43–44
  sake fruit, 268–69
  sea scallops with spicy vinegar, 26–27
  spareribs, 166–67
  special scallops, 6–7
Chocolate
  bread pudding with hazelnuts, 249–50
  chocolate chip ice cream, Jack Dan-
    iel's, 256–57
  cream, 236
  mandarin ice cream, 258
  mousseline cakes, 243–44
  soufflé, 251
  three, terrine, 252–54
  truffles with brandied apricots, 272–73
  white, ice cream with wild strawberries
    or raspberries, 259–60
Chocolate chip(s)
  cookies, 271–72
  ice cream, Jack Daniel's chocolate,
    256–57
Cilantro, stir-fried chicken with garlic
  and, 176–77
Clam(s), 132
  David Hartman's fresh pasta salad
    with mussels and, 96–97
  and mussel soup, 62–63
Coffee buttercream, hazelnut marjolaine
  with, 246–49
Concassé, 293
Concord grape sherbet, 264
Cookies, chocolate chip, 271–72
Corn
  cakes, 185–86
    quail on, with Zinfandel sauce, 184–
      85
  on the cob, 196
  muffins with jalapeño peppers and
    fresh rosemary, 207–8
  soup, cream of, with Gulf oysters, 58–
    59
Court bouillon, 50

Crab
   in black bean sauce, 134–35
   rolls, fried spicy, crab soup with, 67–
       68
Cranberry(ies)
   and pears, sautéed, grilled pigeon
       with, 181–82
   sauce, 165–66
Crayfish (crawfish), 132
   bisque, 60–62
Cream
   chocolate, 236
   garlic, 135–36
   pastry, 224
Crème anglaise, 263
Crème brûlée
   ginger, 269–70
   tart, 227
Crème fraîche, 293
Croquant, 294
Croutons
   goat cheese, 20–21
   spinach salad with duck liver on, 34–
       36
Cucumber sauce, 18–20
Curried oysters with cucumber sauce
       and salmon pearls, 18–20
Cuttlefish ink for black pasta dough,
       102–3

David Hartman's fresh pasta salad with
       mussels and clams, 96–97
Deglaze, 294
Desserts, 219–77
   candied lemon slices, 238
   chocolate bread pudding with hazel-
       nuts, 249–50
   chocolate chip cookies, 271–72
   chocolate soufflé, 251
   fruit, Chinois sake, 268–69
   ganache (chocolate cream), 236
   ginger crème brûlée, 269–70
   hazelnut marjolaine with coffee butter-
       cream, 246–49
   pastry cream, 224
   pears poached in Zinfandel, 270–71
   puff pastry Baumanière, 228–29
   three chocolate terrine, 252–54
   truffles
       bourbon, 274
       cassis, 276–77
       chocolate, with brandied apricots,
           272–73
       mint, 275
   See also Cake(s); Ice cream; Pie(s);
       Sherbet; Tart(s)
Détrempe (flour mixture), 228–29
Dill sauce, 89–91

Duck
   breasts, grilled, spicy pasta with wild
       mushrooms and, 86–87
   Chinese, with plum sauce and Chinois
       pancakes, 178–79
   legs, roasted, with Napa cabbage and
       pancetta, 38–39
   prosciutto, asparagus with, 50–51
   sausage, pizza with, 113–14
Duck liver(s)
   foie gras with sautéed apples, 4–5
   sautéed, pheasant breast with, 182–83
   spinach salad with, on croutons, 34–
       35

Egg nog ice cream, 260–61
Eggplant
   Japanese, 198
   Louis Blanco's three cheese calzone
       with, and basil, 124–25
   pizza with chanterelles, leeks and,
       122–23
Eggs, scrambled, with fresh truffles, 23–
       24
Ehman, Bart, 43, 149
Elephant ear (wood hue) mushrooms,
       197
Emulsion, 294
Enoki mushrooms, 197
   New York steak with shiitake mush-
       rooms and, and new onions, 152–
       53
Epstein, Jason, 292
Escoffier, 75
Ethnic cuisines, mixing, xii
Evans, Linda, 107

Farmer's bread, simple sourdough, 214–
       15
Fennel, red snapper with, 142–43
Fettuccine with mushrooms, 79–80
Fiddlehead ferns, 196
Fish, 131–33
   fumé, 294
   mesquite grilling for, 133
   preparation of, 131–33
   soup, 54–56
   stock, 70
   wine with, 133
   See also Shellfish; names of fish
Foie gras
   ravioli with, and truffles, 91–93
   with sautéed apples, 4–5
Foyot sauce, 153, 154–55
Free-range chickens, 149
Fruit
   Chinois sake, 268–69

rice tart with, 230–31
See also names of fruit

Game, 150
    pheasant breast with sautéed duck
        liver, 182–83
    pigeon, grilled, with sautéed pears and
        cranberries, 181–82
    quail on corn cakes with Zinfandel
        sauce, 184–85
    squab
        with leeks and pomegranate sauce,
            186–87
        salad rolls, 32–34
        sautéed, with panfried noodles,
            188–89
Ganache (chocolate cream), 236
Garlic, 196
    chicken with, and parsley, 168–69
    cream, 135–36
    lamb in lettuce leaves, 31
    stir-fried chicken with, and cilantro,
        176–77
Ginger
    almond cake with, 240
    cake, 245–46
    crème brûlée, 269–70
    sweet, lobster with, 145–46
    vinaigrette, 140–41
Glassman, Dr. Harry, 285
Glaze, 294
Glossary, 293–94
Goat cheese
    angel hair pasta with, and broccoli,
        77–78
    Black Forest ham and, pizza, 112–13
    chicken breasts stuffed with fresh
        herbs and, with chanterelle and
        Maui onion vinaigrette, 174–75
    croutons, 20–21
    salad with arugola and *radicchio*, 40–
        41
    Swiss chard and, ramekin, 21–22
Golden caviar
    angel hair pasta with smoked salmon
        and, 78–79
    pizza with smoked salmon and, 115–
        16
    sauce, 14–15
Grapefruit tequila sherbet, 265
Grape sherbet, Concord, 264
Green beans, 198
Green bell peppers, 198
Green onion sauce, sweet, 171–72
Grilled (grilling)
    baby chickens with truffle vinaigrette,
        169–70

duck breasts, spicy pasta with wild
    mushrooms and, 86–87
fish, 131–32
mahi mahi in red onion butter, 137–
    38
mesquite, xii
    for fish, 133
new onions, New York steak with *shi-
    itake* and *enoki* mushrooms and,
    152–53
pigeon with sautéed pears and cran-
    berries, 181–82
salmon
    with garlic cream and tomato but-
        ter, 135–36
    with leeks and Pinot Noir butter,
        138–39
trout, fresh herb pasta with, 87–88
tuna with mint vinaigrette, 139–40
veal chop with vinegar butter and aru-
    gola, 159–60
veal liver on a bed of onion marma-
    lade with mustard seeds and vine-
    gar sauce, 160–62
vegetables, 194
Gulf oysters, cream of corn soup with,
    58–59

Ham, Black Forest, and goat cheese
    pizza, 112–13
Haricots verts, 198
Hazelnut(s)
    chocolate bread pudding with, 249–50
    marjolaine with coffee buttercream,
        246–49
Herb(s), 193
    chicken with Acacia Chardonnay and,
        172–73
    chicken breasts stuffed with goat
        cheese and, with chanterelle and
        Maui onion vinaigrette, 174–75
    pasta
        dough, 100
        with grilled trout, 87–88
    for pizza, 108
    See also names of herbs
Honey
    almond ice cream, 261
    -glazed baby pork ribs, spicy, 24–25

Ice cream
    banana, 254–55
    caramel, 255
    chocolate mandarin, 258
    egg nog, 260–61
    honey almond, 261
    Jack Daniel's chocolate chocolate chip,
        256–57

Ice cream (*continued*)
  maple walnut, 262
  raspberry, with raspberry sauce, 263–64
  white chocolate, with wild strawberries or raspberries, 259–60

Jack Daniel's chocolate chocolate chip ice cream, 256–57
Jalapeño peppers, corn muffins with, and fresh rosemary, 207–8
Japanese eggplant, 198
Japanese tree mushrooms, 197
Johannisberg Riesling, veal with almonds, pine nuts and, 158
Julienne strips, 294

Key lime pie, 238–39
Kohl, Helmut, 281

Lamb, 149, 150
  garlic, in lettuce leaves, 31
  rack of
    Chinois, 43–44
    with rosemary and artichokes, 162–63
    with wild mushrooms, 164–65
  salad
    Mondavi, 29–30
    roast saddle of, 45
    Sonoma, 39–40
  sausage, 120–21
    pizza, 119–20
Lazar, Irving "Swifty," 290
Lazar, Mary, 290
Lazaroff, Barbara, xii, 3, 281
Leek(s)
  and chervil, cream of, soup with white truffles, 56–57
  grilled salmon with, and Pinot Noir butter, 138–39
  pizza with chanterelles, eggplant and, 122–23
  squab with, and pomegranate sauce, 186–87
Lemon
  pie, 236–37
  slices, candied, 238
Leroy, Gus, 107–8
Lettuce leaves, garlic lamb in, 31
Lime pie, Key, 238–39
Liver, *see* Duck liver; Veal liver
Lobster(s), 132
  ravioli with fresh dill sauce, 89–91
  salad, warm, with white truffles, 48–49
  with sweet ginger, 145–46
Louis Blanco's three cheese calzone with eggplant and basil, 124–25

Mâche, sweetbreads with vinegar butter and, 36–37
Mahi mahi, 132
  grilled, in red onion butter, 137–38
Maida Heatter's breadsticks, 210
Mandarin steak salad, 27–29
Maple walnut ice cream, 262
Marjolaine, hazelnut, with coffee buttercream, 246–49
Marmalade, onion, 160–62
Marzipan tart, strawberry, 232
Matzoh, my not kosher, 211
Maui onion(s)
  chanterelle and, vinaigrette, 174–75
  marinated tuna with, and avocado, 12
Meats, 149–51
  benefits of "undercooking," 150
  See also Beef; Ham; Lamb; Pork; Sweetbreads; Veal
Meaux mustard sauce, 153, 155
Menus, 281–92
Mesquite grilling, xii
  for fish, 133
Mint
  truffles, 275
  vinaigrette, 139–40
Mirepoix, 294
Mise en place, 294
Mitterand, François, 281
Morels, 197
Mousse, 294
  artichoke, 200
Mousseline, 294
  cakes, chocolate, 243–44
Muffins, corn, with jalapeño peppers and fresh rosemary, 207–8
Mushroom(s), 197
  fettucine with, 79–80
  wild
    rack of baby lamb with, 164–65
    soup, 53–54
    spicy pasta with, and grilled duck breasts, 86–87
  See also names of mushrooms
Mussel(s)
  clam and, soup, 62–63
  David Hartman's fresh pasta salad with, and clams, 96–97
Mustard sauce, Meaux, 153, 155
Mustard seeds, grilled veal liver on a bed of onion marmalade with, and vinegar sauce, 160–62
My not kosher matzoh, 211

Nakasone, Yasuhiro, 281
Nap, 294
Napa cabbage, roasted duck legs with, and pancetta, 38–39

New onions, grilled, New York steak
    with *shiitake* and *enoki* mushrooms
    and, 152–53
New York steak
    salad, mandarin, 27–29
    with *shiitake* and *enoki* mushrooms and
        grilled new onions, 152–53
    Szechuan beef, 156–57
New York strip, roasted, with two
    sauces, 153–54
Noodles, panfried, sautéed squab with,
    188–89

Okra, 198
Onion(s), 198
    green, sweet sauce, 171–72
    Maui
        chanterelle and, vinaigrette, 174–75
        marinated tuna with, and avocado,
            12
        new, grilled, New York steak with *shi-
            itake* and *enoki* mushrooms and,
            152–53
    red
        butter, 137
        marmalade, 160–62
Oustau de Baumanière, L', 107, 228,
    287
Oyster mushrooms, 197
Oyster(s), 132
    curried, with cucumber sauce and
        salmon pearls, 18–20
    fresh pumpkin and, soup, 65–66
    Gulf, cream of corn soup with, 58–59

Pancakes, Chinois, 180
    Chinese duck with plum sauce and,
        178–79
Pancetta, roasted duck legs with Napa
    cabbage and, 38–39
Parsley, chicken with garlic and, 168–69
Pasta, 75–103
    angel hair pasta
        with goat cheese and broccoli, 77–
            78
        with smoked salmon and golden
            caviar, 78–79
    black pasta with smoked scallops, 95–
        96
    chanterelle ravioli with grilled chanter-
        elles, 82–83
    cooking procedures for, 76
    David Hartman's fresh pasta salad
        with mussels and clams, 96–97
    dough
        black, 102–3
        fresh herb, 100
        regular, 98
    spicy, 99
    spinach, 101
    fettucine with mushrooms, 79–80
    fresh herb pasta with grilled trout,
        87–88
    lobster ravioli with fresh dill sauce,
        89–91
    panfried noodles, sautéed squab with,
        188–89
    pigeon breasts Chinois, 80–81
    pumpkin ravioli, 93–95
    ravioli with foie gras and truffles, 91–
        93
    spicy pasta with wild mushrooms and
        grilled duck breasts, 86–87
    with sweetbreads and artichokes, 84–
        85
Pasta machines, 75–76
Pastry cream, 224
Pears
    and cranberries, sautéed, grilled pi-
        geon with, 181–82
    poached in Zinfandel, 270–71
Peas, 196
Pecan
    pie, 234–35
    and walnut bread, 212–13
Pepper, 198
Peppers, *see* Bell peppers; Chili peppers;
    Jalapeño peppers
Pertini, Alessandro, 281
Pheasant breast with sautéed duck liver,
    182–83
Pie(s)
    apple, Spago's individual, 221–22
    Key lime, 238–39
    lemon, 236–37
    pecan, 234–35
Pigeon, 150
    breasts Chinois, 80–81
    grilled, with sautéed pears and cran-
        berries, 181–82
    See also Squab
Pine nuts, veal with Johannisberg Rie-
    sling, almonds and, 158
Pinot Noir butter, 138–39
Pizza, 107–27
    beer with, 109
    Black Forest ham and goat cheese,
        112–13
    with chanterelles, eggplant and leeks,
        122–23
    cheeses for, 108
    dough, 110–11
        basic rules for, 108
        whole wheat, 123–24
    with duck sausage, 113–14
    herbs for, 108

Pizza (*continued*)
　　lamb sausage, 119–20
　　　　filling for, 120–21
　　with shrimp and sun-dried tomatoes,
　　　　118–19
　　with smoked salmon and golden cav-
　　　　iar, 115–16
　　spicy chicken, 117–18
　　toppings for, 109
　　wines with, 109
　　See also Calzone
Plum
　　sauce (purée), 178–79
　　sherbet, 266
　　tart, 225–26
Pomegranate sauce, 186–87
Porcini mushrooms, 197
　　calzone with artichokes and, 126–27
Pork, 149, 150
　　baby chops with cranberry sauce, 165
　　　　–66
　　baby ribs, spicy honey-glazed, 24–25
　　spareribs Chinois, 166–67
　　See also Ham; Pancetta
Potatoes
　　baby, 196–97
　　red skinned, 197
Poultry, 149–51
　　benefits of "undercooking," 150
　　See also Chicken; Duck; Game
Principal, Victoria, 285
Prosciutto, duck, asparagus with, 50–51
Pudding, chocolate bread, with hazel-
　　nuts, 249–50
Puff pastry Baumanière, 228–29
Pumpkin
　　and oyster soup, 65–66
　　ravioli, 93–95
Purée, 294
　　plum, 178–79

Quail, 150
　　on corn cakes with Zinfandel sauce,
　　　　184–85

Radicchio, goat cheese salad with arugola
　　and, 40–41
Raspberry(ies)
　　ice cream with raspberry sauce, 263–
　　　　64
　　white chocolate ice cream with, 259–
　　　　60
Ravioli
　　chanterelle, with grilled chanterelles,
　　　　82–83
　　with foie gras and truffles, 91–93
　　lobster, with fresh dill sauce, 89–91
　　pumpkin, 93–95

Reagan, Ronald, 281
Red bell peppers, 198
　　roasted chicken breasts stuffed with
　　　　yellow bell peppers and, and
　　　　sweet green onion sauce, 171–72
Red onion(s)
　　butter, 137
　　marmalade, 160–62
Red skinned potatoes, 197
Red snapper, 132
　　with fennel, 142–43
Reduce, 294
Red wine with fish, 133
Regional cooking, xii
Rice
　　fried, vegetable, 201
　　tart with fresh fruit, 230–31
　　twice fried, 17–18
Robert Mondavi Winery, 29
Rogers, Kenny, 107
Root, Waverly, 131
Rosemary
　　corn muffins with jalapeño peppers
　　　　and, 207–8
　　rack of lamb with, and artichokes,
　　　　162–63
Roux, 294

Sake fruit, Chinois, 268–69
Salad(s), 4
　　chicken, Chinois, 52–53
　　goat cheese, with arugola and *radic-
　　　　chio*, 40–41
　　of grilled chanterelles or *cêpes*, 42
　　lamb
　　　　Mondavi, 29–30
　　　　roast saddle of, 45
　　　　Sonoma, 39–40
　　mandarin steak, 27–29
　　pasta, with mussels and clams, David
　　　　Hartman's, 96–97
　　spinach, with duck liver on croutons,
　　　　34–36
　　squab, rolls, 32–34
　　stir-fried scallop, 8–9
　　warm lobster, with white truffles, 48–
　　　　49
　　watercress, with barbecued chicken
　　　　breast, 46–47
Salmon, 132
　　caviar (pearls), curried oysters with
　　　　cucumber sauce and, 18–20
　　cured fresh, 15–16
　　　　with golden caviar sauce on toasted
　　　　　　brioche, 14–15
　　grilled
　　　　with garlic cream and tomato but-
　　　　　　ter, 135–36

with leeks and Pinot Noir butter, 138–39
smoked
  angel hair pasta with, and golden caviar, 78–79
  and caviar on buckwheat cakes, 13–14
  pizza with, and golden caviar, 115–16
Salsify, gratin of, 199
Sauce(s)
  black bean, 134–35
  caramel, 256
  cranberry, 165–66
  cucumber, 18–20
  dill, 89–91
  Foyot, 153, 154–55
  golden caviar, 14–15
  Meaux mustard, 153, 155
  plum purée, 178–79
  pomegranate, 186–87
  raspberry, 263–64
  sweet green onion, 171–72
  vinegar, 160–62
  Zinfandel, 184–85
Sausage
  duck, pizza with, 113–14
  lamb, 120–21
    pizza, 119–20
Sauté, 294
Scallops, see Bay scallops; Sea scallops
Sea scallop(s)
  Chinois
    special, 6–7
    with spicy vinegar, 26–27
  salad, stir-fried, 8–9
  smoked, black pasta with, 95–96
Seviche, bay scallops and shrimp, in tortilla cups, 9–10
Shellfish, 131–33
  See also names of shellfish
Sherbet
  Concord grape, 264
  grapefruit tequila, 265
  plum, 266
  tangerine, 267
  tea, 267
Shiitake mushrooms, 197
  New York steak with, and enoki mushrooms and grilled new onions, 152–53
Shrimp
  bay scallops and, seviche, in tortilla cups, 9–10
  pizza with, and sun-dried tomatoes, 118–19
Simmer, 294
Snow peas, 196

Sonoma lamb salad, 39–40
Soufflé, chocolate, 251
Soup(s), 4
  clam and mussel, 62–63
  court bouillon, 50
  crab, with fried spicy crab rolls, 67–68
  crayfish bisque, 60–62
  cream of corn, with Gulf oysters, 58–59
  cream of leek and chervil, with white truffles, 56–57
  fish, 54–56
  pumpkin and oyster, 65–66
  tortilla, 64–65
  wild mushroom, 53–54
  See also Stock
Sourdough farmer's bread, simple, 214–15
Spago's brioche loaf, 208–9
  toasted, cured fresh salmon with golden caviar sauce on, 14–15
Spago's individual apple pies, 221–22
Spareribs Chinois, 166–67
Spinach
  leaves, baby, fried, 146
  pasta dough, 101
  salad with duck liver on croutons, 34–36
Squab
  with leeks and pomegranate sauce, 186–87
  salad rolls, 32–34
  sautéed, with panfried noodles, 188–89
Squash, baby summer, 195
Stock, 294
  brown veal, 71–72
  chicken, 69
  fish, 70
Strawberry(ies)
  marzipan tart, 232
  wild, white chocolate ice cream with, 259–60
Striped bass, 132
  in ginger vinaigrette, 140–41
Stripes, 294
Sugar dough, 222–23
Summer squash, baby, 195
Sweat, 294
Sweetbreads
  pasta with, and artichokes, 84–85
  with vinegar butter and mâche, 36–37
Swiss chard and goat cheese ramekin, 21–22
Swordfish, marinated and glazed, 144
Syrup
  maple walnut ice cream, 262

Syrup (*continued*)
simple, 244
Szechuan beef, 156–57

Tangerine
chocolate mandarin ice cream, 258
sherbet, 267
Tart(s)
crème brûlée, 227
plum, 225–26
rice with fresh fruit, 230–31
strawberry marzipan, 232
walnut, 233–34
Tea sherbet, 267
Tequila sherbet, grapefruit, 265
Terrine, three chocolate, 252–54
Thatcher, Margaret, 281
Thulier, Raymond, 287
Tomato(es)
butter, 135–36
sun-dried, pizza with shrimp and,
118–19
Tortilla(s), 11
cups, bay scallops and shrimp seviche
in, 9–10
soup, 64–65
Trout, grilled, fresh herb pasta with,
87–88
Trudeau, Pierre Elliot, 281
Truffles
black, 49
ravioli with foie gras and, 91–93
vinaigrette, 169–70
dessert truffles
bourbon, 274
cassis, 276–77
chocolate, with brandied apricots,
272–73
mint, 275
scrambled eggs with, 23–24
white
cream of leek and chervil soup with,
56–57
warm lobster salad with, 48–49
Tuna, 132
grilled, with mint vinaigrette, 139–40
marinated, with Maui onions and avocado, 12
Turnips, baby, 197–98

"Undercooking" meats and poultry, 150

Veal, 149, 150
chops, grilled, with vinegar butter and
arugola, 159–60
medallions with Johannisberg Riesling,
almonds and pine nuts, 158

stock, brown, 71–72
Veal liver, grilled, on a bed of onion
marmalade with mustard seeds
and vinegar sauce, 160–61
Vegetable(s)
baby, 193–98
fried rice, 201
grilling, 194
stir-frying, 194
twice fried rice, 17–18
See also names of vegetables
Vinaigrette
black truffle, 169–70
chanterelle and Maui onion, 174–75
Chinese, 176–77
ginger, 140–41
mint, 139–40
Vinegar
butter, 36–37, 159–60
sauce, 160–62
spicy, Chinois sea scallops with, 26–27

Walnut
maple, ice cream, 262
pecan and, bread, 212–13
tart, 233–34
Watercress salad with barbecued chicken
breast, 46–47
White chocolate ice cream with wild
strawberries or raspberries, 259–
60
White mushrooms, 197
White truffles
cream of leek and chervil soup with,
56–57
warm lobster salad with, 48–49
White wine with fish, 133
Whole wheat pizza dough, 123–24
Wine
with fish, 133
with pizza, 109
See also names of wines
*Wolfgang Puck's French Cooking for the
Modern American Kitchen* (Puck),
194

Yellow bell peppers, 198
roasted chicken breasts stuffed with
red bell peppers and, and sweet
green onion sauce, 171–72

Zinfandel
pears poached in, 270–71
sauce, 184–85
Zucchini, baby, with and without blossoms, 194–95